CW01513299

Praise for Lucy Martin

'A vivid blend of polic
suspense' T.M. Logan

'A switchback ride of a read' Cara Hunter

'Dark, tense and absorbing' Simon McCleave

'A gripping detective thriller that grabs you from the start.
Readers are in for a treat.' Paula Greenlees

'A white-knuckle ride police thriller with danger around every
corner' Penny Batchelor

'A taut, dark thriller that grips you from the first page - sharp
writing with an addictive plot.' Victoria Dowd

'Refreshing to see such brilliantly strong female characters
lead the way in this twisty novel' Emma Christie

'Utterly absorbing - characters who leap off the page and a
dark undercurrent I couldn/t shake off.' Marion Todd

'Gripping, twisty and insightfully observed, a satisfying and
compelling crime thriller.' Philippa East

'A dark mystery that's both compelling and chilling.,
characters I loved and loathed and prose that made every
scene authentic.' Caron McKinlay

'A rollercoaster of a ride, I devoured every page…' Claire
Dyer

'An intricately plotted dark thriller with a compelling
storyline and unique set of intriguing characters.' Sarah
Clarke

LUCY MARTIN

Last to Leave

Lucy Martin

For Will

PROLOGUE

She knows.

How much of it she's actually processed, what she's actually put together and what she's made of it – that's the question.

But right now the only answer I'm getting is from the ants.

It's a thing psychologists talk about (and I've met a few of them in my time) called *automatic negative thoughts*. Our minds jump to the worst conclusions with no real evidence to bear it out. It's the best acronym I've ever come across, because the thoughts are just like real ants – creeping in out of nowhere, and suddenly they're all over the place; eating you up, driving you mad. You can try ignoring them, you can stamp on them as much as you like, throw boiling water on them, douse them in floury poison, but that's just a temporary fix. These ants know better than to let you find their nest. You're going to need to spend a couple of years dealing with them – learning to retrain your brain, to separate whatever the trigger is from what *ends up* happening by inserting a healthy dose of logic to dissociate the two. Once you've worked out what's going on in that split second where you go from calm to rage, you eventually learn to spot the signs. Then, the next time it happens, you can step in like the cops finding a couple of drunk teenagers in the park. Pull the little fuckers apart, get them to explain themselves and send them on their way.

I don't have a couple of years. I've got less than an hour.

I push the ants away and ask myself with all the rationality I can scrape together: *If I'm right that she knows everything, then the consequences are unthinkable – can I afford to take that risk?*

The results tumble into my mind's eye like dominoes, each slapping down on the next in a cascade of nightmares. It wouldn't take much to flick the first one over. It also wouldn't take much to step in and stop it happening.

My secret isn't the sort of thing you can keep to yourself. I can't take the risk.

I'm outside her flat now. After a minute or two, she appears at the window three floors up, throwing open the balcony doors and stepping outside. She leans on the railings and waves to someone below. For an awful second I think she's read my mind – I've blown my cover – but a woman waves back and my heartbeat returns to normal.

You wouldn't have thought of her as a party girl. More the solo type, a do-gooder, all Zen and yoga and food banks and spirituality. But not today. Today's a birthday gathering, with balloons and the pop of champagne corks and I'm right there with her, watching everything.

I try to stay composed, thinking about – and at the same time *not* thinking about – what I have to do.

Then before I know it, the party's over. She thinks she's alone. I make my move.

It will be easy to get away... I visualise the aftermath where I slip out of the fire exit unnoticed and disappear into the ether while they search for someone with a grudge, or the architect of a botched burglary.

I'm in the room. There's a knife in my hand and a wave of adrenaline washes through my body. She's tidying up, humming to herself as she piles up the sticky plates from the table. The crash and scrape of china and metal slice through my head. I want to run like a coward, down the main stairs and jump in a cab to the airport. Make a new life in some remote Chilean mountain village with goats and no running water, where nobody knows me and my past is a figment of somebody else's imagination.

It's now or never. I grip the knife handle tightly, take a step towards her as she heads for the balcony doors. *Stop!* screams the coward in my head. *You don't have to do this.*

I spot her reflection before she sees mine, but before I have time to absorb what this means our eyes meet in the glass, and now the flash of light from the blade catches her eye and she spins round to face me, hands aloft, face aghast. The betrayal. I can't bear hearing her scream, but I have no other choice.

Nothing goes to plan. I panic. It's messy. Then I freeze.

The scratch and fumble of a key in the door. Someone's back.

CHAPTER ONE

Adam Lloyd First Account

When you see a body on the ground and you don't know if they're dead or not, your heart stops and a million thoughts crash through your mind at the same time. Thinking back, I have no idea what any of them were. It's like when a book falls into the bath. Even when it all dries out, whatever's left is just an illegible mess.

It must have been around ten past five. Max finishes football at four-thirty and it usually takes twenty minutes or so to get him home but with the roadworks, it's down to a single lane after the Wakehurst turn-off, so the journey took twice as long and I'd stupidly forgotten to factor that in. There were a whole bunch of C-U-Next-Tuesdays flying up the outside lane and forcing their way in at the front, so that meant it took even longer. And it was bloody hot, for October. Rain one minute, sun the next, can't make its mind up. So the air-con was on full blast and I had to turn the radio right up to hear the news. Another prison break-out in Yorkshire, and I have to keep on top of all that for work purposes of course. Max was in the back seat, too engrossed in his gaming to chat, which was just as well as I was getting pretty stressed by this point. I'd tried to explain to Hannah that I had dinner plans in London after dropping him back home, so the schedule was tight. The Home Secretary, in case you want to check that out. Needless to say, I never made it to the restaurant.

Eventually I pulled into the entrance to Mulberry Court. Stupid name for a block of flats. What the fuck is a mulberry anyway? Anyway, the parking area is more of an in-and-out drive with a few residents' spaces round the edge. You pay more for one of those, otherwise it's try your luck on the streets, so it's in the private spaces that you'll find your Porsches and MX5s, a few VW Polos. None of your SUVs though. It's mainly couples living in the flats, a few youngsters, but it's not ideal for bringing up a family. Most of them move out to Latchworth Village and get a proper driveway, a hot tub and a couple of Labradors. Not exactly what I aspire to, but then it takes all sorts.

Even without getting out of the car it was pretty obvious something had happened, so I swung back round and parked facing the main road, in case Max decided to look up from the screen. Turned out to be a good decision. I told him I'd just be a sec and jogged over to where a bunch of people were standing clustered around something, like the sort you'd see watching some street magician in Covent Garden. Not sure why that popped into my head – probably wishful thinking. The sun was reflecting off the wet tarmac right into my eyes, like it was trying to put me off and send me back. I was seeing blobs in front of my eyes, so I slowed down, probably subconsciously delaying the moment.

That was when it hit me – *boom*.

It was as if my entire brain had been replaced by the horror of what I saw. First, her bleeding and twisted body on the ground. Then it was the recognition, landing like a hammer-blow to the head. Then the refusal to believe, the denial that this could be her. Meanwhile, there's some peroxide-haired woman kneeling on the tarmac shrieking down the phone something like, *'I think she's dying. Come quickly.'* I was paralysed – disbelief, dread, confusion. All at once, sweeping me away like a tsunami.

Max could have got out of the car at any moment and my priority was to avoid having to tell him anything at all. Saying there'd been an accident would only have made him wrestle past me to see. He had the normal curiosity of an eight-year-old boy, after all. And telling him anything else – well there was nothing else in my head. I assumed she'd been hit by a car. They come swinging round that bend into the one-way system and seem to forget that where there are cars, whichever direction they're going in, there are usually people as well.

I don't know if it was the right thing to do, even now. Who knows, and frankly who has the right to judge, when we're talking about a situation they haven't faced? But I decided to be thankful to Minecraft or whatever it was, for a change, that it could absorb my – *our*–son's attention to the exclusion of all else, and I just ran back to the car, climbed back into the driver's seat and re-started the engine. At that point Max should have noticed something was wrong, should have asked where we were going, wasn't I supposed to be bringing him home? But nothing, just a kind of noisy sucking in of air – too obsessed with his video game to be aware of anything beyond the screen.

I parked up again just around the corner from the flats outside the paper shop and told Max not to move, that I'd just be just a minute getting a pint of milk. He gave me one of his usual grunts, and I leapt out and ran the thirty yards or so back to the courtyard.

The blonde woman was hunched over the body on the ground, still spluttering tearful replies to the 999 operator. *'Yes, I think I feel something, I'm not sure...'* I squatted down beside them both to offer whatever comfort I could, but that wasn't much. I've never even done a First Aid course.

I must have sounded like some bit part from a TV drama. Something like: *'Stay with me, Hannah, it's all going to be fine.'* Blah blah blah, pointless platitudes. But thank God at that point we heard the sirens and the ambulance swung around the corner. Two paramedics leapt out, waving us away and pulling medical equipment out of bags. I stepped back and bumped straight into a group of mullet-haired teenagers who had gathered to spectate. Phones out. No shame. As you can imagine the red mist came down then and I almost went for one of the kids – who just put his hands up in some kind of fake surrender. Bloody snowflakes. That's one of the things I'm going to change about this country as soon I get the chance. Toughen up the younger generation. Of course I didn't hit him. I'm not completely insane. And hardly a fair fight. I know my way around a boxing ring.

I had a brief conversation with the paramedics, told them that I'd only spoken to Hannah a couple of hours earlier on the phone, that I was bringing Max back from Wakehurst Park etcetera. Then I said it all again to the police who arrived a few minutes later – described our exact journey, road by road, just so they could find me on all the cameras if they wanted. And now I'm telling the whole story again for you guys. Doesn't anyone take any fucking notes around here?

When they'd taken her away in the ambulance, lights flashing, sirens wailing, I found Max where I'd left him, still glued to my iPad. He didn't look up when I opened his door and leaned in and told him there'd been a change of plan, that Mum had had an accident and needed to go to hospital. He wanted us to go with her, then and there, so I had to make a decision and I didn't have a lot of choice. Taking him to the hospital wasn't a great idea, but leaving him at home meant asking creepy Giselle next door to babysit and she'd just bank it as a favour. I wasn't in the mood for doing any deals. I said Delilah could come over and keep an eye on him but he said he didn't want her, he wanted to see Mum. He stared me out like I was suggesting throwing him into the lion's den. Parenting is fucking tough sometimes and patience isn't my strong point. Coaxing and cajoling was always Hannah's job. I tried to imagine what she'd do, and we compromised on going up to the flat to get a snack and a drink for him before heading to hospital.

We took the lift to the third floor, where I got down on my knees and groped around for the spare key which was in its usual place, under Giselle's doormat. Hannah was convinced no burglar would ever cotton on to her hiding place, but to my mind, any would-be intruder worth their salt that found a key under a mat would try all the locks in the block before conceding defeat.

Giselle poked her head round the door as I got back to my feet, and gave me her usual look of utter disdain. 'I always hear when someone picks up the key,' she said, like it was some kind of warning to me. 'You never know who might try their luck.'

I looked her in the eye to show her I wasn't intimidated by anything she had to say. 'Hannah's had an accident,' I said, knowing she'd regret her sneer now she'd heard that news. But she just opened the door wider and stared at me like I was making it up. I stared right back at her, because she's a sight to see, Giselle, all pre-Raphaelite tresses and what you might politely describe as an ample bosom, draped in a pink tent that could house a small family. Her cleavage stands out like two coconuts on a balcony. It's hard to take your eyes off them, even though she's never been what I'd call an attractive woman, not by a long chalk. What she was doing living in that place – the mind boggles how she pays for it. I'll leave that to your imagination.

She repeats my words back at me like a bloody retard. *Sorry*, I mean like someone with learning difficulties. Will that do? Living with learning difficulties. Got to keep on top of the old lingo in my job, apparently. And that's not one of my strengths either. Anyway, she's acting all concerned when everyone knows she doesn't give a monkey's arse about any of us. It's all a show for the social services. Ask anyone.

'*An accident?*' she goes, with a frown that cracks the screed of brown make-up on her face like an earthquake. It's the kind of frown that says *I don't trust you to know what's going on, you scumbag excuse for a man.* Giselle had never had time for me, although she seemed to have plenty of time for other men. How they put up with her I have no idea, and what they get up to – well I don't want to go there...

I wanted to give her a whole lot more than she bargained for, tell her that Hannah was unconscious and losing blood from a gash in the back of her head, but Max would have heard and panicked and life wouldn't have been worth living so I told her we were just grabbing some things and going to the hospital.

'Are you sure that's what Hannah would want?' I know! She actually said that. I was lost for words, so she went on. 'The boy can stay with me if that's easier.'

I dug deep for some sort of fake gratitude and told her there'd be no need. She slammed the door shut and I unlocked Hannah's flat, I mean *our* flat, but she owned it – owns it – technically. We decided to do that for tax reasons. It was only ever intended to be a temporary stopping place until we made a decision about – well, lots of things.

Anyway, I walked into the living room and that's when I noticed the balcony doors were wide open. That in itself wasn't unusual, as being on the third floor meant that unlike with her key habit, it was hardly a realistic option for an opportunist. Also, with Mulberry Court being built around a courtyard, there would be plenty of spectators to any attempted break-in.

Still, it's not ideal, leaving everything on show to the world. I'd say anyone would have done the same in my shoes. It was natural to go to shut those doors before doing anything else. Security, weather, privacy – I don't know which reason was foremost in my mind, but it was the first thing I did. Had I known what I knew a few hours later, of course I wouldn't have touched them. Or anything else.

I made Max a sandwich because he said he was starving and wanted it right then and there and moved some crap off the table so he had space to eat. I genuinely didn't see the blood on the floor, or the broken glass. There was always tons of shit all over the place. It wasn't my job to do an inventory.

I know you're going to judge me for this, but you have to believe me. At that point, I honestly had absolutely no idea that my home was a crime scene.

CHAPTER TWO

DS Ronnie Delmar read through the first page of Adam Lloyd's initial statement. First just the once over to get the gist of what he was saying, then again to see what he *wasn't* saying, because that was always where the truth lay, in her experience. First accounts, where a witness was encouraged to relate their whole testimony in an uninterrupted flow, told a much richer story than the punctuated stutter of a traditional interview. After the first account, detailed questions would follow. Listen, repeat back, question the detail. Scanning the transcript, it looked as if DC Baz Munro had made a decent job of it.

'Flat white, sarge?' Baz had set the Styrofoam cup on the table before she had a chance to answer.

'I'd prefer a chilled sauvignon and a family pack of chilli heatwave Doritos.' Ronnie took a sip of her coffee and grimaced, her eyes still glued to the screen. 'Tastes even more disgusting than usual. Maybe it's something to do with coming in at the weekend.'

Baz perched on the arm of the chair facing her which was piled high with files. 'DI reckons the press are going to be all over it. The wife of a Home Office lawyer, destined for Tory greatness.'

Ronnie brought her cup to her lips, then put it down again, remembering the disappointment of a few seconds earlier. 'But Home Office lawyers are still civil servants, and civil servants can't stand for parliament. How did he get around that?'

'They can if they leave the civil service, they just can't do both jobs at once. House of Commons Disqualification Act 1975.'

Ronnie looked up in surprise. 'You've been doing your homework.'

Baz seemed pleased. 'You mean how does a Slavic immigrant know so much about English law?'

Ronnie checked his expression which gave nothing away. Was he implying she was racist? She pushed the thought from her mind and pasted a smile on her face. 'Well first of all you're not an immigrant if your Russian grandparents came over here in the fifties and your mother married an Englishman. Your father was English. What I *meant* is I'm impressed with your knowledge. Accept the compliment. I'll be more direct with them in future.' He was smiling. She could relax again. 'So, back to our Adam, with his political ambitions now officially sanctioned by statute – where were we?'

'I was just going to say that Lydia wants all hands on deck.'

'Of course she does. Those of us that spend our time actually solving crimes rather than bringing the force into disrepute need to work twice as hard, as usual.'

'Ouch.'

'I don't mean you, Baz. Unless you've got

something to tell me.' It was a forced attempt at humour when the subject couldn't have been less funny, and Baz seemed unamused.

'I reckon Halesworth CID is free of bad apples, sarge. God knows they've sent us on enough courses now to ram the point home. It's a whistle-blowers' market these days I'd say. Can't believe anyone would dare overstep the line now.'

Ronnie wasn't so sure, but now wasn't the time to debate it. She angled the screen to share it with him. A clean-cut tanned face stared back at them, eyes unfocused, a half-smile playing on his lips as if he didn't know what kind of photo he was posing for. 'So what did you think of this Adam Lloyd? First impressions?'

'He seemed genuine to me.' Baz frowned at the screen and shrugged. 'He was happy to come in and tell us all about it for a start. Always grateful for a compliant witness.'

'Many a murderer has been at the forefront of the search party. Some of them get a thrill out of helping to solve their own crimes, being at the centre of the investigation into themselves. Don't read anything into his keenness.'

Baz's hands went into his pockets in sulky defence. 'I still say take him at face value for now, and who knows? It could easily have been suicide or even an accident. Someone fell from a block in Tower Hamlets the other day trying to pass a joint to the guy on the next balcony.'

'Mulberry Court is a far cry from Tower Hamlets,

but I take your point. I'm sure SOCO will be able to enlighten us very soon on that, but given the stats on women being attacked by their partners I'd say we're most likely looking at attempted murder. So, if and when we find a weapon, we'll be checking it for Adam Lloyd's prints.'

But Baz wasn't going to give up without a fight. 'You'll accuse me of doing my homework again, but it's apparently about sixty percent of women that are killed by a partner or an ex, and when it comes to prints, Adam *lived* there. His prints and DNA will be all over the flat, and probably on whatever was used as a weapon.'

'He did, but does he still live there? The address he provided is for a flat over in West Dean.' Ronnie flicked over to Google Maps on her laptop and spun the screen round to show him.

Baz opened his mouth and closed it again. The colour drained from his face. 'Sorry, sarge. Can't believe I didn't spot that. I suppose I just assumed.'

Ronnie frowned. 'Don't be sorry. I wouldn't have checked either if he hadn't come across as such a tosser. Made me wonder how anyone could put up with him.' That was an understatement. The way Adam Lloyd spoke screamed 'arrogant, entitled, upper-class arsehole', but she might try and keep those particular words at bay for a little longer.

'That bad?' Baz looked genuinely surprised. 'What gave him away?'

Ronnie looked at him in disbelief. 'What *didn't*?

Not only did he not express any distress at all – barely an hour after his wife was mysteriously left for dead – but he didn't seem to give much thought to *how* she came to be unconscious and bleeding on the tarmac below her balcony.'

'He was in shock. Assumed she'd been run over, to start with, didn't he say?'

She had to admit it was useful having a man to unravel the thoughts of a male witness. Since finding herself single after fourteen long years of marriage, Ronnie had got used to not having to worry about how the male mind worked. Traditionally masculine thinking had its benefits – she could definitely do with honing her ability to focus in on one thing to the exclusion of all else – but if this Adam had really assumed his wife had been run over and thought no further than that, it was a good thing he wasn't working in CID. She scrolled down to a later paragraph of the transcript and turned her screen to face Baz once more.

'What about the fact that, even having assumed she'd been hit by a car, he didn't actually rush off to the hospital with her, but went up to her flat, where who knows what evidence he tampered with, then hung around for another twenty minutes or so whilst his wife's life was hanging in the balance? I mean, he shouldn't have been that easy to get hold of for a statement. He should have been long gone. What was that all about?'

Baz stood up to his full height, taking the wide-legged stance of a man not about to give ground. 'Like

I said, he's in shock, he's got the kid, he's thinking ahead. I think Amber would be impressed if I was forward-thinking enough to make a picnic.'

There was probably no need to launch a debate about it. 'I suppose it's a reason.'

She sat back and refocused. She and Baz needed to get their banter back. Something had thrown their usually easy connection off-kilter. She made a mental note to get him and the others to the pub after work one day, when things had blown over, or sooner. A little loosening of the barriers wouldn't go amiss all round, particularly when everyone was looking over their shoulder for the grim reaper of HR. Career insecurity in the station, the elephant in the room, was mostly unspoken, wrapped up in glossy banter, tied with the ribbon of bravado, sometimes with the added swizzle stick of humour. New cuts were being made every day, so there was no point admitting to anything remotely related to mental health issues, however unmanageable the workload became. It wasn't as if there was any money left for counselling.

'You have to laugh or you'll cry.' It had been one of her father's over-used platitudes, but even humour could only do so much to alleviate stress, and then there was its dark side – the gallows humour and all it entailed that had soured the reputation of the police across the country. Memos had gone round the department each time another headline left its ugly mark, but no sooner had one wound healed than another scar reopened. For the PR and HR teams it was a game of 'whack-a-mole'.

For Ronnie it was more of a rumbling undercurrent, a reminder she had built her professional home at the foot of a career volcano.

But meanwhile, there was a job to do, and hers was to investigate a brutal attack on a young mother. She needed to get back to the facts, make a plan, start the ball rolling. 'What's the football club called that little Max goes to?'

Baz flicked through his notes. 'Wakehurst Park Little League. Sounds rather cute.'

'Let's get hold of them to corroborate the alibi.'

'Right you are, sarge.' He took out his phone and tapped a message with his thumbs. Ronnie was mesmerised for a second. She held a secret admiration for anyone who could do better than the one-finger texting she'd never moved on from. 'How's Hannah doing in ICU?'

'She's unconscious but hanging on. The next few days will be the test but they say they're hoping she'll make enough of a recovery to make her life worth living.'

'Who's going to be the judge of that I wonder?' The words had slipped out, echoes of some sort of cross between her mother and her DI, before she had a chance to think. The medical profession seemed happy to force the most meaningless of lives upon people who might, if asked, choose to give up and let go. Still, it was another negative comment bringing more bad energy between the two of them and she berated herself for the second time in less than a minute.

'Well, you know what I mean.' Baz clasped his hands behind his head and brought his elbows forward, closing his eyes for a second. 'Brain damage or no brain damage is the question, I think.'

'Of course. Well, fingers crossed.' She managed a placatory smile. 'If it turns out to be murder, they're bound to bring in the DCI, most likely with a whole team to take over the job, and then we'll have our hands tied.'

Baz made a face. 'If that happens, let's just hope we're so far down the line with the investigation that it's more efficient to keep us on board and the supervision down to a light touch.'

'Here's to that.' Ronnie raised her cup of coffee. 'Let's get moving then.' She slid a notepad across to him and offered him one of the two biros in front of her. Then, sitting back in her chair, she tapped her own pen on the desk in rhythm to her words, one tap for each item on the list. 'We need to trace Hannah's movements over the last few days. Who she saw, where she went, what she did – all of that might throw some light on how she came to find herself under attack in her own home. I want to know who her friends were, who might hold a grudge, or worse. Was she in debt? Did she owe people money or favours? Was there some part of a deal she hadn't gone through with?'

'Sounds like we're going to need a few more bodies on the case. I'll bring in Overton for the data gathering. He's a sucker for an all-nighter.'

'No all-nighters Baz. We don't want the boss

throwing the rule book at us on rest breaks. Jules Mayer is off on secondment for the next few weeks, more's the pity. She'd be perfect.' Jules was the brightest of the lot of them, and destined for a speedy rise through the ranks but had none of the self-importance that a lot of other DCs might have had in her position.

Baz glanced through the partition doorway to the main office where a handful of officers were hunched over desks and computers. 'Jen Connolly?'

Ronnie's eyes lit up. Jen was a new addition to the CID team, eager, hardworking, intelligent, and not afraid to stand up for herself. 'Great. Bring her up to speed and get her on Hannah's backstory. Then next on the list is the football club. Get them to confirm Max was there and what time he left. Then you and I need to visit the crime scene and see what they can tell us.'

Baz turned on his heel to leave.

'Wait, one more thing.' Ronnie flicked to a new screen on her laptop. 'Before I meet you there, I need to brief the DI and go through the other two statements. We've got this one from the buxom keyholder neighbour and another from the other friend that Adam mentioned as a potential babysitter.' She scrolled down to the name at the bottom of the transcript. 'That's it. Delilah. Funny, I've always loved that name. Despite the song.'

Baz looked puzzled. 'Lost on me, that one.'

'In this case, you may be better off in blissful ignorance. I'll see you at Mulberry Court in...' She looked at the time on her phone. It was going to be a late night. 'I'll see you when I see you. And by the way, Baz, in case you hadn't noticed—' She pointed at a sign on the door that read, in letters that looked easy enough to remove and replace at a moment's notice, *Detective Sergeant Veronica Delmar.* 'For the record, I'm half-immigrant too.'

The door clicked shut and she was alone. It was unusual to be in the office on a Sunday these days, but there was no reason why criminals should stick to standard working hours, and to be fair it was still unclear whether a crime had even been committed. Baz might be right. Hannah Lloyd could easily have jumped or fallen. It would take time to get the tox screen results back and with the testimony of the neighbour Giselle that had just landed on her desk, a drug habit wasn't out of the question. She took another sip of the murk that passed for coffee and regretted it. Tasteless unless laced with sugar or vanilla syrup, which she kept in her desk drawer for occasions like this one. She plucked it from the debris of staples and post-its and poured a generous shot into the cup. The carbohydrate rush was a godsend, giving her tired, weekend brain its energy back.

Re-energised, she spun her chair a few degrees to consider each of the options. Accident, suicide or attempted murder? There was no denying she had a habit of leaning towards crime over misfortune in most of the cases that crossed her desk. It was ingrained in her after nearly twenty years of policing to assume the worst, but that inclination towards distrust could be as distracting as it was useful. She still felt powered by her gut instinct, despite her father's second piece of questionable advice when she first joined up. *'Trust your gut, but remember sometimes it's not enough.'* It was the ultimate hedging of bets, like saying it was going be sunny unless it wasn't, but hedging bets had been Fred Delmar's *raison d'etre*. Poker and gambling of any sort was his life-blood, and in Ronnie and her sister's view at least, had had something to do with the tragedy that ended his life. He owed a lot of people a lot of money, then one day, having taken his boat out to go fishing off the Kent coast, he'd gone missing at sea. It didn't take a detective to work out that foul play was a possibility, but given the complete lack of either witnesses or evidence, it was the one mystery she might never find the answer to.

And since then she had spent her days fighting for justice for other people – in this case it was the turn of Hannah Elizabeth Lloyd, and after that poor woman's thoroughly unpleasant husband, the next person of interest on the list was her rather unusual neighbour, Giselle Gaillard.

CHAPTER THREE

Giselle Gaillard First Account

I think I must have seen her fall. I didn't call the police straightaway because I don't like to get involved where it's none of my business. I've done nothing wrong, I've nothing to hide and I don't see why I should go looking for trouble where there isn't any. Plus I had no idea at the time it was her, or even a person. Could just as easily have been a duvet cover flying off the railings in the wind. It's been sunny enough to dry washing outside for weeks. Climate change and all that. Can't see a problem with it myself. Bring on hot summers.

I had just filled the kettle at the sink and if I'd been an inch further back into the room I'd have missed it. I put the kettle back down on its stand and went to open the balcony doors to get a better look but then I changed my mind. Sometimes it's better just not to know things. I made my tea and sat down at the table. It must have been a few minutes before I heard the sirens, but I still didn't go outside to look. By that point I just didn't feel I could. Plus, it would have been rude to stare, especially from my vantage point. My tea went cold. I suppose it was as if time was standing still while I waited for something to happen. I had an idea that I'd climb into bed and pretend to have been napping, but then there was scuffling outside my door and that's when I opened it to see Adam Lloyd and the boy looking for the spare key.

He was the first one to break the news to me. Just like that, with no emotion, not upset or anything. *'Hannah's had an accident.'* He didn't say she'd fallen, and I didn't want to tell him what I'd seen, so we left it at that. He said they were going to the hospital but needed to pick up a snack first and some water, and I offered to have the boy because a hospital's no place for a youngster like that, but he looked at me as if that was the stupidest idea he'd ever heard. You can't do anything kind these days without being treated like some kind of weirdo.

I won't pretend that Hannah and I ever really saw eye to eye over anything much. She's been my neighbour for three years, I look after her key, occasionally I mind the boy if she's working and that good-for-nothing husband of hers can't have him. But there's not much about her or her life that I liked. Not that I want to speak ill of the dead. Is she dead? I don't even know. At least she had a party just before she went. Like a funeral while you're still alive. There were a few of them round there in the afternoon at some point. I heard shrieky women's voices singing happy birthday. I had to bang on the wall to get them to shut up. Not that I usually complain about noise. There are plenty of worse things in the world, I can tell you.

Like losing your child, then living next door to someone who's no better at looking after hers but gets to keep him.

They took my Leo six months ago now. It's only foster care, but it's like losing a limb. There's not a day that goes past that I don't think of him. I miss him so much it hurts like a dagger in my heart. I get supervised meetings once a week, but that's going to be unsupervised soon if I keep going to my group. Never thought I'd manage this far but when they take away what you love most in the world, what choice do you have but to manage?

Leo's foster family are a bit snooty, a bit well-to-do for my liking. He'll probably come home with all sorts of ideas about eating sushi and playing table tennis but he's going to have to realise we cut our coat according to our cloth around here. No fancy trainers and organic oat milk in this house. The council are paying the rent here, for now at least, which makes me laugh because there's no way I should be living it up in a posh block of flats like this one. They keep saying they're going to move me out but there's not enough housing to go round so it's been three years and I'm still here.

Bloody social workers are on my case every day. I'd like to see how they cope being a single mother. But that *Darana* comes swanning round here with no notice and expects me to drop everything to sit down and chat about how much better I am now. I call her Piranha. Suits her much better. She asks about support networks and I tell her I'm working on that, but then when I actually am working on it she goes mad with the questions. I had my odd-job man round the other day for a bit of support, he was just leaving as she arrived, and she wanted to know everything about him – who he was and whether we were in a relationship. 'Course I said no because we aren't. But if we were, she'd want him police-checked and all sorts I'm sure.

It's been a nightmare trying to pay the bills since I lost my job at the hotel, but I managed in my own way and I'm proud of that. I've even got some interviews lined up. Piranha wanted to know all about them – how was I going to get there? What childcare plans would I put in place? I'll find a way. I've been going to that group therapy class that she forced on me. Learnt all sorts about the way the mind works, how to control thinking patterns. I'm no expert at mental health or much else come to that, but at least there's nobody wanting to push *me* out of the window... that I know of. I presume that's what happened? I can imagine that Hannah had a few enemies. Pleased with herself, she was. Her Max is apparently much too good for my Leo so they could never play together. She's always wearing that smug little smile, looking down on the rest of the world like we're not worthy. And I can't see any reason why she'd be smug. Non-stop rows with that husband of hers. Calls herself a yoga teacher but it's not doing much good if you ask me. She could do with some Valium.

I actually offered her some, not long after they moved in. I opened my door to see her sitting on the stairs weeping buckets, great big shopping bags on the doormat full to bursting. She'd locked herself out.

Adam was away on some conference. The boy was in his sports kit, looking like he was about to cry as well. That's why I offered to have the spare key, so she didn't need to worry about that again. I told the social workers that. About the key, not the drugs. You never know. It might count in my favour if I do good deeds. I don't tell them everything, but then it's none of their business how I spend my time, as long as it's nothing illegal.

As I said. I have nothing to hide.

CHAPTER FOUR

DI Lydia Burnett was the only one in CID with a proper office since the latest round of cuts had been made. Shut off from the rest of the open plan area, its plush furnishings included an antique oak desk and a brown leather swivel chair. With seascapes adorning the walls in heavy frames, and a retro angle poise lamp leaning over her paperwork, it was a world away from the ocean of grey plastic that filled the space outside it. Lydia was on the phone when Ronnie put her head around the door but beckoned her in nonetheless and motioned for her to take the seat opposite.

'I'm on hold,' she said, covering the phone's mouthpiece. 'SOCO are looking at Hannah Lloyd's flat. The evidence suggests she was pushed. I'm just waiting for confirmation.'

Ronnie nodded and sank into the chair that was harder than it looked. Why did she never remember that? Lydia clearly didn't want her guests getting too comfy. Ronnie edged to the front and mimed a response, pointing to an imaginary watch. 'I'm due to meet DC Munro at the scene, ma'am. I'll debrief when we're back.'

'Just a second. They won't be long I'm sure.' She held a finger up to indicate the number of minutes Ronnie should wait. 'Any thoughts so far, from the statements you've read, any new medical reports?' Her face looked blank where there should have been raised eyebrows. Ronnie had always suspected she wasn't a stranger to the Botox clinic, but today the extreme smoothness told its own story. It must have been a very recent visit.

'You mean do we think it was accident or assault? The medics say most of her injuries appear to be from impact as she hit the ground but she also has a significant knife wound to the chest. Latest from the hospital says it's not clear whether the head injury is life-threatening but the next 24 hours will be crucial.'

Lydia lifted the phone to her ear again. 'Yes, I'm still here.' Then she raised her head at Ronnie in another mute bid for her attention. 'Was anyone still in the vicinity of the flat at the time the incident occurred? I understand she had company until shortly before the attack.'

'A birthday lunch, apparently. Any one of the three women she'd spent the afternoon with is potentially in the frame. We're talking to them all, as well as the husband and a neighbour, but nothing concrete yet.'

Lydia covered the mouthpiece again and pointed her pen in Ronnie's direction. 'We need to interview all visitors of course, including the delivery man, as well as friends, neighbours and family.' She had apparently forgotten she was speaking to a DS who after fifteen years in the force was more than capable of drawing up a to-do list. Ronnie dug out her best smile and made as if to note down the tasks which were all well under way.

'The husband had been out all day and was collecting their son from a match that finished around four-thirty. There should be camera footage to back up his journey home. If forensics can give us a better idea of the time of the incident, then we could be closer to eliminating him from our enquiries. There could be just minutes in it. There's also a next-door neighbour who thinks she witnessed the fall but can't pinpoint the time. An hour or so beforehand she had heard 'Happy Birthday' being sung.' She glanced at her notes. 'Sounds like somewhere in between 'Happy Birthday' and the fall, most of the guests left.'

'Most of them?'

'Delilah Byrne, another statement that's just come in – she's adamant she wasn't the last one to go home.'

'Can we check that?'

Lydia was never this hands-on. Normally Ronnie would be trusted with the basics. She wondered what was going on behind the scenes. A visit from the commissioner perhaps? Until she knew, playing along was the only option. 'Checking CCTV around the flats now, ma'am, and talking to the other residents, but nothing yet.'

Lydia clicked her pen, eyes fixed on a point on the opposite wall. 'Tell me about the neighbour.'

'She was at home alone, her relationship with Hannah was pretty frosty and she had a key to the flat.'

'Unlucky for her. Opportunity and no alibi.'

'Absolutely. Not sure she'd want to get into

trouble with the law, though. Single mother – lost her child to the care system a few months ago when she got nicked for pushing benzodiazepines onto frazzled housewives.'

'Spotted a gap in the market?'

'Exactly. Social worker says her justification for it was that she could see women all around her falling to pieces, and seeing as she'd found them so helpful herself, she was apparently doing the world a favour. There was no evidence she was selling them or she'd be doing time by now.' Ronnie paused for breath, wondering for a minute why she was being so defensive about Giselle's behaviour. Maybe she sympathised with her at some level. 'Anyway, her remorse and recovery have been exemplary and they're on course for getting the kid back home. But she needs to be squeaky clean if that's going to happen, so she's unlikely to take a risk like this, however frosty relations were.'

'Fair enough.' Lydia didn't seem entirely convinced. 'If she wants the kid back, that is.'

Ronnie gave her a look. Lydia didn't have children, and neither, it appeared, did she have any concept of what it was to have them. In Ronnie's experience, being a mother of twins was joy and pain in equal parts, but now they were seventeen and the most troublesome years had passed, the pain mostly came from imagining ever losing them.

Lydia seemed to realise her misjudgment. 'Alright, we presume she does, but anyway...'

'No stone unturned, ma'am.' Ronnie slid a file

onto Lydia's desk. 'I wanted you to take a look at this one. It's Delilah Byrne's statement. Supposedly a friend of Hannah's, but I'm not getting the feeling that all was good between them. Also, she seems convinced that Hannah and Adam's relationship wasn't all it appeared to be on the surface, and she makes a reference to Hannah's reckless spending habits. It makes interesting reading.'

Lydia turned the pages with her free hand while the other kept a loose hold of the phone. 'Ah, this is the one who says she wasn't the last on the scene. I'll take a look at her statement while you're over there. Anyone else?'

'Delilah mentioned a couple of others and we're trying to get hold of them. Hannah's sister-in-law and one of her yoga students. Uniform have been doing house-to-house to see if anyone on the estate knew her at all, but no joy yet.'

'Any other family?'

'No parents alive. She hadn't been well, suffering with depression and anxiety since her mother died. One brother, James Garrett. He's been informed but we haven't spoken to him yet. James' wife is the one Delilah says stayed on after she left.'

Lydia held up a finger and spoke into the phone. 'Yes, I'm still here.' There was a pause, while her expression changed and she looked up at Ronnie. 'OK, DS Delmar will be with you shortly.' She ended the call and clasped her hands in front of her face as if in supplication to a deity – the god of please-don't-let-this-be-true.

'News?' Ronnie held her breath in anticipation. It didn't look good.

Lydia's hands slid back to the table which she gripped with whitening knuckles. 'They've found the weapon. So, we're looking at attempted murder, or if she doesn't make it – well, I don't need to spell it out.'

CHAPTER FIVE

Delilah Byrne First Account

For *fuck's sake* I should be with Hannah in the hospital, not sitting in a bloody police station. Someone needs to be with her, and I doubt it's Adam she wants sitting by her deathbed. After what he's put her through, and what she's had to put up with. Always at work. Never at home. Absent father, absent husband. I mean obviously there's another side to it if you talk to him. I've been a solicitor for long enough to be familiar with the witness statement procedure. I'm just supporting the sisterhood.

The three of us trained as solicitors together ten years ago. Adam went on to work for the civil service and I followed him. Bit of a cushy number after slaving away in private practice, to be honest. And now Adam's paving the way for yet another change of career. Trying to extricate himself from the civil service so he can become an MP, which might be just what they need as a family – a new beginning in a new constituency, if he wins the seat of course. Obviously it's a fairly safe one as he's a first-timer, and in the depths of the countryside where Max can climb trees instead of three flights of stairs every day. Bless him. He's also my godson of course. I think Hannah and Adam both saw me as too ambitious to ever settle down and have children so they very kindly gave me the next best thing.

Max is more than enough for me, children-wise, and I want everything to be as good for him as it can be. He could have done with having siblings, like any kid, but I think Hannah struggled enough with the whole parenting thing anyway. Rocky childhood, her mother always playing her and her brother off against each other. She left the firm a couple of years ago to become a yoga teacher, then when the mum died, she went into a kind of slump, which is odd given that she presumably inherited a fortune. Her mum was loaded and the brother got nothing. Then, Adam, well, he wasn't the best husband after that, if you know what I mean. I kind of get it. Hannah had inherited millions and it made her so miserable that she was about to hand the bulk of it over to some charity in India. Seems an odd thing to want to do. Charity begins at home and all that. So that's when things started to get a bit tense.

It feels mean commenting on people's relationships. I've been trying to stop doing it, but since this is official and I can't lie, well, I won't. Hannah and Adam ended up in a pretty bad place. Hannah retreated into herself a bit. She completely stopped sharing stuff with me like she used to. She didn't want to come out drinking on a Friday night with the rest of us and she wasn't interested in gossiping about other people which ought to be a good thing, but it doesn't leave you with much to talk about. Adam must have found that lonely, isolating I suppose. Still, it doesn't give him the excuse to treat her like he did, and as I said, I don't imagine he's the one she wants hovering over her while she's fighting for her life.

It's her birthday today. I haven't forgotten the irony of that. There were four of us there for lunch, or brunch. I'm never sure what the difference is but we ate around midday – me, a woman from Hannah's yoga class called Ali and Hannah's sister-in-law Meghan. So her brother's wife, but not her brother. They don't seem to have much contact – not surprising really given she's supposedly squandered all the cash, or is about to, but she still sees his wife, so that's something.

It was a strange kind of afternoon. It was a pretty odd gathering to be honest. There was a time before the slump when she would have invited the whole neighbourhood. She knew everyone, through Adam, through yoga, so she wasn't short of friends. Odd to have just three people at your birthday party. I was a bit surprised to be in her top three mates, as we've drifted apart so much recently, but I think she might have been trying to build bridges.

Ali T was good fun. I hadn't met her before but she really livened things up in the short time she was there – hooting with laughter at everything, talking too loudly. Larger than life, in every way. Like you wouldn't want to come up against her in a dark alley, or at least you'd want her on your side. Must be six foot and a bit of a gym bunny by all accounts. She was chatting away about Fitbits and Pilates most of the time. She brought a birthday cake she'd made herself (who does that anymore for God's sake? What's wrong with Colin the

Caterpillar?) then she got her phone out to play the 'Happy Birthday' music and sang along with the harmonies. A bit of an all-rounder it seems. Into everything. A bit too much into everything if you ask me. No wonder she did yoga. She needed calming down. She started the singing, so loudly that one of the neighbours banged on the wall. That was Giselle – absolute caricature of a French Nell Gwynn, ageless, busty, dressed up to the nines at all hours of the day – totally not what you'd expect. To be living there I mean. She should be in a council flat, or in France. Preferably in France.

Then there was the sister-in-law, Meghan, totally the opposite of Ali, sensible and motherly, finding napkins and forks when we'd all have been happy to eat with our fingers. A bit of an edge to her though. I reckon her outer self was a construct from learned behaviours rather than where her true energy lay. You can tell I did a psychology degree before law, can't you? Meghan brought Hannah a present, beautifully wrapped in tissue in a bag with a card and a label she'd actually remembered to write on. I'm more the type for a get-it-today Amazon prime order handed over in its original packaging. There'll be a thank you letter in the post by the time she gets home and probably a photo collage Facebook post to follow. But I wouldn't want to be Meghan for all the tea in China. She's chained to domesticity and there's no escape from that now she's expecting a baby. Not my idea of fun at all. As I said, one godson is plenty.

And that was it. Nobody else turned up, except the delivery guy from the sushi place, and Adam phoned just when Ali was leaving around one thirty. Said she had a flight to catch but I reckon she was just running low on that fairy dust she insists on sprinkling everyone with. Anyway, Hannah went into another room to talk to Adam which gave Ali the chance to slip out without having to make too many excuses. She shouted something about chatting on the phone later and then the door slammed behind her. Peace at last after that.

Hannah came back looking a bit bruised, which didn't surprise me. Most of their conversations end badly these days. Adam gets impatient and frustrated. Hannah could probably stand up for herself a bit more, but she's not like me, or Ali from what I saw of her, and she hasn't adapted to Adam's changing ways. As he's climbed the career ladder, his ego has gone on ahead and taken the steps two at a time. Those were Hannah's words by the way, after at least three glasses of crémant. Apparently it's the new prosecco. Who knew?

I stayed on longer than I wanted to, maybe because I felt sorry for Hannah. Left around four-ish, which was a good decision. I'd only have ended up ploughing through another bottle and regretting it the next day. Hannah hugged me goodbye when I left – one of those hugs that goes on slightly longer than necessary. I remember feeling the gratification of a relationship repaired and restored – not words I'd usually use, but there we go.

And off I went back home. I live out in

Latchworth Village. We pronounce it like the French 'villaaaage' you know, it's so posh there. I'd caught the bus because I knew there'd be booze involved. Even Hannah was drinking, which I hadn't seen for ages. I'd forgotten that. Maybe there's more to life than teaching yoga after all.

So like I say, that was about 4pm. That's what happened so I'd like that to go in my statement word for word. And I'd like a copy of it please, just in case this goes to court. I don't need a solicitor and I don't want some CPS barrister trying to trip me up on the witness stand.

And that's everything – hang on, except one thing. I just remembered.

When I left Hannah's place there was one person left. Meghan Garrett. But I presume you'll be speaking to her.

CHAPTER SIX

Mulberry Court, constructed in a hurry some ten years earlier in response to yet another housing crisis, formed three sides of a skewed rectangle, partially enclosing a floodlit tarmac courtyard where a central fountain and neatly landscaped surround helped create an oval driveway for vehicles to flow in and out. No Parking signs lined the immaculate flowerbeds and a pair of potted olive trees guarded each of the three main entrances. Each building was four storeys high, with balconies facing inwards or outwards depending on the location of the apartment. Most windows were lit with the glow of lamplight behind closed curtains, but there wasn't a washing line in sight and the plethora of dwarf palms and acers told its own story about the priorities and social status of the residents. It was a part of town blissfully unaccustomed to crime. Undaunted by the incessant drizzle, a small crowd had gathered around the taped-off area. Ronnie elbowed her way through and flashed her badge at the officer on duty who lifted the tape and stepped aside. She had just nodded her thanks when she spotted a scene of crime officer coming out of the main door and heading straight towards her, hood still up to keep off the rain which had moved in with a vengeance after the weather had broken. His face, or what she could see of it, looked vaguely familiar but she couldn't place him. It was only when they were feet apart from each other that the penny dropped.

'Frank Reilly?' The words sounded strange, it was so long since she'd said them.

He did a double take. 'Well if it isn't Ronica Delmar as I live and breathe.' His face lit up and his hands came together in a clasp of joy. 'I'd give you a hug but we don't want any cross-contamination, do we?'

'I can't believe it's really you. Of all the people to bump into!'

'I could say the same about you. We're a long way from Chingford nick.' He pulled at his hood as the rain started coming down harder.

'Thank God. Feels like a lifetime ago. How are you? Looks like you had the same bright idea to go suburban.'

'Never looked back.' He grinned. 'Life's good. How's yours? Or is this a bad day to ask?' He glanced upwards to where a cluster of white suits were examining the railings and glass panels of the third-floor balcony.

Ronnie followed his gaze, grateful for the chance to return to business. 'You're right that it's not the best day to rave about my quiet life away from the rat race. But luckily there are plenty of positives, like being able to park my car in a space more than an inch longer than it, and breathe without being poisoned by diesel fumes.' She glanced over her shoulder where his eyes had wandered to a car parked at the kerb, then back at the building, as the reason for their being there slammed back into her mind. 'So, tell me, what's the scene like upstairs?'

'Doesn't look good if I'm honest. They'll brief you when you get up there. Sorry – you caught me mid-flight. I'm needed at home, but let's touch base soon. How can I find you?'

She handed him her card. 'Definitely let's do that. It's been way too long,' and then as an afterthought added, 'And please call me Ronnie, won't you? Can't have the other staff laughing at my childhood nickname.'

'Sarge, a word?' An officer appeared at her side, giving a cursory nod of acknowledgement to Frank who took his leave miming a phone call and pointing at an imaginary watch on his wrist. Ronnie turned to the worried face of DC Overton.

'It's DC Munro, sarge. He's been waiting for you up there since they found the weapon. Keeps asking why you're not here yet. I think the wife's on his case. Sunday night and all that.'

'I'll be right there.' Everyone had someone waiting for them at home except her. Sunday nights were the worst for that. Ronnie pushed through the revolving door and took the stairs two at a time, regretting it by the time she reached the open door to flat thirty-six. Baz grinned as he pulled his mask down under his chin. Not too impatient then. That was good.

'There's a perfectly good lift you know.'

'I'll remember that for next time,' Ronnie panted, pulling on a pair of gloves and overshoes. 'What've you got? Catch me up and then go home. You've done more than your fair share today.'

Baz led her into the sitting room, which had been soco'd within an inch of its life and bore no resemblance to its original purpose. Amongst the glasses and bottles that littered the surfaces and some of the floor, numbered yellow cards indicated the presence of key evidence. More suited CSIs were examining walls and flooring, door frames and handles, zip-locking evidence bags and swabbing for DNA. It always surprised her how long the crime scene investigation took, even in a small empty room where you'd imagine there was nothing to find. What in years gone by must have been a few minutes with a magnifying glass could now take a whole team of experts the best part of twenty-four hours or longer, but the good news was that every extra minute spent by them was guaranteed to make the detectives' jobs easier. Frank Reilly, in his time considered to be the best scene of crime officer in East London, had been a godsend in her first months at Chingford and she hadn't forgotten the way he'd taken her through the forensic process, explaining the intricacies of lifting prints, fibres and DNA from the most unlikely sources. They were lucky to have him on board here, that was for sure.

Baz swept his hands through the air in a gesture of helplessness.

'Hard to say at this point what the hell went on, until our esteemed colleagues give us their verdict. Looks like a disturbance, then some hapless attempt at tidying it up.' He indicated the dining table, where an assortment of used glasses, cutlery and crockery had been pushed aside to reveal one strangely empty corner. 'Unless you have another idea?'

Ronnie shrugged. 'The look of it would fit with Adam's story, moving things around to make space for Max to eat, wasn't it?'

'Yes, and that was rather unhelpful of him, as is the fact that his prints are everywhere, and his shoe prints are in the blood on the floor. We presume they're his, as he admits to being here and the prints are size ten trainers which would match. But again, we need to confirm that.'

Ronnie exhaled deeply. 'Any other prints that don't belong to either of them?'

'Yes, plenty. And what we're most interested in of course is this.' He held up an evidence bag containing a black-handled chef's knife.

'The weapon used on Hannah?'

'Very likely. They need to compare her injuries to the blade and we need to trace the fingerprints, but we could be onto something.'

Ronnie frowned. 'I know every criminal has their own MO, but I've never really understood why anyone would leave the weapon at the scene. Why save us time looking for it?'

'A knock at the door, an unexpected interruption? But yes, you'd think it would at least be wiped clean of blood and prints.'

Ronnie let the thought settle. Baz had a point, but

there was another one that made more sense. 'Yes, *if* they wanted the prints removed. But if there were other prints on the knife already, they might have found their perfect weapon.'

'How would they know there were prints on it?'

'If it looked as if it had been used, whoever used it was most likely not wearing rubber gloves, unless it was a whole other type of party.'

Baz chuckled. 'OK, fair point.'

'Then there's the danger of spreading the DNA onto the cloth you wipe it with...' She was on a roll now. 'And then there are all the questions that arise from wiping it rather than just putting it in the dishwasher. Might be worth leaving it, letting the multiple prints and DNA issue run its course and make identification too inconclusive.' Baz was nodding, but not processing her words as fast as they were coming out. She should slow down, but when thoughts came flooding in like that, delaying their expression would more often than not mean the idea slipping away. Baz would catch up in his own time.

'We'll need to see her phone, laptop, iPad, all the tech. Get Harry's team onto it ASAP.'

'On it.' Baz held up the evidence bag with a tablet and iPhone inside, looking delighted to have been one step ahead on the action plan.

'Of course you are. I'm beginning to sound like bloody Lydia. Tell me to shut up.' She pulled open the dishwasher door. Empty. 'Setting it to run with just a knife in it might have looked a little odd, and I doubt they'd have had time to deal with all this stuff.' She cast her eyes around the detritus strewn across the worktops. 'Looks like my house *after* the kids have cleared up dinner. Let's get an assessment from the forensics. See if they've got anything more.'

She caught the eye of a SOCO and waved them over. The mask was pulled down to reveal a tired middle-aged face not unlike Frank Reilly's. It was strange how all white men of a certain age seemed to have the same look about them. She held up her badge and forced what she hoped looked like a genuine smile.

'DS Delmar, Halesworth CID.' The words sounded odd as she said them. It might have been partly the fact that it was a Sunday evening at work and she had an empty flat to go back to, but she definitely wasn't feeling herself. All she wanted was to go home, fall asleep and wake up to a new clean slate where Hannah Lloyd was planning her birthday celebration, where they all still had chances.

'Pete Knowles. How can I help?' Raised eyebrows from the white suit. The expectation of a response, when all she wanted was for him to start talking. She needed to elicit some sort of report on the state of things if he wasn't going to volunteer any facts.

'I didn't get a chance to ask the boss on his way out. What's your overall assessment of this one?'

The white suit stared ahead into the middle distance while the brain computed the question and produced an answer. 'A lunch party, then some subsequent interference with the scene, possibly innocent, possibly in an attempt to confuse things. Hard to tell at this point if that was the assailant or a subsequent visitor. We need to check the blood we've found is Hannah's, but there's surprisingly little spatter for what could be an attempted murder.' He indicated a small shadow on the back of a chair and another on the wall by the French windows. 'The majority was found here on the floor and some spots going towards the doors.' He pointed at the numbered yellow plastic markers that led from the middle of the room to the balcony.

'Did he clean up? Or she?'

'Possibly, but we'd usually see evidence of that, and it would be odd to clean up so scrupulously, yet leave obvious traces of blood as well. There are prints on the outside of the glass barrier on the balcony, consistent with someone trying to stop themselves falling.'

Ronnie blinked away the vision of Hannah being forced over the edge at knifepoint. 'I see. Anything else?'

'The other issue is that the knife had been moved by the time we turned up. Presumably by the victim's husband seeing as he had access to the scene before we got here. That's not clear yet but we should know very soon. So, if you'll excuse me...'

As he edged away to rejoin the crew of investigators, Ronnie tried to piece together the puzzle, but there were too many anomalies, and they'd hardly even started. Knowles was right, the spatter was minimal but obvious, and yet Adam not only hadn't mentioned seeing the blood on the floor, but presumably had picked up the knife as well and hadn't bothered to remember that either.

Baz read her mind as they peeled off their suits in the hallway. 'You're thinking Adam was either incredibly unobservant or in a different apartment entirely.'

'Dead right. He must have picked up the knife to move it, and how could he not have noticed the blood on it?'

'I suppose he was preoccupied, having just found his wife on the tarmac.'

Ronnie noted what she took to be the taking of sides, and picked her words carefully. 'Surely he should have been even more on the look-out for something that might give a clue as to how she ended up there?'

Baz looked uncomfortable. 'Some people just don't notice stuff. They only see what they want to see, or they see things but it doesn't register properly.'

'But this guy's a solicitor. They're paid to notice stuff. Whose team are you on, Baz?' She regretted it as soon as she said it, but the accusation didn't seem to bother him in the slightest.

'I know what you're thinking, but I'm just making sure we're seeing all sides of the story. Talking of which...' He pulled his phone out and flicked through his notifications. 'There's a missing link in this particular mystery, and he's being brought into the station tomorrow morning.'

'A missing link?' Baz had a habit of talking in riddles but today it was annoying her more than usual. She took a slow breath in and out to bring some calm back. 'You must mean Max.'

'Yep. Thought you'd want to hear what the boy has to say. He's staying at the aunt and uncle's tonight, then Adam's bringing him in before school.'

'Well, let's hope Daddy and Auntie Meghan haven't spent too much time practising his lines with him.' Ronnie checked her phone. It was time to call it a night. 'Now where's that lift?'

CHAPTER SEVEN

Max Lloyd First Account

It was me that picked the knife up off the floor while Dad was shutting the doors to the balcony. It had started raining but when he shut the doors it was all quiet which was much better. It was a normal kitchen knife, the one you cut up potatoes with, or a cake, but it shouldn't have been on the floor so I picked it up in case someone stepped on it. Then I saw red on it. I thought ketchup, then I remembered Mum hates ketchup. Says it's full of sugar and bad stuff. But before I could say anything, Dad turned round and saw me holding it in my hand. He looked properly terrified, like I was going to murder him or something, and then his face went all calm again and he took it off me and put it up on a high shelf.

I wanted to go to the hospital as soon as Dad told me what had happened, but he said we had to get me something to eat, then he got angry because Mum had no sandwich food in the house. He can be a bit scary when he's angry so I tried to help and found the cheese that doesn't look like cheese because Mum wraps it up in this special re-usable plastic. I wasn't hungry but I took the weird cheese sandwich and put some stuff in a rucksack so I'd have something to do while we were waiting. Then we were about to go when there was lots of knocking on the door and some policemen came in shouting questions about who we were and what we were doing there. They said it was a crime scene and that Dad shouldn't be interfering but he shouted back at them asking what was he supposed to do and saying that he had no idea. One of the policemen said he had to make a statement and then he stormed out so I just followed him with my bag.

Dad didn't speak the whole way to the hospital but that was fine by me. I can play Minecraft on the iPad and that always makes time go faster. This time it helped me stop thinking about the knife and worrying about Mum. Then Dad was cross about the hospital car park because it was full of cars driving round really slowly, then reversing as well sometimes to let someone out of a space. He was thumping the dashboard and at one point he wound down his window to shout at someone, then closed it again as if he'd changed his mind.

I wasn't allowed in to see Mum straightaway. A nurse with ginger hair offered me squash in a plastic cup and asked me questions as if I was three years old or something but I just showed her I was fine with my videogames so she let me get on with it. When Dad came out of the Intensive Care ward, he looked as if he'd had some really bad news. Like Mum does when she's been talking to her friend Delilah on the phone. It doesn't happen much now because Delilah isn't her best friend anymore, Mum says. She won't say why but usually when someone says that it's because the other person has done something wrong. Maybe Delilah said something bad about her on social media. Mum's always on Twitter and Instagram. She says it's for her business. She has to keep tweeting and showing pictures of herself in yoga poses. Then sometimes she gets bad comments from people but she doesn't get upset. She says they're just jealous because she's so lucky to have a lovely boy like me. But those Instagram people don't know about me, so that can't be true. Except Delilah. She knows, and she doesn't have any children. Maybe she's jealous of Mum. I'd never thought about that before.

When they let me into the room I couldn't speak for a minute. All the adults were looking at me which made it even worse. There were computer screens beeping and tubes everywhere, one going into her mouth, lots of others coming down from plastic bags stuck to a pole and disappearing under the blankets where her arm was. Mum had her eyes closed and looked as if she was dead except for the breathing sounds. The nurse said something about calling us back as soon as Mum woke up and Dad seemed to be happy with that so we left. Dad was cross again about the cost of the parking, but I thought the hospital deserved the money if they were going to look after Mum with all those tubes.

He dropped me with Auntie Meghan after that because he had to go and give a statement to the police. He said it wouldn't be long but it felt like ages. Auntie Meghan kept trying to make me eat stuff but I wasn't hungry after the weird sandwich. She said I mustn't worry and Mum would be fine, but she didn't look as if she believed herself. Uncle James asked if I wanted to watch a film with him but I said no thank you. I just wanted to sit on my own until Dad came back. Uncle James was pacing up and down the hall for ages and Auntie Meghan was trying to calm him down but he told her to just leave him alone. He must have felt like I did.

I'm not sure what went wrong with Mum and Dad. I know she used to have the same job as him. I went to after school club every day and sometimes stayed with Giselle if they were working really late. I was glad when she left being a lawyer to do the yoga stuff. She even picked me up from school so I didn't have to go to the club anymore.

But at the same time, when I was in year two, Dad was there less and less. He was coming back smelling of beer and sometimes not coming back at all, which made Mum cry a lot. And then just before my birthday when I was going to be eight, Granny died. I didn't actually like Granny very much but she always gave me nice birthday presents. The rest of the time she said lots of mean things about people. Mum was always trying to make her happy but it didn't work. When she died, Mum said it was like all the chances to make her happy were gone, and now what could she do? She said she didn't want the money from an unhappy person but she had found some children in India who needed clothes and food and wanted to give it to them. I felt sad for the children but a bit sad for me too because there are lots of things I need and she says they cost too much money. We could have used the Granny money for them. I don't mind where the money comes from if I can get an iPad of my own just like Dad's. Dad asked me to find out how much money Granny left, but Mum wouldn't tell me. She said I bet you're asking because Dad told you to and it's none of his business.

Dad was trying to be a politician. He started living in a flat which he said was for when he had to work late on the election campaign, but Mum said he was just trying to leave us without us noticing. One time she went up to see him at the flat as a surprise. I went on a sleepover with Ben from school, but she rang up even before we'd gone to bed to say she was back and could she come and pick me up. I asked Ben's mum to tell her I was already asleep but she put me on the phone so I had to tell her not to myself. Mum said it looked like she was right that Dad had other plans for his life, and that I shouldn't expect to see much of him anymore. I was awake all night worrying about it but when she came to collect me from school the next day, she was all smiley again and told me not to worry and that everything would turn out fine.

Since then, Dad takes me out at weekends, to football and then for an ice cream as well if he has time. Sometimes I stay over at his flat, but even when he's there he's always working on his computer or talking on his phone. He always has it on speaker so he can do other things at the same time, but it means I have to shut the door if I'm trying to watch TV. I do look forward to seeing Dad but at the same time I miss when we were all together. They say they're not getting divorced but Ben told me they're only saying that not to upset me.

I don't understand what happened to make Mum fall off the balcony. She always tells me not to climb up on the railings. Do they think someone pushed her? The only person I've ever seen push her before is Dad. Only once. He said he'd never do it again.

CHAPTER EIGHT

The station was quiet for a Monday morning. October half-term meant that a few of the officers were on childcare duty, and Ronnie took a peculiar delight in crossing her name off the list that was doing the rounds of the office. 'No time off for me. Kids are old enough to look after themselves this year.' It felt strangely liberating to be free to work whatever hours she chose. The Ocado app remained untouched, the shoe rack in the hall kept hold of its contents and phone chargers stayed where she put them.

The flip side of the peace and quiet at work was the fact that there was more going on for the remaining staff, so she and Baz had their work cut out if they were going to make any progress with the Lloyd case, let alone make sufficient headway to discourage DCI intervention, should things take a more serious turn. She took a seat at an empty desk and picked up a pen and paper. Foremost in her thoughts was little Max, the eight-year-old caught up in what might end up as a murder enquiry, now back living with his father, but the question *for how much longer?* was already on Ronnie's mind. If Adam was arrested and charged with Hannah's murder at any point, then Max would be on social services' radar in no time, unless the aunt and uncle were happy to take him on, and even then, they'd have to be cleared from the list of suspects before anything could be put in place. Max's interview was a textbook success. With very little prompting, he had spoken for several minutes and given them more detail than any of the others so far. His testimony, especially his keen observation of the relationships going on around him, had already pushed all the characters in the drama onto the main stage. She should be grateful, but it just gave her more information to wade through.

Her phone buzzed with a text. Baz was on his way up to the office and he'd just heard back from the lab. That was all. No doubt he wanted to tell her the details face to face. Seconds later, the office door opened and swung shut behind him. His expression was uneasy. Things obviously weren't as cut and dried as he'd have liked. A second later the door opened again and Jen Connolly slipped into the room behind him, clutching a file and a notebook.

'Mind if I join you?' She shut the door quietly. 'I've been going through Hannah's last movements.'

Ronnie had forgotten how soft and quiet her voice was, a real asset when it came to calming down a tricky situation, or even a heated debate in the office. She had been a popular addition to the team, fresh-faced and devoid of artifice, beautiful in what Ronnie thought of as an old-fashioned way, wavy brown hair scraped back in a chignon, shirt buttons done up to the top. 'Of course, Jen, come in.' She pulled out two chairs for them both.

'Baz, let's hear it. What have you got?'

'It's not the best news,' he began, taking a breath and holding it visibly.

Ronnie wondered what the best news could be – perhaps Hannah making a sudden recovery, having fallen rather than been attacked, or the blood on the knife turning out to be stage blood used in Hannah's birthday am-dram production of *Macbeth*? There weren't many happy endings that she could imagine from what they had so far.

'It's Hannah's blood on the knife.'

'No surprises there.'

'And we found Adam and Max's fingerprints on it, as well as Hannah's.' He sat down heavily and spun his chair to face her.

'That's to be expected. We know they both handled it, and I bet Adam's shoe fits the print in the blood on the floor.'

'That's all correct, sarge.'

'You sound as if there's more to come.' She was used to Baz using dramatic build-up to his revelations – a habit she found varyingly endearing and frustrating. Today for no reason that she could put her finger on, it was more the latter.

'There is more. This is the bit I don't like, if I'm honest. There were other prints on the knife from outside the family. There's Delilah's – we have hers on file from the interview and two other sets of prints which we have yet to identify.'

Ronnie thought for a second. 'Didn't Delilah say they all cut themselves a slice of cake? So they could belong to the other women at the house that day – Ali from Hannah's yoga class and her sister-in-law Meghan Garrett.'

'And one of them is currently on the other side of the world...'

'I think if we get Meghan and the three of them to confirm they all used it then we can work on the assumption the last set of prints is Ali. What about Giselle, anything on her?'

'No trace of her in the flat at all so far.'

Ronnie let the information sink in and thought aloud. 'So we have six suspects.'

'It would seem that way.'

'Jen, any more on Hannah's recent movements?'

Jen opened her notebook. 'No deviation from her routine until yesterday. CCTV of her going to all her usual classes, we have ANPR data showing her doing the school run and her diary mentions some appointments on the Saturday.'

'Can we speak to the people she met at those appointments?'

'Done that. Turns out it was a possible new venue for the yoga classes. A studio in West Dean that's just opened. They said she was very keen. Apparently there are hardly any places available for hire with the right feng shui or something. Hannah was going on about that a fair bit.'

'Nothing wrong with a bit of good energy. What about the others?'

'There were just the initials FC and a question

mark. Not sure if it's relevant, or what it stands for.'

'Football Club?'

Baz scratched his head. 'Yoga at a football club? That's hard to picture. But before you ask, no I don't have any better ideas.'

'Where are we with Hannah's phone and iPad? Are they taking it apart for leads? Can we get more insight from those into her friendships with the other women, and her relationship with her husband?'

Jen turned the page of her notebook. 'The tech team are on it now, but nothing so far. She was very active on social media, seemed to have a bit of a following for her online classes, not all of it the kind of following you'd want.'

'How do you mean?' Ronnie's mind flashed back to little Max talking about the Instagram posts. 'Threats of any kind?'

'Still trawling through her feeds but not sure we're going to get sight of the stories and reels because they self-destruct after twenty-four hours and aren't in her archive, whatever that means. Don't use those platforms myself.'

'Strangely enough, having teenagers in my house I am familiar with the workings of these apps, so yes, it makes sense. Let me know when Harry's done his magic. I'd like to take a look at it myself, to get a better picture of Hannah, even if some of the detail is missing.'

'I'll get them to call you as soon as they're done with it. And I'll get back to you asap on the CCTV at Mulberry Court. Lots of comings and goings, and uniform are just trying to match the very blurry images with the residents in the building. So asap might mean tomorrow.' She stood and pushed her chair back into the corner where it had come from, closing the door quietly behind her as she left. Ronnie suppressed a smile. She didn't remember Baz ever doing that. Was it a female thing, always tidying up after yourself, not making too much noise, or was that a sexist observation?

'So, Baz, any joy getting hold of Meghan?'

He straightened up and smiled. Good news was coming. 'She's actually downstairs waiting for us.'

'What? That was quick work.' Ronnie looked at him quizzically. He really was firing on all cylinders today. 'How did you manage that?'

'She couldn't wait. Turned up last night apparently saying she wanted to talk about what had happened. Front desk made the appointment, so bingo – half our work is done, which is a bonus given the absenteeism round here.'

'Desperate to clear her name or point the finger, I wonder?' Ronnie sat back and clicked her pen. It was unusual for a witness to beg to be interviewed, but perhaps Meghan had her reasons.

'Or neither.' Baz wasn't going to be pushed into assumptions. 'What did you think about Max?'

Ronnie flipped open the file of interview notes. 'He shone a bit more light on things. I felt sorry for him, watching his parents' relationship sour in front of his eyes. I do feel some bizarre curiosity about how and why it went the way it did. Nobody's explained that yet.'

Baz cocked his head. 'It's not unusual though, is it? Kids are always witnessing horrible break-ups.'

Ronnie felt the heat of embarrassment and a rush of defensiveness in its wake. She'd become so accustomed to single parenthood that she'd almost forgotten what had come before the dividing of assets and the decree absolute landing on the doormat. Tempers had raged, doors had slammed, harsh words had been spoken without any regard for the thinness of walls and the sharpness of children's hearing. She didn't need to justify it, but the temptation was too strong to resist.

'You're right, the kids are always the ones who suffer the most, but at least in our family the twins had each other, and they were almost fourteen at the time. This is different, I'd say.'

It was Baz's turn to be embarrassed. 'I'm sorry, sarge. I didn't mean it like that. I was just thinking that what the boy had to go through is normal these days. Marriages fail. That's why Amber and I aren't rushing into tying the knot before Nebuchadnezzar is born.'

'Before *who* is born?' She was used to Baz's unusual turn of phrase but this was a first.

'Aha, so I wanted to give him or her a name before the real one is agreed, and, well, that's got to be a unique choice. What's so weird?'

'Nothing at all. It's cute.' She hesitated. 'How is the pregnancy going? I mean, after last time, she needs to take it easy. Plenty of rest.'

'Thanks, doc.' He half-smiled, clearly relieved the tension between them had evaporated.

'And make sure you don't take your work home with you. That's an order.' An order with a heavy dose of hypocrisy, she thought. There weren't many days in her career that she hadn't done that, not only taken work home but let it keep her up at night and send her on the odd adventure of her own, not always entirely within the remit of her job.

'I will try my hardest not to do that. The miscarriage was a nightmare, but this pregnancy seems to be different, and we're further down the line than the first time so I'm feeling positive.'

Ronnie allowed herself a genuine smile. It was a stark reminder that there was life outside work, and life and death hung in the balance outside these walls as well as in the case file. 'Sorry for being bossy.' She stopped short of saying 'It's only because I care,' but it was time to climb out of the rut she had just dug for them. 'Now, talking of expectant mothers, let's get to our witness before she goes into labour.'

***

Meghan Garrett looked as if she was about to give birth any minute. She sank into the chair with a loud sigh and accepted a cup of tea from a uniformed officer whose eyes widened in alarm at the size of the bump. She just grinned up at him.

'Two sugars please. Baby needs the energy for all

the thrashing about she's doing. Only a couple of weeks more of this, thank goodness.'

Ronnie gave her a smile of sisterly acknowledgment of what she was going through as well as what was to come. 'So, in a second I'll start recording. You can take your time. There's no rush. Except...' She glanced downwards and Meghan giggled nervously.

'I'll be sure to get out of here in time for her arrival.'

Ronnie started the tape and dealt swiftly with the introductory admin, before leaning forward to speak. 'Please tell us all you have to say about the events of Sunday afternoon. We'd like to hear it in your own words, then we'll ask you some questions.' She leant back again. Meghan composed herself and Ronnie had the feeling this might be their most useful witness yet.

CHAPTER NINE

'My name is Meghan Garrett. I've been married to James, Hannah Lloyd's brother, for ten years and we have one five-year-old boy, Hugo. Hugo's soon to have a little sister, and I'm not sure what he's going to make of that. Anyway, we live just a short drive away from Hannah in West Dean so it's easy for me to pop round now I'm on maternity leave, and I have ended up seeing a lot of her over the past few weeks. It was Hannah's birthday on Saturday and she only wanted a small gathering, so it was me, Delilah and Ali Tremaine from the yoga class. We got through quite a lot of fizz – or at least Ali and Del did. And Hannah – who doesn't normally drink at all, so I was quite surprised. I mostly just stuffed my face with sushi and cake. We sang 'Happy Birthday' and Ali sang in harmony which was more like a whole other tune and quite put me off the melody if I'm honest. That girl is a bit OTT for me, but this isn't about her... There was a bang on the wall at some point. The neighbour thought we were being antisocially loud. I was quite relieved if it meant that Ali would calm down a bit. But a bit harsh on Hannah. It wasn't exactly a rave.'

'Giselle Gaillard,' Baz said under his breath. 'What's she got against Hannah?'.'

'Ali left first, saying she had a plane to catch.

Alright for some, jetting off to the sun at those inflated half-term prices, then it all kind of slowed down. I can't be doing with staying out too long in my condition.' She patted her swollen belly. 'No chair is comfy enough to sit in for more than five minutes, so I felt I'd done my bit after another few hours. We chatted about superficial stuff mainly. A bit of news stuff, outrage at the stories of migrants drowning in the Channel, dishonest politicians, which made Hannah squirm a bit because Adam has political aspirations, so it's only a matter of time before he goes bad. Then there was the chat about what series we're watching on Netflix. You know the sort of thing. Once you get into that and everyone starts recommending stuff and saying 'Oh my god I can't believe you haven't seen this or that latest thriller', then you can't wait to get back home and switch the telly on. Screen FOMO. Is that a thing?'

Ronnie smiled to herself. Meghan was a tell-it-like-it-is woman. The best kind, but she was running out of steam. She was struggling to get comfortable in the plastic chair, the grimace on her face saying everything for her.

'Are you OK to continue? Shall I ask someone to get you a cushion?' Ronnie doubted whether such a thing existed in the building but Meghan shook her head.

'No, I'll be fine if we can get this done quickly.'

'You were saying. You left at what time?'

'Ten past four. I remember checking my phone and being surprised I'd been there so long. I went home, put my dressing gown on and put my feet up and James brought me a cup of tea. He said he'd do dinner and I said I wasn't hungry but managed to eat half a horse anyway. Still...' She stroked her stomach again and smiled. 'Not much longer thank goodness. Normality will return very soon. Then we got the call from the police. A bit of a shock, obviously.' She looked from Ronnie to Baz and back again. 'That's it. Over to you guys for the quiz now.'

Ronnie began uncertainly, slightly wrong-footed by Meghan's mastery of the handover.

'I hear Ali brought a cake. Did Hannah cut it and make a wish?' She tried to make the question seem as irrelevant as possible but only succeeded in sounding sarcastic. Meghan frowned and looked up and to the right, perhaps in demonstration of the dubious theory that correlated eye movement with truth-telling. Most people Ronnie interviewed seemed to flick theirs in all directions, as if hoping to hit the right one eventually, or mask a mistaken glance in the lying direction with a concerted look the other way.

'I don't remember who cut the first slice. Hannah, I presume. It was chocolate and salted caramel. My absolute favourite, which is a shame because I've got to stop over-feeding baby or we'll both be on a diet for the rest of our lives. I spend my whole time sitting in peoples' kitchens inhaling calories in six-figure sums these days.'

'Did you handle the knife at all?' Baz was right to ask for clarification, but then Meghan reacted as Ronnie had suspected she might.

'Why, does that make me a suspect? Was she stabbed?' Her expression transformed from thoughtful to terrified. 'I did cut myself an extra slice. I knew it was a bad idea, but didn't realise quite how bad.'

Ronnie leaned forward, with what she hoped was a calming expression on her face. 'Don't worry, this interview is entirely voluntary. You can leave at any time. Are you OK to answer a few more questions?'

Meghan murmured a barely audible 'yes'.

'How would you describe Hannah's relationship with her husband?' Baz threw her a look as if to say she was being too forward, but Meghan answered without hesitation.

'Well, that's a tricky one. And that's really what's been bothering me and what made me come down to the station in the first place.'

'Go on.' Ronnie looked at Baz with her best *I told you so* expression.

'I'd been wondering for a while what was going on with the two of them. Hannah had said, in dribs and drabs during our chats over the last few weeks, that he'd become a lot moodier lately, staying at work late, business trips overnight. To me he was showing all the signs, although you don't want to say these things out loud. It was up to her to bring up the possibility.'

'Of what? That he was having an affair?'

Meghan made a face as though the word was too taboo, too distasteful to pronounce herself. 'Yes, if you like. I mean, it was up to her to come up with those actual words.'

'And did she?' interrupted Baz, suddenly interested.

'She seemed to be deliberately holding back. I knew she wouldn't be able to keep it a secret forever. Then the next thing you know he's moving out. A "trial separation", she said but we all know those aren't trials at all. I said they should try Relate. James and I did a few therapy sessions and found them very helpful.'

'I see.' Ronnie pondered the situation. 'So at that point, she hadn't mentioned actual infidelity of any kind.'

'Not as such. She just said things like *he can do what he likes, as long as he leaves me and Max out of it* and when I asked what kind of thing, she just said *oh you know, he's got these political ambitions, so that's where his focus is.*'

'So still no mention of another woman?'

'No, and that did surprise me. And that's the reason why I stayed later than the others on Sunday. To see if she'd be more open after a couple of drinks.'

Baz perked up again. 'So both of the other guests left before you? Are you saying you were the last to see Hannah alive?'

Meghan looked searchingly at Baz as if to assess his ability to take in what she was about to say. Ronnie recognised the look as the one Tilly would give her when asked how a party had gone. *Do you really want the truth?*

'Everyone left before me, but I wasn't the last to see her alive. That would be Delilah.'

Baz's eyes widened, then narrowed as he processed her words. 'She came back?'

Meghan nodded slowly, a small smile playing at the corners of her lips. 'I was leaving. Hannah had made it clear she didn't want to talk about Adam anymore, said he was bringing Max home in half an hour and she needed to tidy up and make dinner. So I took my cue to go. I took the lift because I can't manage stairs without passing out, and I'm not sure if you've been in the Mulberry Court lift but it's half glass on one side, so you have a partial view of the stairs as you go up and down. That's how I saw her, jogging up the stairs between the second and third floors. She looked as if she was in a hurry to me, but it was hard to tell as I was going down at some speed myself.'

Baz rubbed his eyes, then blinked them open and refocused as if in an attempt to shed new light on the thickening plot. 'How do you know it was Delilah you saw, if you were, as you say, going down at some speed?'

Meghan laughed again, but this time a different kind of laugh entirely. More of a cackle. 'Have you met Delilah? She's hardly one to sink into the background, disappear into a crowd. She's unmistakeable. Look at her hair for a start. It's got to be a wig.'

Ronnie hadn't had Meghan down as the jealous type. 'How do you two get on?'

Meghan flinched at the question, then seemed to bring herself back to the room. 'Me and Delilah. Oh, we get on fine, as far as we have to, but we don't meet that often, so I suppose you could say the friendship hasn't been truly tested. And I don't mean to be bitchy, just saying she's easy to recognise even from a fleeting glance, and I wouldn't cross the road to talk to her. You know what the song's about, don't you?'

Baz pricked up his ears, spotting his chance. 'Ah yes, the song. What's it about?'

'A husband who comes home and finds his wife cheating on him, so he stabs her.' Meghan let the smile spread. 'I mean, why name your daughter after someone with that kind of a reputation? And then there's Samson and Delilah. She's no better.'

'Thank you, Meghan. I'm sure we all have namesakes with colourful pasts. Shall we get back to the matter in hand?' Ronnie made a note on the pad in front of her to come back to that relationship when the heat had dissipated. Meanwhile, she wanted to know more about Meghan's background with Hannah, and her role as sister-in-law.

'Your husband James and Hannah weren't speaking. Is that right?'

Meghan looked up, startled. 'Who told you that?'

Ronnie glanced at Baz. 'Is that not true, then?'

She shifted in her seat. 'It's not that they don't speak, it's just that there was a bit of a falling out when their mother passed away last year.'

'What kind of falling out? Over an inheritance, by any chance?'

Meghan's eyes narrowed. 'Yes, something to do with that, but it wasn't anything that was going to last. Anyone would feel affronted at being excluded from a parent's will.'

Ronnie raised her eyebrows. 'I see. Well yes of course, that's understandable. Not something I could contemplate doing, without a very good reason.'

'There is no reason at all, in the *world*, to exclude your own child from your will!' Meghan exploded, then immediately pursed her lips as if regretting her words. Ronnie let her stew for a moment before asking her next question.

'And probate, presumably all done and dusted?'

'How would I know?' she snapped. 'Hannah was sole executor and sole beneficiary. Prosecutor, judge and jury. I'd say ask her that question, but you might struggle to do that for a while.'

Baz smiled at her references to the legal world and leaned forward to interject. 'These things can take years to sort out, so it may well be that there were pensions or suchlike that hadn't been assigned to their beneficiaries. Not everything goes through the will.' Then, perhaps feeling the hardness of Meghan's gaze, he added, 'But that will become clear in due course, I'm sure.'

Ronnie looked at Baz who motioned for her to continue. The next question had been a long time in the build-up, and hopefully their conversation about inheritance had been enough of a distraction to clear the decks for it. She made sure she had Meghan's attention, then spoke slowly and deliberately, watching the effect of her words.

'Going back to Delilah – when it comes to her

relationship with the family, did it ever cross your mind that it was *her* having an affair with Adam?'

Silence filled the room for too long than was comfortable. Ronnie held her nerve. *Pause and pounce*, Frank Reilly had told her on the day of her first witness interview, and since that day, she'd never been afraid of waiting as long as it took for an answer to a question. It was a battle of wills. Eventually, Meghan re-composed herself before clearing her throat and making her final pronouncement. She gave a slight flick of her neatly coiffed hair as she said it, reminding Ronnie of a dressage horse prancing out of the ring. 'It didn't just cross my mind. I was convinced of it. But I've been convinced of other things that have turned out to be wrong. Haven't we all?'

Ronnie met her gaze, sat back to let the words sink in. Meghan had just summed up the life of a detective in a nutshell.

'Absolutely we have.' She shuffled her pages and scraped her chair back from the table, indicating the end of the interview. 'Thank you, Meghan, you've been very helpful.'

CHAPTER TEN

Back at her desk, Ronnie scribbled notes with her phone clamped to her ear. 'That's very helpful. We'll be in touch if we need anything more from you.' She ended the call just as Baz appeared, waving his notepad and smiling a half smile that said *I have news*. He leant against the partition wall with an air of confidence that filled her with hope.

'So the medics and forensics are now in agreement that it was the same knife that wounded Hannah. The blade is consistent with the injury.'

'Okay, that's good, I think. At least there's one part of the story that fits together.' She swivelled her chair in a full circle, coming to a halt with a heavy sigh.

'You sound beaten. I feel we're getting somewhere.'

She sat up straighter. Beaten wasn't good. Beaten sounded like losing. 'I'd say it's more that we're getting to *too many* places and that's what I'm worried about. There are just too many leads here.'

'You mean after listening to Meghan?' Baz sat down and steepled his fingers under his chin. 'She did seem furious on his behalf about the inheritance, or lack of.'

'And that's a pretty big motivator if you're broke and about to have another baby. So yes, it does rather bring her into the mix, and pointing the finger at Delilah wasn't exactly subtle. Clumsy I'd say. Panicky.'

'Agreed. Is it enough to get a warrant to search her house? There could be clothing, traces of Hannah's blood in the house, or in the car? How about the husband? Just as likely to be him, if not more likely, and sending the wife in as a willing witness is always a good tactic if you want time to get your story straight.'

Ronnie raised a finger to interrupt his flow. 'Jen's getting him in now. But meanwhile, something else has just come in. About Adam. We're going to have to get him back in, soon as, under caution.'

Baz's confidence gave way to confusion in a nanosecond. 'I thought he was no more under suspicion than any of the others with prints on the knife, surely? They've all made their mark, just waiting for the one who flew off to the tropics.'

'They were all pretty much neck and neck until ten minutes ago. But our Adam just got himself a head start.'

'But the timing doesn't fit for him to be at the flat. You're not making this about his relationship with Delilah are you? I mean we have no proof of it for a start, and if we did it might be relevant, but circumstantial, surely? Not a motive in itself.'

'Indeed, but it's a motive nonetheless.'

Baz interrupted before she could go on. 'That would give Delilah the same motive, assuming there was something going on between them. And Delilah wins hands down on opportunity. Last to leave, according to

Meghan. Sneaking back to Hannah's flat. She's got to be our prime suspect.'

Ronnie nodded, waiting for a break in the flow, and at the same time acutely aware she was adopting Baz's irritating habit of letting the facts dribble out at a frustratingly slow pace.

'Actually she doesn't. Win hands down, as you put it. Even if Meghan is right, and she saw Delilah from the lift, it turns out Adam had just as much opportunity as she did.'

'Opportunity? How would he have time between the last party guest leaving and collecting Max from football?'

'Well, firstly you're *assuming* he collected Max at 4.30.'

Baz shook his head. 'I don't follow. That's when it finished, isn't it?'

'But it's not when he arrived to collect him. I just spoke to the coach, if you can call him that. Sounded more like one of my son's schoolfriends. Anyway, apparently Adam was ten minutes late arriving, which, given that he was supposedly at his West Dean flat earlier in the day, and since the lane closure he spoke about only affects the traffic coming *back* from the football club to Mulberry Court, means he had at least a twenty-minute window of opportunity.'

Baz took a long breath. 'So he goes in there, does the business, frames the lot of them. I didn't see that coming.'

'Nor did I.'

'The timing's too tight, surely?'

Ronnie twiddled the pen in her fingers. He had a point. It would have to have been a slick operation. 'Yes, it's tight, but possible. We'll know more when we get clarification from the CCTV. Should be able to eliminate Adam that way. But until then I think we have to keep him at the front of our minds.'

'What about his motive?' Baz looked around the room as if in search of an escape route. 'I mean, he's possibly not the most faithful of husbands, but we don't have actual proof, do we?'

'On its own, no, you're right.'

'What else is there?'

'They're still married, wherever he happens to call home. She dies, there's every chance he will inherit.'

'Unless she's changed her will.'

'Nothing was found relating to a will at the flat. If she died intestate, husband gets the lot.'

'OK, but since we're not sure about the terms of any will, or about exactly how much she's worth, can we make that presumption? There was an inheritance, yes, but she could have spent it for all we know, donated it to the needy of Calcutta. Wasn't that what Max was upset about?'

'Absolutely, we don't know that yet. We're looking at her bank accounts now. But there's more. The reason Adam Lloyd might well want to get rid of his wife was that she knew exactly what he was up to and was about to blow his affair with Delilah out of the water.'

Baz folded his arms defensively. 'How do you

know?'

'It's all on here.' She leaned down and plucked an evidence bag from the box by her desk. 'Harry's team came back, found nothing as Jen said, the reels and stories have evaporated into the ether. But then we did a little digging together.'

Baz looked lost for words. Ronnie pulled on a pair of gloves, extracted the phone and scrolled down the screen. 'Easily forgotten, but this is where the best secrets are kept.' She held the phone out towards him.

Baz leaned over to look and let out a moan of defeat. 'Drafts? I'd never have thought to look. Never use them myself.'

Ronnie paused mid-scroll. 'Here it is, deep down inside the folder nobody looks at. The messages you start writing then change your mind. Mostly they're just the beginning of a message to someone who then gets back to you, so your words are superseded by another conversation. Or you change your mind about sending it.'

'Surely it should still have been spotted?'

'No title, no addressee, wouldn't come up on a search of the phone for Adam's name because she doesn't mention his name in it at all. See for yourself.' She slid the phone over to him across the desk.

'But are you suggesting she actually sent it in the end? In which case it should be in the sent folder, and if she didn't, then how does that give Adam reason to get rid of her?'

Ronnie was ready for the question. 'She may have

sent it by other means. She could have used another email address we don't know about, sent it anonymously, or sent it from here and deleted it from deleted items. She might have told him face to face. This could have been her attempt at writing the speech. She could have said it all to him on the phone, written a letter even. There's only so far you can dig. The important thing is we know she knew.'

Ronnie scrolled to the end of the message. It was the rantings of a woman scorned.

'So, we assume she's seen him with someone else and she was never going to forgive him.' Baz zoomed in on the last words and recited them aloud.

I haven't decided what to do or who to tell yet, but I can imagine it wouldn't go down well at party HQ.

'So what do we do with this?' His voice was almost a whisper. 'I mean, it's a threat. We don't know if he even got to know about it. But if he did, then I suppose...'

'We can search Adam's flat. That's the quickest way to get into Adam's phone and laptop. He might have cleaned up the hard drive, but there's a small chance we'll find something he's forgotten to delete.'

'I'll get Overton on the warrant for that.' His tone was resigned.

'There's one more thing, Baz. I want to go back to Mulberry Court.'

'Pete Knowles was the guy we met there. I'll give him a call to sort out another recce.' He glanced at the time on his phone. 'But won't they have finished by now?'

Ronnie tapped her pen. 'You're probably right. I'll try the crime scene manager. Turns out he's an old friend from way back, lost his daughter when she was the same age as mine – left a nightclub one night and was never seen again. He's seen the worst of life, which may be why there's more of a human side to him than that Knowles guy. I'll find out if he'll come down and talk me through how he thinks it all happened, blow by blow. I need the scene in my head so I can see if Adam fits into it. Then we go to see the man himself with the full picture of how *and* why he attacked his wife.'

***

Frank was waiting at the main entrance to Hannah's block when Ronnie pulled up in her Audi. He walked towards her as she climbed out of the driver's seat, all smiles.

'Ronnie! What a delight to see you again so soon. I am honoured you chose me.'

Ronnie beamed. 'I know I could have asked Knowles and saved you the trip but he's a bit tricky, don't you think? Probably superb at his job, just no bedside manner.'

'I know what you mean.' He stood aside to let her lead the way. 'But it's pretty rare to get the perfect mixture of the two in a job like this one.'

'Fair enough. Oh, and thanks for getting my name right. Not sure I want my past coming back to haunt me.'

Frank laughed. 'As long as it's just your name you want to keep under wraps. We can't be doing with any more police scandals.'

'I wish I could laugh at that, but you're right. Thankfully not too many skeletons in my cupboard.' She pressed the door code and held it open for him. 'Thanks for coming down here at short notice. Shall we?'

Hannah's flat looked much the same as it had done the previous day, minus the white suits and evidence bags. Frank opened the balcony doors and a rush of cold air chilled the room. Autumn was well under way and fighting a losing battle with the first inklings of winter. Didn't Adam Lloyd mention noisy air conditioning in his car? A shadow of doubt crossed Ronnie's mind again. Another detail that didn't sit well with the rest of it. The sooner they could search his flat, the better.

As Frank pulled back the drapes Ronnie sent a message to Overton to make sure the warrant was his first priority, then let out a breath she didn't know she'd been holding. It was happening more and more these past few weeks. The slightest whisper of stress and her body and mind went into fight or flight mode – muscles tensing, mind racing for an answer that inevitably eluded her until she stopped chasing it. When it happened in the middle of the night, she would end up lying awake for hours, mentally combing through every area of her life to examine the source of the anxiety, and often fell back to sleep from sheer exhaustion. It was time to see a doctor about it, but this wasn't the week to ask for a morning off. If things escalated, she'd need to be firing on all cylinders. A decent bottle of red wine and a Netflix mini-series would be her medicine until the case was solved.

Frank's chirpy voice roused her from her thoughts. 'Ronnie? Something on your mind? You've gone all distant.'

'No, it's nothing. Just a random thought that can go back in its box. Ignore me.'

'I didn't get a chance to ask you yesterday, had to dash off to another job. How's your legend of a mother? I bet she still misses Fred. I know I do.'

Ronnie felt her shoulders relax.

'I'm sure she does, but she keeps it to herself most of the time.'

'Course she does. She's a diamond, your mum. Nothing can break her.'

Frank had been the best of family friends before he'd been a colleague. He and her father would spend weekends fishing off the Kent coast, coming back with stories of near misses and mercy releases to explain their empty handedness. Years later, he'd been one of the key figures in Ronnie's journey into policing, introducing her to the idea of going into the force in the first place, then playing the role of stalwart cheerleader through thick and thin, her man on the inside, her promoter. When Fred Delmar went missing at sea, Frank was the first on the scene, playing the role not only of investigator but family supporter and campaigner for the search for Fred's body to be extended and sustained beyond what was deemed an acceptable amount of time.

'Mum's moved over this way now, distracting herself with the grandkids, you know. Spending a fair bit of time down in Sussex at the moment though going through decades of memorabilia in the attic before putting the house on the market. We'll miss that place so much. The twins used to love it down there.'

'They must be grown up by now, those two.'

'Almost eighteen, although they don't act like it most of the time. Tilly's alternately lovestruck and heartbroken, Eddie's too interested in gaming for my comfort, but they are amazing human beings. It hasn't been easy doing the single parent thing, but I've had Mum and Serena on hand for emergencies...' She hesitated. 'Sorry, Frank. I totally forgot. They never found Jessica, did they?'

Frank shook his head. 'Don't you worry. Long ago now, and I know you know how it feels, what with your dad and everything. They never found Jess, but then you never lose hope, do you? Hope is a duplicitous friend – a lifeline and a torture all at once.'

Ronnie stared out of the window at the gathering clouds. More rain was on its way. 'Do you still think she'll come back?' It was the clumsiest, most cack-handed of questions, but it was out there, and again, Frank didn't seem to mind.

'Well if I'm really honest, Ronnie, I don't think

she's coming back.' He let out a long sigh. 'And coming to live down here was some sort of attempt to stop living in the past. I got divorced, then got married again to a lovely lady I met online called Helen. You must meet her one day.' His expression clouded briefly, then brightened.

'So, I think you wanted to go through the motions, so to speak? It might take our minds off our own misfortune to focus on someone else's for a while. Shall I show you the way I think our victim met with her fate?'

On the scene with all the props to hand, the events seemed to make more logical sense. Frank demonstrated with the ease of an expert how, if Hannah was approached by her knife-wielding attacker somewhere in front of the balcony doorway, she could have then staggered backwards, making it easy enough for her assailant to give her that final push over the edge.

'I know they found her prints on the outside of the balcony glass. That will tell you if she tried to stop herself from falling. Rules out suicide at least.'

Ronnie pictured Hannah making a last grasp for safety and shook the thought away.

'Sorry,' Frank said, flatly. 'These things are never easy. Unfortunately we've got a real lack of shoe prints between the location of the assault and the balcony edge due to rainfall, and the husband's prints which were obvious and plentiful could easily have been left on his return to the flat after he'd found Hannah on the ground, so they just muddle the scene. What about you? Do you have a theory?'

'At the moment, too many of them,' said Ronnie, hands behind her head and eyes skyward in search of inspiration. 'And a handful of suspects, all of whom were here within an hour of the incident and whose prints are on the weapon.'

'All of them?' Frank steepled his index fingers, under his chin. 'That's a problem for you. What about motive? Do you think any of them wanted to hurt her?'

'We have a few ideas, but the husband is still number one on my list. We're getting a warrant to search his flat. We think we'll find some key evidence on his phone or laptop that might give him a considerable motive to hurt Hannah.'

'Husband is usually the first port of call. Makes sense. What about the other prints?'

'Looks as if the same knife they used to cut the cake was used in the attack, and all three women who were here used it to cut their own slice. Then we have a neighbour across the hallway, no prints, but motive – if you count petty jealousy, and opportunity.'

'Sounds like a good start to me. One man's petty jealousy is another's reason to kill. We never know how deep the waters run. So what's the plan?'

'Well, it's purely speculation on the boss's part for now, but there could be something there with this Giselle Gaillard.' Ronnie questioned for a second whether she could afford the time to download all the facts of the case when there was a flat to be searched and an interview to carry out, but it was helpful to organize her thoughts, and running over things with Baz wasn't going to achieve that until he stopped jumping to Adam Lloyd's defence. 'She was in her flat alone at the time. She and Hannah aren't exactly each other's biggest fans. Giselle thinks Hannah looks down on her, which may or may not be true, and there's been some trouble with drugs, so her son is in care until she gets clean, which she seems to be now. Adam made some reference to her having undesirable male visitors, but that could be a handyman, for all we know. She mentioned one of those in her own statement.'

Frank's eyebrows shimmied up his forehead. 'So what are you thinking motive-wise?'

'I don't know, but if Hannah knew she was using again, that could scupper Giselle's chances of getting her son back.'

'Murder sounds like an even quicker way of ensuring you never see your child again, I'd say, and do you know she was using again?'

'No evidence to suggest she is.' Ronnie glanced at the door to make sure they weren't being overheard. 'But most people would have a lot to lose if convicted of murder, not just her.' She pulled out her phone and read a message from Baz telling her they had Lydia's authority to go through Adam's flat. 'Looks like I'm needed elsewhere. We have a search to carry out. Thanks again for coming down here at short notice. I appreciate it.'

Frank had only just pressed the button for the lift when the neighbouring door opened to reveal the voluptuous and extraordinary figure of Giselle Gaillard.

Delilah was right. She was the image of Nell Gwynn, or Nancy in *Oliver Twist*. She seemed taken aback for a second, then looked Frank up and down appreciatively and turned to Ronnie. 'DS Delmar isn't it? I thought I heard something. You never know these days who might be lurking around outside.'

'You're absolutely right about that,' Ronnie said, distractedly. She'd expected a French accent, or at least hadn't expected south London glottal stops and missing 'g's on 'ing's.

'Terrible business,' she said, nodding at Hannah's front door. 'Any nearer to finding Hannah's murderer?'

'She's still alive, at this moment, so no murderer to find, but with any luck she'll be able to tell us herself who assaulted her at some point soon.' She studied her for a reaction but was met with a look of pure blankness. Presumably another frequenter of the Botox clinic. 'Remember to give us a call if there's anything else you remember, however irrelevant you might think it is. Anything at all.'

'I will, don't you worry.' The door slammed.

CHAPTER ELEVEN

Adam Lloyd made no attempt to hide his irritation at the sight of the police at his front door. A frown spread across his forehead and his eyelids flickered, as if to bat them away. He was taller than Ronnie had imagined, at least a decade older than his wife, greying at the temples and looking every inch the senior civil servant. It was another reminder that leaving interviewing to the DCs somehow left senior detectives at a disadvantage. The video recordings were never quite the same as seeing a witness in real life.

'What do you mean, a warrant? There's absolutely no justification for that.'

'I'm afraid the judge thought differently, Mr Lloyd.' Baz held up the stamped Magistrates' authorisation, while Ronnie walked past Adam into the hallway and looked around.

'It shouldn't take too long, sir, but we will need you to come back to the station with us for an interview under caution. And we should read you the caution right now just for good measure.'

As Baz recited his practised lines, Adam's face exploded with disbelief and anger, each battling for priority as his mouth dropped open and his hands went up first to his hips, then behind his head. 'What the...? It's no bloody wonder no-one has confidence in the police. Not only did I have no motive to try to kill Hannah, but I couldn't possibly have done it. You've seen me on the traffic cameras haven't you? I was on the... road with my son at the time it happened.'

Ronnie waited for him to finish before ushering him into the kitchen diner and motioning for him to sit. 'We have camera footage of your car en route from the sportsground to Mulberry Court at various points between 4.45 and 5.10.'

'Exactly, so how the hell could I have been at the flat?'

Baz leant over the worktop so Adam had no escape. 'Because you arrived late to collect Max.'

'Oh come on, a couple of minutes.'

'At least ten minutes according to the coach,' Baz said, checking his notes. 'With Hannah's accident timed at between four and five, there's every chance you could have been there after everyone else had left, and before you went to collect Max. The roadworks only affect the traffic in one direction. It would have been a fifteen-minute drive.'

'Have you seen my car on any cameras between Mulberry Court *to* the football club? You can't have, which means you have no evidence.'

'No, but we haven't seen it on the route from your flat to the club either. You must have taken the side roads, wherever you were coming from.' Baz was on a roll. Ronnie sat back and let him continue. It struck her that Adam was more comfortable being questioned by a man. He had no response to Baz's last question, and with that, she got to her feet and glanced around the room. The search wouldn't take long. Nothing on show on the pristine white worktops, and from what she could see through the half-open door, not much going on in the sitting room either. All the better for keeping the costs down.

'We have a couple of officers outside who are going to take a look around the flat while you talk to us down at the station.'

'What's wrong with here?'

Ronnie relished the question. If it was so inconvenient for him then he should have thought twice before lying to the police about his whereabouts and picking up the knife. 'Let me see, firstly we like to do things by the book as the public rightfully expects, we have access to the correct recording equipment, and you have the right to a solicitor, which we can arrange from there. Shall I go on?'

'I am a bloody solicitor. How many times...?'

Ronnie gave him a look she usually reserved for the twins when they used to claim they never learned anything at school and might as well stay at home, before reminding him that his speciality was not criminal law, and that it was in his best interests, not her own, for him to get all the help he could. 'Oh, and we need to look at your phone and your laptop as well.'

Adam got to his feet with a roar of dissent that Ronnie had already braced herself for. 'No! You have absolutely no right to take them off me. Confidential information. There's no way you're getting your hands on my laptop.'

Baz and Ronnie exchanged glances. The good thing about interviewing an experienced solicitor was that you could quote statute case law at them without fear of a blank face response and Baz did just that, reciting the section of PACE on police powers of seizure, like a lion licking his lips while his cornered prey paced up and down the kitchen, growling. The phone and laptop were slid into an evidence bag and Adam Lloyd allowed himself to be bundled into the back seat of the Ford Focus.

Less than an hour later, seated on a plastic grey chair opposite the two detectives in interview room one, Adam brought his fist down on the table with more force than was necessary every time they asked if he was absolutely sure he didn't want a solicitor.

'All I want is to just get this over with so I can get back to work.'

'Of course, Mr Lloyd, and you'll probably be wanting to go to the hospital as well.' Ronnie couldn't resist the taunt, but it did nothing to make her job easier. Adam looked up for long enough to glare at her before focusing back on the middle distance and saying nothing.

'So what is it you do exactly?' Ronnie took up her pen and fixed him with an expression of innocent curiosity. 'A lawyer, with aspirations to politics? Is that it?'

He eyed them both with distrust and made them wait a few seconds before he spoke. His tone was suddenly calmer, more composed. 'I'm a government lawyer, I work in the Home Office, as you know. We work from a central base in Surrey and support all the various areas of the department – immigration, anti-terrorism, Border Force, policing.' He gave Ronnie a half-smile that made her shudder inwardly.

'And the plan is what exactly, after this?'

'Well, as you probably know, civil servants can't run for parliamentary office, so I've handed in my notice with a view to making a career in politics.'

'So if you win the seat at the next election, it will be all change. New house, new school for Max, new everything?'

Adam threw Baz an exasperated look that failed to forge the bond of brotherly misogyny it was intended to, if Ronnie had read the signs right. Adam turned to her with another half-smile and folded his arms. His calm voice was still in charge, in sharp contrast to the look in his eyes which betrayed his inner fury. 'That's not how it works. I'd have a house in my constituency but I wouldn't live there full time. Nobody does. Too much upheaval for the family.'

Ronnie smiled back at him. 'I see. So the rest of the time you'd expect to continue living at Mulberry Court.'

What was left of the smile vanished from Adam's face. The answer was accompanied by another thud of fist on table. 'Yes. Where are you going with this?'

'The thing is, Mr Lloyd, as far as we understand it, you've already moved out of the family home, and it technically belongs to Hannah.' Ronnie's eyes were fixed on his face, but he wouldn't meet her gaze.

'Who is my wife. It's our home.'

She decided to leave exploring the various definitions of home for another time. If his home was somewhere he didn't actually live or own, that was a road she was happy to go down. 'Fair enough. And as you're still married, you'd stand to inherit it automatically if she died intestate... along with a small fortune she inherited from her mother last year.'

Adam jerked backwards but the chair, fixed to the floor, refused to budge, making him look as if he'd just had a collision on the dodgems. Once he'd settled, Ronnie tried a new angle.

'So you don't deny you've moved out?'

Adam shook his head, then mumbled a 'no' as Ronnie pointed to the tape.

'And you don't deny you'd stand to gain financially from Hannah's death?'

'No, but I have plenty of my own money. Why would I want hers?' His voice was raised again. It didn't take much to rile him. He was a marionette responding instantly to the tweak of a thread above his head. Ronnie sat back and folded her arms, determined to hold on to the power she had as his puppet master.

'I don't know, but people usually like having more money than they actually need, in my experience.' She left a few seconds gap for impact. 'And you have a son, whose education, if it's to be as good as yours...' She glanced down at the notes Baz had just slid towards her.

'Is going to cost an arm and a leg.' Baz finished her sentence with the perfect English idiom and looked suitably proud of himself.

Adam stared ahead at the wall, seemingly determined not to make eye-contact. He spoke through gritted teeth.

'You don't commit murder to pay school fees.'

Ronnie smiled at him. 'You'd be surprised.'

'And how do you know about the money?'

Ronnie turned to an earlier page in her notebook. Jen Connolly had checked Meghan's story with the Lloyds' family solicitor, so they were good to go on that one. Then there was the money itself. She hadn't seen the bank accounts. But they'd know soon enough, and Adam didn't need to know what information they had and what they were still awaiting. 'As we understand it, Hannah was the sole beneficiary of her mother's will, and it was a pretty sizeable estate.'

Adam blinked. 'That may be true, but I have no idea of the figures and I certainly never saw any of it. Max says she wanted to send it to some charity in India.' The disgust on his face was clear.

'But you don't know if she's done that yet.'

Adam leaned back, hands covering his face. Ronnie glanced at Baz, who instantly struck a new pose, stroking his chin, one ankle resting on the opposite knee, and took up the questioning.

'So, Mr Lloyd. As you know, Hannah had some friends round on Sunday to celebrate her birthday. Her sister-in-law Meghan Garrett, Ali Tremaine from the yoga class, and a friend of yours and hers called Delilah Byrne.'

'If you say so. I wasn't there. I wouldn't know.'

Baz ignored his attempt to flick the issue away. 'I was wondering how well you know these people. Let's start with Meghan. She's family, so...'

'Obviously I know bloody Meghan.' Adam surged forwards towards Baz, then sat back again suddenly. 'She simpers around Hannah the whole time. Couldn't ever get rid of her. And I work with Delilah. We both used to work with her until Hannah dropped out. But I don't know this Ali. Never met her. Never heard of her.'

'Tell us about the phone call you made to Hannah that afternoon.'

'What about it? I rang, she answered, we spoke, she hung up. She always hangs up first. Gives her a feeling of power.' Ronnie absorbed that. Normally it took one to know one when it came to second-guessing power trips.

'Does it work? Does she get the power back?'

Adam blinked, apparently considering the idea for a second before answering. 'No, I wouldn't say that. I always get a rise out of her by having the phone on speaker. Irritates the shit out of her. That's more power back to me.'

So there was a real battle going on between these two. She wondered if that's how it was with her and Simon. She wasn't aware of it, but now she thought about it there were definitely ways in which she would try to take the control back from him at any opportunity. In the first few years of separation it was like living on a knife edge, never knowing how safe you were, constantly imagining being laughed about by the ex in the arms of his new lover. The thought of it sent a shiver down Ronnie's back and she wondered if it was like that for Adam.

'Was there a party going on in the background when you called?' Baz asked.

'There might have been music on. I don't honestly remember.'

'No voices that you heard?'

He looked stressed, confused. 'No. Just hers, loud and clear blasting through the flat like a ship's steward announcing the evacuation procedure. Can't say I was sorry to be hung up on.'

'What was the conversation about?'

Adam frowned. 'I rang to let her know I'd be round there later when I'd collected Max. Asked her if she'd made a decision on changing the arrangements for the weekend after.'

'Why was that?' Baz was on him before he'd finished his sentence.

'I had something on with work. These things happen. Plans have to change.'

'The Home Secretary again?' Ronnie interrupted.

'Will you fucking lay off my private life? It's not relevant to anything. I may not be a criminal lawyer but I know I'm under no obligation to share my diary with you.'

He was right, for now, but it had been interesting

watching his growing discomfort. Maybe there was more where that came from. Ronnie leaned forward briefly to check her notes.

'Mr Lloyd, there's one more thing.' She looked up and met his eyes. 'Did Hannah ever threaten you?'

His eyes flicked left and right before meeting hers again. 'Threaten me? What the fuck do you mean by that? Looks more like someone was threatening her, doesn't it?'

Ronnie was unperturbed by his burst of anger. It was absolutely what she expected of him. 'As you said, you have political ambitions now, need to keep your nose clean, so perhaps something like an extra-marital affair getting out wouldn't be ideal. Did your wife find out you were seeing someone else and threaten to go public with it?' She sat back and folded her arms to gauge his reaction.

'No she fucking didn't, and I wasn't seeing anyone. I'm not seeing anyone else.' He corrected himself emphatically, mirroring Ronnie's body language to show her he wasn't beaten yet. She decided to let him think whatever he wanted. She had what she needed, for now.

'Well, that about wraps things up, and don't imagine you're the only one we're re-interviewing. We have a statement from Delilah for example, but there are a few things we need to clear up with her as well.'

Adam seemed to sit up and take notice. 'Oh? Anything I can help with?'

'Not unless you're familiar with her private life.'

She watched the panic flash across his eyes before he regained his composure and raised one groomed greying eyebrow.

'Sounds like I should leave it to you then.' He was good. But Ronnie could be better.

'Sounds like you should. We're good at things like that.'

Adam waited a beat before looking at his watch. 'Much as I'm enjoying this little chat, I have to pick my son up from school in half an hour. If you need me for anything else...'

'We know where you are.' Ronnie finished his sentence for him and was already up and holding the door open.

Baz caught Ronnie up in the corridor after the interview. 'I like your style, sarge, but seems like he was ready for you there.'

Ronnie turned to face him in the doorway. 'Exactly. If there was nothing in it, if it was the first time anyone had mentioned it, he'd have been shocked or upset or something. But he was prepared. He knew we'd ask. Probably wondered why we didn't come out with it straightaway.' She pushed open the door and almost bumped into Jen Connolly, her tiny frame dwarfed by an armful of files. 'Ah Jen, just the person. Why don't you both sit down with me for a moment? I want to know what new info we've got on Hannah.'

Jen flopped into the swivel chair opposite Ronnie's desk, forcing Baz to relieve the chair in the corner of its burden of paperwork and drag it forward to join her. Jen clasped her hands in her lap and spoke with the calmness of a storyteller on a meditation app.

'Well, as you'd expect, no criminal record, no cautions, nothing on the database. And no enemies to speak of. She taught all her yoga lessons in the church hall that week, showed up at school with Max every morning, never late to collect him. The other mums in the class didn't notice anything odd about her. The teacher says Max was behaving the same as normal.' She looked up for a reaction. 'Nothing of note. No dark side to this woman at all apparently. You want me to keep at it?'

Ronnie was making notes as she spoke. 'What about bank records?' Better late than never. If Hannah had put her philanthropic dream into action, it might be hard to prove Adam had a financial motive, but then again, if she hadn't told him, then the motive still stood.

Jen pulled out her notebook and flicked through the pages. 'There was a transfer from an executor account two months ago. The money's in there. Two million pounds of it. No power of attorney in place though, so the money's not moving for a while. Those street kids in Calcutta might have to wait a little longer for their hand-out.'

Ronnie pondered the news. It wasn't necessarily a disappointment that Hannah's background check hadn't thrown up any surprises, and the inheritance was a breath-taking sum. The next of kin of a victim might kill for a lot less. Which reminded her of James Garrett.

'Where are we with the brother?'

Jen handed her an interview transcript. 'Came in this morning. He wasn't in a great state, mentally, which could have been guilt I suppose.'

'The guilt of attempted murder or at the fact his estranged sister is lying in a coma in hospital, with his chances of reconciliation dwindling with every day that passes?' Ronnie mused aloud.

'Or just the distress of it all, who knows? Anyway, he didn't know how much Hannah had inherited, didn't want to in fact. Could have been a bluff, but he was so downbeat, so deadpan, there was nothing to pick up on.'

'Alibi?' Ronnie tapped her pen on her pad. James sounded like a dead-end but Lydia would be wanting all the boxes ticked.

'Watching the rugby with a neighbour who has corroborated.'

'Any other witnesses to that?'

Jen shifted in her chair. 'No. I could run his plates through ANPR, see if he's on the road anywhere?'

'No point. Meghan had the car.'

'What if he was in there too, biding his time?'

Ronnie stopped and blinked. She hadn't thought of that. James driving Meghan to Hannah's, popping back for some alibi time before going back to collect her, waiting for the sign that everyone had gone, getting the alert that Delilah was on her way back. Meghan must have been delighted to see that. She props the door open for him, he nips up the stairs, out by the fire exit and makes a run for it before anyone's even noticed the body on the tarmac.

'This should all be on the CCTV, when we finally get some news on that. Why is it taking so long? The times are pretty tight.'

'Apparently it's a combination of grainy images giving no clue as to who's who, and some building work being done in one of the flats, which means there are a whole lot of comings and goings that need to be checked against what have turned out to be very patchy memories. And we're not talking men in hard hats carrying tools, there's a visit from building control, designers, you name it.'

'On a Sunday afternoon?' Ronnie was perplexed. It didn't make sense.

'Backlog, planning team tells me. Flexi-working experiment after a whole heap of complaints about delays, and then there's being there when the place is free of the actual builders.'

'Okay, but let's try to develop this hypothesis.' She scribbled notes as she spoke, glancing up with each point she made. 'James has a financial motive to get rid of his sister. He's a state school teacher and the main breadwinner for a family that's about to take on a new member. He may not have known how much Hannah had inherited but how much do we know about the backstory to their relationship with their mother? This might sound a little extreme but I'm just thinking aloud. What if he's the one looking after her, being the dutiful son while Hannah swans around sorting yoga venues and spying on her husband's philandering? He hasn't had contact with Hannah for months. Of course he's sorted out an alibi but that might crumble under pressure. It's a path we need to explore, but its value depends heavily on the CCTV footage. I get the issues there, but go back and get them to look specifically for someone coming in that front door just as or around the time of a heavily pregnant woman leaving. Then we might have something.'

Jen nodded, scribbling to keep up. 'On it, sarge.' She stood to leave, just as Ronnie's phone pinged with a message from the officers on the house search.

'Damn, nothing at all of any use in Adam's flat. Let's hope Harry Grogan has better news.'

***

The tech team at Halesworth was a one-man band, and the one man seemed to change on a regular basis. Ronnie knew better than to question why. The ongoing cuts which had already been responsible for the merger of their original force with neighbouring Latchworth were a constant reminder of the state of policing in the home counties and weren't over yet. The current incumbent of the role, an eager, conscientious young graduate from the local college with a mission to prove his worth and move into fast-track CID. His office wasn't much more than a broom cupboard containing one desk cluttered with laptops and phones and two screens set at an angle to each other.

'What do you have for us?' Ronnie leant over his shoulder to see the screen he was working on. 'Anything juicy? Any communications with Hannah?'

Harry scrolled up and down again, too fast for anything to be legible. 'Nothing that jumps out. Looks like he had a habit of deleting everything from deleted items as well as inbox. There's the odd message from Hannah, but the bare minimum, arrangements for Max, admin stuff. I can take you through it if you like but I don't think you'll find what you're looking for. Oh, and before you ask, I've checked the drafts.'

Ronnie smiled. 'Good. We live and learn. What about Delilah Byrne? Anything to or from her?'

'Again, there are messages about files and cases, very vague, nothing personal.'

'Damn.' Ronnie walked to the door and leaned her back against it. 'Back to square one.'

A phone buzzed and Baz reached into his pocket. 'Talking of Delilah...'

CHAPTER TWELVE

Ronnie pushed open the door to interview room one where Delilah Byrne sat smiling a Hollywood smile and holding her mane of dark hair in a pony tail above her head. She let it drop as they entered, and her smile faded, unreciprocated. Ronnie went through the motions of reading out the caution and reminded her she was entitled to legal representation but Delilah waved the idea away.

'Thanks but there's no need, for now.' She placed both hands demurely in her lap. 'How is it that I can help you, detectives?'

Baz opened the questioning this time, asking Delilah to describe the events in her own words again, which she duly did, offering a story that only differed in respect to the focus on the merits of shop-bought cake. She spoke and he took notes while Ronnie studied Delilah's glossy appearance and unruffled manner. There was something mesmerising about her she couldn't put her finger on, a kind of ridiculous confidence, as if she knew she had the world eating out of the palm of her hand, but Ronnie had a grenade in her armoury and was itching to throw it. Baz caught her eye and let her take over.

'In the statement you gave our officers on Sunday, you mentioned leaving at around 4pm. Is that what happened?'

'Yes. I mean I didn't check the time, but it was some time around then.'

'And you didn't go back later at all?'

Delilah's smooth forehead was momentarily furrowed by a frown. Ronnie mentally put her on the no-Botox list. 'Later?' She was playing for time. Ronnie reformulated the question.

'Did you go back to the flat at any point that afternoon?'

There was the shortest pause before she got her reply. 'Oh, you know you're right. I did go back.' Her smile resurfaced. 'I'd completely forgotten about that. I realised I'd left my scarf there and I went back for it. It was one of those decisions – do I? Don't I? I thought better to go, because you never know how long it will be till next time...' She drifted off, perhaps realising what she was saying – that there might never be a next time now.

'So, tell us about that. Did you call Hannah before you went back?' Ronnie tried unsuccessfully to hide her impatience. Delilah had gone from fascinating to irritating within the space of thirty seconds.

'I called Hannah from the bus stop but she didn't pick up. I walked back there. It was only five minutes or so, then I ran up the stairs because I realised by then I was going to be late for another thing that evening if I didn't get a move on. I rang the doorbell and Hannah answered it, not looking particularly happy to see me I have to say.'

'What gave you that impression?'

'The expression on her face. She probably wanted a bit of time on her own before Max came back, which is understandable. She also didn't open the door very wide, just enough for me to see her face. I told her I'd left my scarf, said sorry and what a dufus I was, and she reluctantly stood aside for me to come in. I'm not sure she said anything at all. The scarf was on the chair where I'd been sitting. I picked it up, said thank you and sorry a few more times, which isn't like me so she must have really been giving me the evils. Then I left.'

'Did you see anyone as you were leaving? Anyone hanging around the building at all?'

'Not that I remember. There were probably people about, there always are, coming and going, but I was just doing my thing, living in my bubble. If I'd known there was going to be a quiz afterwards I'd have taken more notice. And with any luck, someone must have seen me. A camera or something?'

'We will be talking to everyone who lived in Mulberry Court to establish exactly where they were between four and ten past five that day. As you can imagine, it takes time to track everyone down, especially visitors, delivery drivers, and people who don't want to be found, for whatever reason.' They'd know if they'd seen you, she thought, but there was no need to say that out loud. 'What was it you were going to that evening, may I ask?' She leant on the table, chin in hand, as casual as she could manage. Delilah smiled as if she had seen the question coming a mile off.

'Just drinks with a friend.'

'Name?' Baz reached for his notebook and looked up at her, pen poised.

'Fran Butler. I'll give you her number if you like.'

Baz and Ronnie exchanged glances. Was Fran an alias for Adam? Was Delilah in fact the fictitious home secretary in his story? 'Yes please,' Ronnie continued. 'And what was your relationship like with Hannah and Adam, generally?' Ronnie left a pause after each name, watching Delilah's expression.

'On the whole I'd say it was very good, in the circumstances. As I said, after her mother passed away she got quite depressed. It was a complicated relationship, but it was still her mother.'

Baz pricked up his ears. 'How did her relationship with her mother compare to her brother's? Did either of them pick up the lion's share of the looking after, for example?'

Delilah sat back in her chair, looking as if she really didn't care about which sibling had done the shopping trips and daily phone calls. 'I don't think she had much to do with her, but she did what she had to, in between working and being a mum. Maybe she didn't do enough and felt guilty about that, I don't know. All I do know is that she hid herself away for ages and no-one could get through to her. I think I mentioned that in my statement.'

'You're sure that was all bereavement-related?'

Delilah looked momentarily affronted before re-composing herself. 'I'm not a therapist but I think it's a fair assumption, don't you?'

'I don't know. I don't know Hannah like you do. I was wondering if there was anything else bothering her.'

'I'm sure her home life wasn't helping, but I can't tell you how she felt about that because those are details that were never shared with me.' Her face settled into defiance, head slightly lowered, a bull ready to charge.

'Did Adam try to get through to her?'

'Of course he did, but by then it was probably too late. The ship had sailed, the horse had bolted.'

Baz's eyes lit up briefly at her creative use of the English language. He leaned forward to meet the charge head on. 'Do you think she was depressed because her relationship with her husband was going wrong?'

Delilah regarded him with something almost like contempt. 'It's not for me to comment on their relationship with any authority. Who knows what came first, the depression or his behaviour, but it's no secret that Adam wasn't interested in her anymore. He had his heart set on politics and was basically living a new life away from his family. Enough to make anyone upset, wouldn't you say?'

Baz sat back, admonished, and Ronnie took the reins back.

'Delilah, I have one more question for you. Forgive me for being direct. Were you and Adam Lloyd romantically involved?'

Ronnie was ready to wait as long as it took but she didn't have to. The answer was inaudible through the splutter that preceded it.

'What? Are you seriously suggesting that I would have an affair with my friend's husband, when there's so much at stake for us both? Don't be ridiculous.'

For Ronnie it was as good as an admission, but her words needed more clarification.

'What do you mean by *so much* at stake?' she asked. 'I'd have thought it wouldn't be much more than the obvious, his family life, access to his son?'

'Well, there's his political career for a start – he can't be blighted by scandal before he's even begun!'

'That's odd, because it seems that Hannah had some sort of information on his love life that she was considering going public with. We aren't sure that Adam ever received the message, but this is what she wanted to send to him.'

It was Ronnie's turn to sit back. Baz passed the print-out of Hannah's draft email across the table and watched the colour rise in Delilah's face as she read it. Whether it was the shame of being caught out, or something else, wasn't clear, but it wasn't the expression of someone emotionally unaffected by the words in front of her.

Eventually Delilah passed the paper back to Baz and leaned forwards, clasping her hands and looking Ronnie straight in the eye. The colour had gone from her cheeks. She was back in control.

'I have nothing to say. I know nothing about what Adam was up to in his spare time, and neither do I care. He's an attractive man, probably considers himself single. Personally I don't see the problem if he's seeing someone else. It's not ideal, publicity-wise, but hardly a deal-breaker.'

Ronnie let her believe she was believed, before adding, 'And what about you? What would you lose, if the two of you were in love?'

Delilah smiled. 'Well, my sanity for starters. It's enough having him as a boss, cracking the whip in the office all day.'

Ronnie scanned her notes and compared them to the list of questions she'd written earlier that morning. Delilah sat straight in her chair, hands on her lap, and it was a minute or so before either of them spoke.

'So, am I free to go or are you going to arrest me?'

Ronnie looked up, then checked the time on her phone and glanced at Baz questioningly. He shook his head.

'I have no more questions for you just now, Delilah, so yes, you're free to go, but we may need to speak to you again. Thank you for your time today.'

'It's no problem at all,' she beamed, all conflict forgotten. 'It's been a pleasure.'

CHAPTER THIRTEEN

From the second-floor window, Ronnie watched Delilah leave the building. It was accidental, but it would have been hard not to watch, because as the heavily pregnant Meghan had said in no uncertain terms, Delilah was hard to ignore. It wasn't just her looks either. Her confidence was dramatic, unapologetic, and she had a sense of entitlement bordering on the psychopathic.

Ronnie turned back to her desk and replayed the DVD of the interview. She had seemed beyond incredulous at the suggestion that she and Adam were having an affair, but then again she was obviously more concerned with the detrimental effect on Adam's political ambitions than losing her friendship with his wife. Her unanswered phone call to Hannah checked out, and the scarf story was credible, but could it easily be a smoke screen for something else? Did she call Hannah to talk about the man they were both, or *had* both been sleeping with, fuelled as she must have been by alcohol and maybe ready to confess? Did she turn back, frustrated by Hannah's lack of response and run up the stairs looking for a solution to the love triangle? Was that when Hannah met her death? But that would have meant Delilah leaving the building at some point after the fall, which would mean that she, and in fact anyone leaving via the front door, would be forced to almost walk past Hannah's body on the ground. Impossible.

'DS Delmar?'

It was Jen Connolly, leaning round the cubicle wall that separated her office from the rest of CID.

'Ah, just the person. Any more joy with the CCTV?'

'We've got a definite on Delilah coming out, only a minute after Meghan.'

'Good, I think.' She had nothing personal against Delilah but it was hard to be grateful for information that brought them no closer to the answer. 'So nobody else coming *out* of that door that we can't account for?'

'Everyone coming out has now been identified, even the sushi delivery boy.'

'Even up to, say, five thirty, by which time we know Hannah had fallen and Adam would have gone in there?'

'Yep, *and* we only see Adam coming out when he said he did.'

'So no chance he was there earlier than he said?'

'Not looking likely.'

Ronnie's heart sank. Every avenue was turning out to be a dead end. 'What about fire escapes? That would be another way out. Are there cameras on those?'

'Yes, and nothing to see.'

She put her head in her hands for a minute, then looked up, her mind working in fast motion. 'What about going in?'

'Still in progress. As you know, there was some activity on the top floor with the building work, but we've accounted for them now, then it was a few residents coming back home, the odd visitor to a resident's flat. So far.'

Ronnie let it sink in before speaking her thoughts aloud. 'I don't think that counts them out does it? Being a resident or a visitor to a resident would give you the best opportunity. Nipping back down the corridor to your flat to clean up?'

'All the residents are being interviewed, sarge. That should cover all eventualities.'

'OK, so unless something startling comes up from that line of enquiry, it's back to the drawing board.'

'Before we do that, sarge, we have a visitor ourselves waiting downstairs. Giselle Gaillard. Says she'll only talk to you. Nobody else.'

Ronnie picked up her notebook. 'I know who she is. Get them to bring her to room two and I'll be down straightaway.'

Giselle looked even more incongruous in a police station – a vision of tearful desolation, swathed in a pink silk and sequinned scarf over a corset-style bodice and off the shoulder puff sleeves. Her skirt swished with every movement, and her whole body convulsed with every few words she said. Ronnie brought water and tissues and guided her to a chair at the table. The words came in a staccato hiccupping torrent, between nose-blows and the wiping of black streaks from her cheeks, with Ronnie at a loss to know how to react.

'Hannah's ruined everything for me. Apparently she's gone running to the social telling them all sorts of lies about me and now I can't ever get my son back.'

'Hang on, how could she have...?' Ronnie tried to protest that Hannah couldn't be to blame as she was in intensive care attached to who knew what monitors, tubes and machines, but Giselle wasn't done yet.

'Exactly. How *could* she? She can't get away with this or my life is ruined forever. Please say you'll do something.'

It was a while before she was quiet enough to listen to Ronnie's questions, and then the story came out in fits and starts but was just about intelligible.

'Turns out Hannah told them all this stuff about me and now they want to carry out some kind of investigation. Supervised visits only with Leo, more interference from the social. But she's lying. You've got to believe me.'

'What exactly is she alleging you've done?'

Giselle looked up through mascara-clogged lashes, streaks of blue and black coursing down her ageless, fake-tanned face.

'She told them something about me bringing the neighbourhood down and encouraging undesirable visitors.'

'What sort of undesirable visitors?'

'Clients. You know.' Giselle's eyes bore into Ronnie's, willing her to understand without the words being pronounced.

Ronnie's jaw dropped. 'Prostitution?'

Giselle gave the faintest of nods and stared at the floor.

'Did she claim to have evidence?'

'I don't think that matters. Any doubt about my character will be investigated, which means more months, maybe years until I get Leo back.'

Ronnie struggled to put the story together to make a coherent narrative. It didn't make sense. Apart from anything else, Hannah was lying unconscious in a hospital bed.

'How did she contact social services? Presumably before the accident?'

Giselle blinked and flicked her eyes left and right. 'They said a message came in yesterday. Online. Email I think it was. Does it matter? She's probably got a phone with her now and she's firing off her vitriol from her deathbed.'

'I doubt it. She's in a coma, and her phone is here with us.'

Giselle's momentary confusion evaporated in an instant. She wasn't concerned by the practical impossibility of what she was suggesting. 'Oh, it was her alright. They read it out to me. I could imagine the words coming out of her mouth, every one of them. It had her name all over it.'

'Was there anything specific she mentioned? Names, dates, times?'

'Not really.' Giselle pulled out an embroidered handkerchief from her sequined purse and blew her nose hard before folding it carefully and stuffing it back in. She was a mixture of so many traits – dramatic but fragile, self-possessed and unstable all at the same time. 'They wouldn't read me the whole thing. Just said they were investigating the matter and would be in touch again soon.'

'Did she accuse you of touting for business in a public place?'

'No, online. Is that a public place?'

'Not yet. Although there are plenty of campaigners who believe that it should be.'

Giselle's mascara-streaked face remained impassive. 'I haven't done that, ever,' she whispered, blinking back the tears and looking back up at Ronnie. 'But the social will believe anything. What can I do?'

Ronnie made a note to contact social services to get hold of the message. Whoever had sent it must have had access to Hannah's account. That could easily have been Adam, but what would his motive be? He had nothing to gain from exposing Giselle as a sex worker. Or did he? Ronnie couldn't find a scenario in her head where that might be the case, unless he wanted to frame her, which was a decent enough reason, if you thought you were going down for attempted murder.

'Let me get onto social services and find out what's been happening.'

'Please make them see it was lies. I don't know what she had against me but I swear to you on Leo's life...'

They were strong words.

'I'll let you know when I've spoken to them.'

'Thank you, detective,' she sniffed, rising from her seat and gliding towards the door.

When she relayed the exchange to Baz later, he was as incredulous as Ronnie had been. 'I mean, she's just not the type.'

'What *is* the type?' asked Ronnie.

'Oh, I don't know.' He reddened under her stare. 'More obvious? More rock and roll?'

Ronnie let the words echo in her head and pictured the image of Giselle that she had from their last meeting, a billowing figure with pouting lips and kohl eyes, her cheeks contoured and highlighted within an inch of their lives. 'I'd say she's all over the rock and roll, just from the eighteen sixties rather than the twenty twenties. But as we know...' She flipped the file shut. 'If I had a pound for every time someone who wasn't the type committed the crime, I'd be a millionaire.'

Baz chuckled and looked at the time on his phone. 'OK if I head off to the hospital appointment now?' Ronnie looked up, confused. Baz slung his bag over his shoulder. 'Twenty-week scan, emailed you about it, sarge.'

'Of course. I'm so sorry.' First she was challenging his assumptions about what a sex worker looked like and then the next minute she'd forgotten his antenatal appointment. 'My head's all over the place today.'

'No worries. I'm looking forward to finding out the sex. Amber's not so sure, so wish me luck with that argument.'

'Good luck.' Ronnie looked up. 'Secretly hoping

for a boy? Someone you'll understand?' Baz blushed, making her feel uncomfortable for the second time in less than a minute. 'Don't worry, we all want our own kind to start with. It eases you into parenthood if you have a vague idea what you're dealing with.'

***

DC Mike Overton was predictably hard at work hunched over his laptop when Ronnie tapped him on the shoulder. 'I don't suppose you've got a minute?'

'Sure, sarge, what can I do?' He was on his feet in a second and following her back to her office, where she motioned to him to sit.

'The thing is, I've got a bit of investigating to do, and I need someone discreet, who's not going to leave a trail or raise suspicion in any way.'

'Sounds like me all over sarge,' he grinned.

Ronnie shut the door and pushed a pad and pen towards him.

CHAPTER FOURTEEN

Jen's background research on Hannah Lloyd was as complete as it was going to get, and although not fascinating, was at least detailed and evidenced, without a single gap in the timeline. She had been teaching yoga at various venues since qualifying two years previously with a reputable national institution. She had a hundred or so clients on her database, ranging from teens to over-eighties, and ran everything from private one-to-one classes in their homes, to countryside retreats, to weekly group sessions at the local village hall and health club. By the looks of her testimonials, her reputation was as flawless as the poses emblazoned across the home page of her website, and her call to action that accompanied it was irresistible. *Find peace with Hannah's Home Yoga course.* Below that, a link to a series of subscription-only YouTube videos promised a new life of flexible fitness and inner contentment, and the whole scenario made Ronnie think of one person.

Serena Delmar, normally be found upside down, in downward dog or a shoulder stand, was no stranger to the yogic life. It had been a while since she and Ronnie had seen each other, what with work commitments and Serena's endless building project at her house, so it made sense for Ronnie to drop by on her way home.

Hearing her car pull up on the gravel outside the cottage, Serena threw open the door and pulled her into a tight hug.

'Veronica, my favourite sister. Come inside and eat cake with me.'

'Not if it's vegan.' Ronnie extracted herself and followed her sister indoors, immediately sinking into an armchair in the minute sitting room. 'But I'll take a cup of tea if there's one going.'

While her sister busied herself in the kitchen, she fired off an email to the local council social care department. They would all have gone home by now but it was worth getting in the next day's queue nice and early. Giselle had been on her mind, and she needed answers.

Serena returned with a tray laden with mugs of tea and plates of carbohydrates.

'So what brings you here, apart from missing my company? Come to inspect the extension?'

'After this I will,' said Ronnie, taking a bite of carrot cake and feeling a rush of sugar-induced pleasure. 'But first I have something to show you.' She passed her the phone and Serena zoomed in on the photo.

'That's Hannah Lloyd. I went to her classes ages ago.'

'Why did you stop going? You love yoga.' The cake was delicious. She should visit her sister more often.

Serena sat back and sipped her tea. 'Can't remember. Maybe it didn't tie in with my work schedule.

I think she was OK as they go. I don't remember anything bad or good. Why do you ask?'

'She's been in an accident. At least we thought it was an accident, but now we know it was attempted murder, or murder if she doesn't pull through.'

Serena fell silent, her face pale, and set the mug back on the table. 'What? Who would want to kill her?'

'If we knew that...'

'So who could it have been? Someone jealous, angry, wanting her silenced? Did she know something she shouldn't? People say all sorts of things to yoga teachers. It comes with the job, getting unsolicited confessions out of people.'

'I hadn't thought about that scenario as such,' Ronnie said, putting her plate down and taking the phone back. 'But that's a lot of people to question if we have to go through her whole database.'

'Did she have any friends that she taught? Could they shed some light on Hannah's relationships with the others?'

Ronnie thought about Ali Tremaine, the last remaining visitor to the flat. 'Yes, there is one we need to talk to.'

'If she and Hannah were close, Hannah may have confided in her about any rogue yogis with ulterior motives for being in the class. There are always a few weirdos in those groups in my experience.'

'Really? What kind of weirdos?

Serena pondered for a second. 'I don't know. Stalkers? Hero worship isn't out of the question.

107

Happens a lot where someone gets over-dependent on a teacher, wants all of their time, all their attention, always bagsies the spot bang in front of them in the class. Some of these women are spookily obsessed.'

Ronnie took a moment to absorb what she had just said. 'OK, I can imagine that would add another level of danger to the job.'

Serena was looking at her intently. 'Don't always assume it's a man, is all I'm saying.'

Giselle? Ronnie tried to imagine it. But Serena was on her feet now, dusting off her hands and holding one of them out to her.

'Now come with me and look at all the new building that's been going on.'

The extension was nothing more than the conversion of a modest side return into a dining area, but in the process the kitchen had doubled in size and had already been filled with Serena's vast collection of herbs and houseplants, hanging and shelved. Flowering shrubs, cacti and spidery ivy trailed across the roof lights. Brightly coloured pots of basil and mint adorned the windowsills. The sight of it all made Ronnie's shoulders untense. She took a seat on a bar stool, closed her eyes and let the aromas of basil and lavender permeate her senses.

'Aromatherapy. I can get you some essential oils if you like it.' Serena knew better than to do any more than make a gentle suggestion, or Ronnie wouldn't be seen for dust.

'I like it. Where do I sign?'

'Anything on your mind, apart from the case of course? Just noticing your stress levels are a tad above the usual today.'

'What makes you say that?'

Serena waited a beat. Ronnie wasn't making it easy for her, but then she wouldn't expect an outpouring of soul-baring emotion. 'Just a vibe. I'm wondering who's annoying you. That's what it usually comes down to.'

Ronnie opened her eyes. 'Well, now you mention it, Baz never usually irritates me, not professionally at least, but when he's approaching the case with a preconceived idea that the husband is beyond reproach...'

'Is he? Doesn't sound like him.'

Ronnie paused. Was she right? Was he biased, or was it her imagination? She met Serena's gaze. 'Maybe not. That's the trouble. That's the issue I have right now – I don't completely trust my judgement. I used to be so sure, so trusting of my gut feeling with a sprinkling of rationality, and that's kind of evaporated over the last few months. Not helped by being part of a national institution that's being dragged through the mangle of press scrutiny. The IOPC seems to be lurking around every corner these days, and it's getting to me. I'm going to start suspecting myself of gross misconduct soon.'

'That's understandable.' Serena made a face. 'Sorry, I know it's not funny, but that atmosphere can be so stifling. I can imagine you must start imagining the worst of everyone. Does Baz have a connection to the case or anyone involved that you don't know about? I mean, of course he'd have to come clean about it, but I bet not everyone does.'

Ronnie baulked at the thought. 'You mean he might have a reason to protect Adam Lloyd?'

Serena shrugged. 'Who knows? Everything's a possibility at this stage I expect, and as you say, with the police being the nation's villains right now...'

'I don't know. I don't want to even go there, feels a bit like jumping on board the demonisation bandwagon. I don't know if it's connected, but alongside all that I'm feeling bizarrely detached, like I don't belong in the job either. Like I'm part of it, so I'm part of the problem. Isn't that what they say?'

'Oh God, please don't think like that. There are plenty of decent police officers out there and you need to stay in your job to keep up the ratio.'

'I think they call it imposter syndrome,' Ronnie said, flatly.

It was a few seconds before Serena responded, but her tone was decisive. 'I think they call it hormones.'

'Hormones? You think I'm *menopausal*? Aren't I too young?'

'Oh my God, why does everyone panic at the mention of the menopause? Because they think it equates to infertility, redundancy, being kicked off the team. But reframe it and it's just another phase of the female life cycle, where you step away from childbearing in favour of your children. You can't look after grandchildren if you're still having your own. It's a selfless sacrifice of womanhood in favour of the next generation.'

Ronnie blinked. It all sounded a bit too much. 'If you say so.'

'I do say so. I might be wrong, but just being aware of that even as a possibility might make you more forgiving of yourself. If you're feeling impatient, having an off-day, just not getting into your groove, let it happen. So what if you're a bit pissed off with your colleagues. Maybe you have a right to be. Don't get sad, get mad.'

Ronnie brightened at the sound of advice she could relate to. 'That's more like it. Permission to rage against the machine.'

'You're welcome. Maybe you need more offloading.'

Ronnie groaned. 'Like counselling? No budget for that these days. And isn't that the whole point of family, friends? I dunno. I'm not going to go sharing my deepest thoughts with a stranger.' The words sounded crass as she said them. They came from a place of disgruntlement, because the person she most trusted with her soul was redirecting her to dump her troubles elsewhere. It wasn't like that of course, and she knew it, but there was a sullen five-year-old inside her itching to storm out of the room.

Serena stood to re-arrange the danglings of a spider plant that had migrated too far to one side. 'Tell me something good. Who's on your side? Who's your ally right now, if not Baz?'

'On my side? Gosh, let me think.' It was definitely

111

time to scramble out of the pit of misery she'd just burrowed into, but for a moment it was a hard question to answer.

'Actually, there is a bright horizon out there. I bumped into Frank Reilly the other day. He's leading the CSI team on the Lloyd case. I had no idea he'd moved down here.'

Serena abandoned her adjustments and clasped her hands at her chin. 'Frank? Well there we go. An angel appears in the darkness. I'll never forget what he did for Mum when she thought the world had ended. Probably saved her life. And maybe having him back on the team will help you get back on yours. Talking of which...' She slowed down to check she had Ronnie's full attention. 'You haven't forgotten about Friday night, have you?'

Ronnie shook her head, racking her brains. 'Of course I haven't forgotten. But remind me again?'

'You're coming here for dinner. Well, you said you'd check with work and you never got back to me, but optimistically I'm going ahead anyway. I've asked Susie Marshall and the boys next door who have been so patient with all the building noise. So I was going to say why don't you bring Frank if you like? Be fun to see him again.'

'Ah, of course. It's in my diary, had just slipped my mind.' She hadn't been in the mood for socialising for a while now, and the thought of sitting with a room full of people making small talk filled her with dread. Serena read her mind.

'I know it's probably the last thing you feel like if you're in a bit of a funk, but you'll know everyone and it will be super-relaxed, I promise.'

'No interrogations about what detectives do all day?'

'I promise to get a full list of questions over to you to approve.'

Ronnie smiled. 'Well if work allows and I'm not chasing down some drug lords...'

Serena looked horrified. 'You don't think that's what it's about, do you?'

'God, I hope not. The issue of narcotics has raised its ugly head but I don't think that's what we're dealing with here.'

'Phew. So, barring work commitments, you're a yes.'

'I'm a yes. I'm sure it's just what I need. I'll see if I can get Frank to come too.'

'Oh, and Ronnie, I know you're not keen on psycho-nonsense or whatever it is you call it, but take this.' She handed her a teal-coloured business card bearing the name and number of a counsellor and psychotherapist.

Ronnie looked up, unsure how to react. 'You know this person?'

Serena nodded. 'Vaguely. A friend of a friend, but a wonderful person, my gut feeling told me, someone you could definitely relate to. Give her a go, if you feel like it of course. No pressure.'

'I'll give it some thought.'

Dusk was gathering when she got home half an hour later. She switched the engine off and closed her eyes, letting silence replace noise and allowing the questions that plagued her fill her mind. Was she going mad? Was she in the wrong job? Had her career run its course? Or had she just collided with the tip of the menopausal iceberg? She turned the teal business card over in her hands, before stuffing it in the glove box and opening the car door. Serena had a point, and she might book a visit to the GP to draw a line under the whole thing, but in the meantime she was going to put every ounce of energy she had into solving the Lloyd case, and no hormonal side show was going to stop her.

CHAPTER FIFTEEN

Next on the list of witnesses was Ali Tremaine – another half-term holidaymaker as it turned out, but perfectly happy to do a long-distance video meeting with Ronnie any time that day. It made a change from the dreary interview rooms at the station, and the glimpse of blue sky and turquoise sea in the background was a much-needed reminder that there was joy in the world, if you looked hard enough for it.

Ali visibly paled as Ronnie told her what had happened. The news clearly hadn't reached her in Mauritius. She was silent and reflective for a few seconds before speaking.

'So that's why she didn't call.'

'She was supposed to call you?'

'Yes, later that day, when everyone had gone. At least that's what I suggested. Maybe she didn't hear. Sorry, I'm in shock. Who would want to hurt Hannah?'

'That's what we're trying to find out. How did you meet her?'

'At yoga. I joined the Thursday morning group in the village hall, eighteen months ago or so I think. She's one of those people that gets you to open up, and I always end up chatting to her after the lesson. She's a good listener, doesn't give much away herself though. I told her about some family stuff and she was incredibly sympathetic. She has a real way with people. Makes you feel like you matter, you know? I was so honoured to be invited to her birthday. Felt like a real privilege.'

Ronnie wondered if it was too much to ask what kind of *family stuff* she had shared with Hannah but was saved by Ali's next remark.

'My mother died last year around the same time as hers. She understood what I was going through because she'd been through it too. She'd inherited some money but didn't feel comfortable with it. We used to chat about what the zen thing to do would be, if you could do some good anywhere in the world.'

'Where did you plump for, in the end?'

Ali looked thoughtful for a second, then her face broke into a broad smile. 'She had some crazy idea of rescuing a whole Indian city from poverty, by setting up some kind of outreach programme to street children.'

Ronnie nodded. 'Sounds very noble. Did you talk about other things related to marriage and family?'

Ali's smile faded. 'I think things were bad with her and Adam.'

'How bad, would you say?'

Ali hesitated. 'OK, I can't lie. Bad bad. Like things seemed to go from bad to worse. I mean, she didn't want to offload, but the things she hinted at made it clear to me her husband was having an affair.'

Ronnie nodded, her face just the right level of interested to encourage more without seeming over-fascinated. 'She didn't give you a name, say how she'd found out?'

'She implied he'd made it so obvious, it was like he was asking her to break up with him.'

Ronnie thought back to the inheritance. By the sound of the wealth Hannah had inherited, Adam stood to gain a lot by divorcing her. Not as much as he would by killing her, but a million pounds or thereabouts. These days the courts were keen for fortunes to be shared, not automatically handed to a wife, even a wronged wife. Adultery meant nothing to a family court judge. She wondered how much Hannah had thought about that route, and how much she might have divulged. 'Did you get the impression Hannah wanted a divorce?'

Ali paused again, as if trying to gather the transcripts of all past interactions with her friend before summing up her feeling. 'Yes and no,' she said. 'Yes, she wanted rid of Adam, but she was no fool. She knew he'd get a lot of her money, so she wasn't going to let him escape easily.'

'So she had a plan of some sort?' Ronnie was on rocky ground with leading questions, but they were tiptoeing around something huge, she was sure of it.

'If she did, she didn't share the details of it with me, but I think she might have been about to.'

'What makes you say that?'

'Her text to me on Saturday morning – *I know you've got to rush off to the airport but is there any chance you can come early? Need a chat before the others arrive* – something like that. I just assumed it was something to do with a new love interest, or some gossip about Adam. I never thought about the money side of things.' She paused, looking somewhere beyond the screen in search of something. 'Anyway, as it turned out, I couldn't make it. Hopelessly late packing and I had to get the night flight to come out here so I only managed a quick visit to say happy birthday. I helped lay the table, knocked back a couple of glasses of prosecco with her and the others then headed off home again.'

She laid the table, so her prints would be on the knife, Ronnie thought.

'So we didn't get the chance to talk privately. I shouted goodbye to her when I had to leave. She had just gone into the other room to take a phone call.'

Ronnie's interest was piqued suddenly. Delilah had mentioned the phone call from Adam. 'You shouted goodbye. Just goodbye?'

'I think I said *let's have a catch up on all the gossip when I'm sitting around with the girls at the airport. Call me.*'

'Gossip, you said gossip?'

'I think so. Why? I mean, it's a turn of phrase isn't it? It's what girls say to each other.' Ali's face looked slightly pleading, eyebrows raised saying *please understand me.*

Ronnie smiled. 'Of course, I was just trying to get the facts. And what would you say her state of mind was on Saturday, while you were there? Did she seem frustrated at not having had the opportunity to chat?'

Ali looked into the distance. 'Hard to say. There were people there I didn't know and I was trying to get the measure of them, while at the same time being my bull-in-a-china-shop self, filling the gaps with mindless chatter, crapping on about nothing so there wouldn't be any silences.'

'I know what you mean.' Maybe Ali needed to learn about *pause and pounce*. Silences could be tamed, if you were confident enough to brave them out. It had always amazed Ronnie how even the most reticent of witnesses had been known to crack under the pressure of absolutely nothing. 'So was there some awkwardness that you felt obliged to compensate for?'

'Possibly. There was a woman called Delilah who was one of those people I couldn't work out. Stunningly, kind of intimidatingly beautiful. But on edge. Like she didn't want to be there. Weirdly, she seemed to like me, gave me her number as I was leaving and said we should go for a drink or something. It was like coming out of a disastrous interview and then being told you've got the job.'

'How was Hannah with Delilah?'

'Nice. Very nice. Although I couldn't work out if it was real or not. It was that slightly triumphant niceness, like when you know someone's got their skirt stuck in their pants and you're not going to tell them.'

So not very nice then, thought Ronnie, and seeing her face, Ali was quick to take it back. 'Not like that. I don't mean it like that. See what I mean about crapping on? It was just a feeling I had that Hannah was kind of enjoying her being there and Delilah wasn't.'

Ronnie looked down at her notes. Ali had given her more than she'd expected, and her mind was already champing at the bit to explore a new avenue of investigation. It was time to wind up the interview, but she hadn't quite finished her line of questioning.

'Going back to yoga classes, was Hannah close with anyone else as far as you know? Anyone there that might have had an issue with her, or an obsession with her?'

Ali's eyes widened, a rabbit in the headlights. 'No. Not that I know of. Do you think she had a stalker?'

'Not necessarily. But we need to ask the question. We're talking to some of her regular clients and we'll be asking them the same thing.' She looked down at her notes and ticked off the question. One more and they were done. 'Then lastly, I just need you to confirm the time you left the flat and who was still there when you went.' She held her breath, waiting for the answer, pen poised to strike Ali Tremaine off her list of suspects and onto her list of invaluable witnesses.

'One thirty, or maybe a couple of minutes after, and Delilah and Meghan were still there.' In the background a small child was shouting '*Auntie Ali come back outside.*'

'Listen, I'd better let you get back to the beach. I'm very jealous of that tan and the weather by the way.'

They said their goodbyes and Ronnie sank back into her swivel chair, turning to face the window – the same one through which she'd seen Delilah leave the previous day. She thought back to Delilah's uniquely self-assured demeanour, and the description Ali had just given of her that told a different story. The evidence was pointing to Delilah and Adam being an item, but even Delilah had said there had been a change in Hannah's attitude to her. Ali had just corroborated that, describing Hannah's fake 'niceness' and Delilah's obvious discomfort with that. What had happened to Hannah that changed her attitude?

Then there was the shout goodbye. The scene in the flat an hour before the murder was taking shape as the different layers were painted on. Each witness added another viewpoint, and what had seemed like the innocent phone call interrupting a gathering of women had now taken on significant proportions in Ronnie's mind. She replayed Ali's words in her head about having a catch up on the gossip when she was at the airport with the girls. She closed her eyes and pictured the scene. Hannah had gone next door to take the call. Ali's voice would have been loud and clear even through a closed door. It was conceivable, even, that someone on the other end of phone could have heard what she said. And if that person picked up on the fact that there was some gossip to be spread, and they didn't want that to happen, who knew what they might do?

It was a long-shot theory that needed thinking about as much as it needed a break from being thought about. Sometimes a complete distraction was the best way to lure the needle from the haystack and Ronnie had just the thing.

Tapping her phone into life, she scrolled through the latest notifications. The twins had been posting Instagram stories of their antics in France which brought a smile to her face, and her mother had made a little more progress with trying to sell the family home in Sussex. It would be an emotional moment for Ronnie, giving up their home on Waterman Lane, but there was no point in hanging onto the past any longer. Her father had been missing for over a decade and there was no reason to think he was still alive. In the family there had been a shared fantasy that he might one day come back to the house, the only place he remembered living – hence the reluctance to get rid of it. But with every year that passed, that hope faded to the point that nobody even mentioned it anymore. Frank had had to let go of any hope of finding his daughter, missing since she walked home from a club alone one night, aged just eighteen. He'd done the unimaginable, and maybe it was time for them to do the same.

She took a long breath in and exhaled until her lungs were empty. It was like clearing the slate, creating a blank screen to work on with fresh eyes. Outside, after days of rain, the street was suddenly bathed in sunshine.

Guilt, the uninvited guest was kicked out. The door slammed in its face. Now her mind raced back to Adam like a sniffer dog magnetised to the drugs haul. Her theory did hold water. Could Adam have heard Ali Tremaine's parting words, and then, for some reason, panicked?

'Sarge? Lydia wants an update.'

It was Baz. Ronnie jumped, imagining him having telepathically registered her thought process. She wasn't ready to share her new theory with her dc just yet, but

she gave him a look that said, *I'm ready for the next fight.*
Little by little, everything was beginning to make sense.

CHAPTER SIXTEEN

Baz and Ronnie sat opposite DI Burnett relaying the past day's progress while she looked from one to the other, nodding and scribbling notes on her pad.

'So, if I may summarise where we are: Hannah is still unconscious in hospital and it's not looking good. Serious brain damage if she survives, so we are looking at a high chance of never getting the truth out of her. Her husband may or may not be having an affair with this Delilah Byrne, but if Hannah threatened Adam the way her draft email suggests, and if this affair going public would spell disaster for Adam's career, then we have a motive. Added to that, if he can get away with it, he stands to inherit a couple of million, which, left to her own devices, Hannah is in danger of hurling into the abyss of the charity sector. However, I'm not entirely convinced. Firstly, he may well have known that when push came to shove she'd keep the cash. Secondly, he'd do pretty well in a divorce, coming out with half of that inheritance if he gets himself a decent lawyer. Thirdly, going down for murder would be somewhat worse for him than living with the scandal we are imagining here. So we'd need to find a credible disaster scenario – more than just infidelity. The public have a reasonable tolerance of politicians taking solace in the arms of a colleague. Just look at the papers.'

Ronnie suppressed a smile. Lydia's turn of phrase was unique. She imagined Adam falling into Delilah's arms in some kind of scene from a Shakespearean tragedy. 'Agreed. They're getting a better press than us at the moment,' she said.

Lydia frowned, her train of thought interrupted, and took a second to re-establish her flow. 'Added to that, if the affair is out in the open before he even gets the job, the disappointment is done and dusted. He might be perceived as happy and stable and a better bet for the seat than someone in a long marriage whose scandal has yet to happen.'

Baz was nodding vigorously in agreement. *Team Adam*, Ronnie thought again, then gave herself a mental slap on the wrist. Lydia was making a perfectly good argument.

'I'm quite taken by the point that he lied about the time he collected his son, and the absence of camera footage to support his alibi. But then I'm surprised he didn't think of that. It's a clumsy mistake, too big a risk to take, not leaving a decent trail. And as far as we know he's not a stupid man.'

Speculation, thought Ronnie. When someone has little time to think or prepare, which is the case for most violent crime, they don't perform to a set of standards.

Lydia was twisting her pen between her fingers in deep thought. 'So I'd say we're only half way there with Adam Lloyd. We need to get closer to establishing the nature of the risk to him of Hannah speaking out. If there's a darker secret they're hiding, then that opens up a new line of enquiry.'

Ronnie reached for her notepad. That was where she and Lydia were in agreement, and it was a line of investigation that would satisfy her as well as her boss.

Lydia moved on to her next point. 'And if we open our minds to the possibility of collaboration, we know that Delilah returned to the flat – she claims in order to fetch a scarf. Do we have any substantiation there, about the scarf itself, or could it still be a smokescreen to hide her involvement?'

'Delilah doesn't dispute her return to the scene, but apart from that, I'd say smokescreen is just about possible,' replied Ronnie. Delilah and Adam as a double-act was beginning to look like a safe bet.

'So, given all that, anything more you can dig out on the backgrounds of Delilah and Adam is first priority. Now let's turn to the yoga student.'

'Ali Tremaine.' Ronnie scanned the previous page of her notebook. 'Seemed genuinely shocked to hear what had happened. They bonded over bereavement. Ali's prints are most likely the last unidentified ones on the weapon because she laid the table but she was off the scene well before the assault.'

'So we can rule her out?'

Ronnie hesitated. Instinctively she didn't want to read too much into Ali's testimony until she had had time to mull it over and explore the link with her parting comments when Hannah was on the phone. 'As perpetrator, yes we can, but the two of them were good friends and I feel we should explore that relationship a little more. It may be that Hannah confided in Ali more than we know at this point. Or was about to. I want to talk to Ali about it again.'

Lydia seemed satisfied. 'And then we have Meghan, the clingy sister-in-law who grassed up Delilah for coming back after she'd left. We take her testimony there at face value, because Delilah doesn't deny coming back to the flat. Her prints are on the knife, as Delilah's are, because they all cut themselves a slice of cake. Do we have any reason to consider her a suspect?'

Ronnie's instinct was an outright no, but she gave it a few seconds consideration before replying. 'Well, there's the possibility that she and her husband James might stand to gain financially from Hannah's death. James is a secondary school maths teacher who barely speaks to Hannah. He has an alibi that could crumble under pressure, and he could have been collaborating with Meghan on the day, or even sent her as an unlikely proxy. Nobody would suspect an eight-month-pregnant woman of murder. Then the only other scenario I can imagine here is that Hannah might have information that could bring some kind of disgrace to the family.'

She could practically see the cogs whirring away in Lydia's brain.

'Financial gain is unlikely, given that we still have no record of a will, and under intestacy laws everything would go to her husband.'

'There may be some bad blood on the finance side given Hannah inherited everything from their mother. I don't think we should ignore it,' Baz piped up.

'That's a third option then, basic revenge for parental favouritism, regardless of the terms of the will, but it doesn't wash with me, yet.' Lydia looked up at them both with a half-challenging, half-amused expression. 'So in your second scenario, what kind of family disgrace did you have in mind, before we go down this rabbit hole?'

Baz cleared his throat, to Ronnie's surprise. He was coming to her rescue at just the right time. 'She could have something on James, something involving children which might lose him his job in the school? That would cause an issue financially, and if they're hard up as well...' He glanced at Ronnie for support, and she nodded and took over the point.

'They're not living in the lap of luxury, and with a baby on the way I don't expect things will get any easier. We'd need to look into his background. It hasn't been a priority as yet.' She couldn't imagine having had the time for that as well as everything else in the three days that had passed since the assault, but that wasn't the point. Things needed to be done, and nobody was going to make allowances for the number of hours in the day.

Lydia dismissed the idea with a flick of her hand. 'By all means do a background check on James, but it's highly unlikely he'd be working in a school with a sex-offender record. So, barring the possibility of Hannah blackmailing her brother for paedophilia, we don't have enough on Meghan or James to make them worth pursuing. Now tell me about this neighbour, Giselle Gaillard? She interests me as she has no alibi, there's no love lost between her and Hannah *and* she had a key to her flat.'

'No prints on the weapon, though.' Ronnie had been through this puzzle over and over with no conclusion. 'So unless she went in with gloves on after the party... It's just about possible, but again we have no clear motive, apart from a peculiar twist yesterday. Giselle came in distraught with the news that Hannah had reported her to the social services, who say they received an email from Hannah on Sunday night, thirty-six hours after she had been admitted to ICU in a coma, which itself is a mystery.'

'Not necessarily,' Baz interrupted. 'You can programme emails to send at a future time. It's not rocket science.'

Ronnie winced with the attack on her technical knowledge, and only managed to stop herself retaliating. Not in front of the boss. It could wait, and Lydia was less concerned with the timing of things.

'An email? Reporting Giselle for what?'

'Soliciting for sex work online, entertaining gentlemen visitors – slightly odd terminology some of it. I'll show you the wording.' Ronnie flicked through her notebook and handed it to Lydia. 'Sorry, illegible scribble.'

Lydia sat back in shock. 'Well, this changes everything, doesn't it?'

Ronnie frowned. Was she missing something? 'How so?'

'If Hannah had information on Giselle, the

exposure of which would destroy her life, then what better reason for Giselle to get rid of her? Sounds as if she just didn't get rid of her in time though.' Lydia was staring at Ronnie as if in wonderment that she could be so stupid as to miss this point.

'I think,' Ronnie began, 'that the risk of Giselle being arrested for murder was just too high, and then she would have lost everything forever, in particular her son Leo. And does Hannah have the power to destroy Giselle? A decent lawyer could put in a good case for her, maybe even get her off. It's by no means a done deal.'

'Giselle might *know* people...' Lydia seemed to flail around for a word to describe the kind of people Giselle might know, but the idea of her having mafia connections just didn't make sense.

Baz looked as if he was having just as much trouble imagining it. 'So Giselle gets someone to do the job for her?'

They were down another rabbit hole. Ronnie clasped her hands in front of her on the desk and addressed the DI. 'We can look again at Hannah's phone to see if we missed any communications between her and Giselle then that might shed light on this. I have no doubt Giselle will have deleted anything incriminating on hers. But it's worth a look there too.'

Lydia looked unconvinced, but it was hard to detect any expression on her face these days. 'What happened about the food delivery? Any joy with them?'

Baz consulted his notebook. 'Nothing to report,

they paid by card online, the food was delivered on the doorstep. He didn't go in, couldn't even manage a description of the person who opened the door. He said all women of a certain age look the same to him.' He looked up at Ronnie apologetically.

Lydia nodded briefly and shuffled her papers together to indicate that their chat was over.

'I think you need to go back to talk to Giselle, DC Munro. Keep it low-key, lots of sympathy and see if you can get anything more out of her. Talk to the social first so you have a reason to go round there. Now that things have gone this far, it may be that she admits to more than she has already – and if you can do some more digging on the Adam and Delilah set-up, look for a second level of jeopardy that would make the risk worth their while, we could find ourselves a little closer to the truth tomorrow.'

CHAPTER SEVENTEEN

The ringtone crept into Ronnie's dream as a fire alarm. She was in a burning block of flats and the residents were trampling over each other in an attempt to escape. Baz and Adam were on the outside, tut tutting at her for putting up flammable cladding on the building. When her mind finally made sense of the noise and dragged her back to the real world she was met by her mother's face on her phone screen. She pressed accept and propped herself up on her pillows. 'What's up, Mum? This is early for you.'

'Veronica?'

'Yes, I'm here. What's happened?'

'Have you got time to come down to the house? There's something I need to show you.'

'Today? I have to work. You know that.' A surge of resentment rose inside her.

'What about after work? It's important. You know I wouldn't ask if it wasn't.'

Ronnie flicked over to her calendar app and then back to FaceTime. 'I can be there by seven, depending on traffic. But can you just give me an idea of what this is about?'

'It's your father.'

Ronnie's stomach lurched. Only the day before he had been on her mind, the idol of her youth, turned gambler by the time he was fifty and dead by sixty-five. For a second, she imagined him having walked through the door. 'What about him?'

'I can't talk about it on the phone.' She sounded subdued. Her voice lacked its usual spirit, the hutzpah that had seen her through years of uncertainty, the inability to physically bury her husband or even consign his memory to a mental graveyard.

'OK, I'll do my best. Shall I bring Serena?'

'I've asked her. She's busy this evening, cooking for you apparently, and a few others coming over tomorrow. She said she'd seen you, that you had a tricky case on your hands. I was just hoping you could spare a couple of hours for me.'

Ronnie fought back the instincts that were beating on the door of her heart, the resentment that Serena was first to be called on in her mother's hour of need, and the exasperation at her use of emotional blackmail to get her way, even her second-choice way. It was a shame Serena couldn't make it. It was always easier to have a third person to dilute their mother's intensity, but clearly that wasn't going to be an option this time.

'I'll see you at seven at the house. I'll text you if I'm going to be late.'

She was about to hang up the phone when inspiration hit. 'Hang on. You still there, Mum?'

'What is it? Don't tell me you've just remembered you're busy too?'

Ronnie ignored her instinct to hang up in fury. 'Actually I was going to suggest something.' She ran through the idea again in her head and decided to share it, even if it was met by the derision that seemed so much in favour today. 'The case I'm doing, the lead CSI is Frank Reilly. We had a brief catch up but I was thinking if you'd like me to give him a call...'

'Bring Frank! Oh, Ronnie, that would be so lovely if he came with you. I'd be delighted to see him again. He saved my life you know.' She tailed off, a new humility in her voice as memories of the past cast a shadow over her words.

'I'll call him. It's a long shot but fingers crossed. I'll see you sevenish anyway.'

***

Baz noticed something wasn't right as soon as they met at the office coffee machine.

'Bad night, sarge? You look like the cat that didn't get the cream.'

He was making up his own similes now. Ronnie forced a smile. 'It's nothing. Busy day, then have to drive down to Sussex tonight to see Mum. Talking of mothers, I forgot to ask how the scan went.'

Baz's face clouded for a second. 'All good. It's a little boy which, as you said, is reassuring in a strange way. They've just got to run a few tests.'

Ronnie put her cup down on the machine and turned to face him. 'What kind of tests?'

'Oh, you know, the usual. There's a tiny chance of a heart defect they've detected and they want to find out a bit more, so Amber's going in tomorrow again.'

'You can take the time off, you know.'

'Thanks, sarge. I might do that if it's OK with you. Not the whole day. Just the afternoon.'

'Of course. Take as long as you need.'

'Oh, and sarge?'

Ronnie raised her eyebrows, her mind already back on the evening road trip.

'Sorry to butt in with that delayed delivery email thing. Didn't want to seem like a show-off. Just wanted to limit the number of mysteries we have to solve.'

Ronnie smiled, not having realised, until he apologised, just how much it had affected her.

'And on the subject of parenting, I'm off to see Giselle. The social said they are following protocol, there'll be an investigation, but nothing's been decided as yet. Also, I asked about her background, and it turns out the boy's dad was a diamond dealer, twenty years older than her, married to someone else, wanted for money laundering a few years back and disappeared, never to be seen again.'

'Well, that's going to leave its mark, for sure. Good luck, Baz. I think you'll deal with her brilliantly. You're the bringer of good news and reassurance. Just keep it low-key, so she feels you're on her side.'

Ronnie watched his retreating figure with a gnawing ache right in her core. When she'd been pregnant with the twins it had been constant back and forth to antenatal appointments, there had been whispers of *gestational hypertension* and worried looks between obstetric consultants and their staff. When she looked back on it, even though it had ended happily with two healthy babies, her pregnancy marked the beginning of the end of her and Simon. Once that first niggle of uncertainty over the twins' health had crept in, it stayed with them like a virus, erupting through the cracks of every disagreement, a chorus of blame and resentment that went back to the very beginning. 'You should have given up work. You knew the risks...' The implication was that she cared more about her career than her children, and she could feel the twist of the knife with the vaguest of references. She wondered how Baz and Amber would deal with the prospect of a baby with a health problem, but that was a thought that needed shutting down before it took hold. It would probably never happen, and more importantly it was none of her business.

The office was displaying all the signs of half-term – clear desks, post-its on PC monitors with scribbled dates of absence and smiley faces, no sign of the usual puffer jackets slung over the backs of chairs or water bottles littering the windowsills, no smell of bad coffee, no raucous laughter at a shared joke. Those who were still due in had taken the liberty of a late start. Office conditions like these were rare, and it made the perfect scene for a follow-up chat with Ali Tremaine.

'DS Delmar, how can I help you?' Ali's face moved in and out of darkness as she found her way indoors. 'God it's hot out there. I needed an excuse to escape from the heat, so thank you for giving me that.' She broke off to flick back dark snakes of wet hair and take a bite of a what looked like a sandwich.

Ronnie did a quick calculation. Mauritius must be around four hours ahead, making it lunchtime. 'Call me Ronnie, please,' she began. Getting her witness to relax was key to getting the truth, and formalities were never going to oil the wheels of honesty. 'I won't keep you long. It's just that something's been on my mind since we spoke and I wanted to get it clear in my head so I don't go...' She hesitated. Reaching for unnecessary idioms was usually Baz Munro's speciality – something to do with his expert grasp of everything British.

'Barking up the wrong tree?' Ali grinned and pushed away another stray snake. 'I know what you mean. I'll do my best to enlighten you. What was it?'

'I want to take you back to that moment you shouted goodbye to Hannah.'

'Yep, walking out of the main reception room, into the lobby, and Hannah was in the study just off the lobby.'

'Door shut?'

'Door shut. Both doors. Fire doors, regulations or something – we always take the closers off but maybe cos Adam's a lawyer and stuff he likes to stay the right side of things like that.'

Ronnie smiled encouragingly. Detail was essential. 'And you heard her talking to Adam?'

'Yes, I mean not exactly heard, because as I said the door was shut and there was music playing in the kitchen, but I knew it was him. She told us it was him before she moved to the other room.'

Ronnie scribbled some notes. 'And, sorry to go on

137

about this but it's important. What exactly do you remember saying? As close to the actual words as you can, Ali, would be really helpful.'

'I said let's have a gossip later, while I'm waiting with the girls at the airport. Call me.'

Ronnie flicked back to her last set of notes from their conversation the previous day. It was going to be a long haul, if Ali gave a different answer each time. Her face had turned away as a voice called from outside, and for a second she was just a silhouette in profile, eyes on more exciting things than a police interview.

'Can you give me an impression of how loudly you shouted?'

'You want me to shout now?' A smile played at the corners of her mouth. 'OK then. Just a sec.'

She leapt up to close the door to outdoors before clearing her throat and composing herself. Her voice was suddenly sharp and shrill, a grating contrast to her dulcet phone voice.

'Let's catch up for a gossip when I'm at the airport. Call me.'

Ronnie looked down at her notes and smiled back at Ali. 'That's great. Now I have a proper picture of it, with a soundtrack.' Ali grinned back.

'You're welcome, DS – Ronnie, sorry. Ronnie is an unusual name. When I first saw it on the text I was expecting a man.'

It wasn't the first time someone had said that. 'Short for Veronica. And yes, I like surprising people.'

Jen Connolly was hovering by the office door as

she ended the call, talking quietly into her phone. She looked up as she said her goodbyes to Ali Tremaine.

'Give me two minutes.' She wanted to hear what she had to say, but she needed to process the information she'd just been given. Three differing accounts of Ali's last words to Hannah, two of which were given within seconds of each other. Was Ali doing it deliberately? If so, what reaction was she expecting? If it was genuinely a mistake, which Ronnie found hard to believe after making her focus intently on the detail, then how trustworthy was her testimony? She looked again at her notes. The words each account had in common were 'gossip' and 'airport'. For now, she'd just have to assume that Ali Tremaine had shouted those words, amongst others, to Hannah through a closed door on her way out of the flat, but the trail was going distinctly cold.

'Sarge? Sorry, I know you said two minutes but DC Munro's on the phone. Says yours was engaged. Even tried your personal phone.'

'I always turn that one off at work. You know the rules.' That was neither true, nor necessary, since they were all supposedly contactable on both numbers. They exchanged a hint of a smile. 'Shall I call him back or is he still there?'

Jen handed her the phone and she clicked the speaker button, motioning for Jen to sit.

'Baz? What have you got?'

'Sarge, I've just spoken to Giselle. She maintains this is the first she's heard of any accusations from

Hannah. I mean, as she told us, they weren't best mates, but there had never been any threatening behaviour from Hannah, and Giselle can't think of a reason she'd do this.'

'Kind of what we expected then. We had no indication there was anything serious between the two of them.'

'I guess, but I'm also thinking she's bluffing. She's building up a picture of herself as vulnerable and helpless – showing up at the station in floods of tears, wrongly accused and trusting the police to fix everything. Hardly likely to commit attempted murder.'

Ronnie put her head in her hands. 'But surely that message was a lead we were always going to follow and it puts her right in the firing line as a suspect. If she'd kept quiet, there would be no spotlight on her relationship with Hannah. She wouldn't even be a person of interest, with no prints on the knife and no motive. She has a lot to lose. I think it was a genuine shock.'

'What about her past? Hardly whiter than white. She sold amphetamines online.'

'To support herself in a crisis, when her benefactor left her high and dry. Look at her behaviour since. Remorse, rehabilitation – she's been the model citizen.'

'We're presuming. What if she's relying on that, on our belief in her turnaround?'

'I'm not sure she's clever enough for that.' Giselle just didn't come across as having the cunning or the arrogance required to attempt to manipulate the police. Ronnie glanced up at Jen who made a face that said she had a point. Baz was silent for a second before coming back with a new argument.

'You'd be amazed how clever a person can become when stuck in a tight spot.'

'I still don't see her as the assailant. It just doesn't sit well with me.'

They weren't going to agree, not until there was some evidence to support what was still effectively a hunch on both their parts, and Ronnie was about to end the call when she thought better of it.

'Baz, I know it doesn't always come across, but I do appreciate your hard work on this case.'

'We've opened a proper can of worms though, haven't we?'

'That's what we're here for, rifling through the worms till we find the answer.'

When the call had ended, Jen handed Ronnie a list of names and addresses. 'These are all the people who came *in* to the building in the hour leading up to the ambulance being called. Of course, whoever it was might have been hiding out there for days. There's only one we can't account for.'

Ronnie looked up with sudden interest. 'An arrival?'

'An arrival in the building we can't match to an apartment. It could still be an individual who had access, if someone was subletting, or if they were visiting someone who wasn't there and might not have known they were out. The image is too grainy to make any sense of, so it's going to take another round of chats.'

'You're about to tell me we don't have time for that.'

'Something along those lines, sarge. The boss says without a decent image we'd struggle to make an ID and any case would fall apart just on that.'

'Fair enough. I need to mull this over.'

She spun the chair round to face the window. By taking her focus outside the confines of the office, there was always the possibility of a thought landing from elsewhere and opening her mind to an idea she hadn't considered. The sky, or what she could see of it above the roofline opposite the station, was her muse, but today its blank grey palette reflected her mood right back at her. She moved her gaze down to Nico's café with its blanket-draped chairs and laid tables set out optimistically on the pavement, then left towards the shops that lined that end of the street; a dry cleaners, an insurance brokers, a mini cab office – all the excitement of a suburban commuter town on a dull October day. Life was in progress, a whole raft of lives, each of them oblivious to anything outside their bubble – a mother navigating her way through the crowds with a double buggy while texting one-handedly, a gaggle of office girls on their lunch break, sandwich bags in hand, an old couple arm in arm pulling a bulging shopping bag on wheels. Here were representatives of the present, the past and the future, briefly inhabiting the same space yet preoccupied exclusively with their private worlds. How soon before one of these people had to call on the emergency services – a sick baby, a spiked drink, the first signs of a stroke? It was only a matter of time, statistically.

Her father's time had come decades too early, and the circumstances of his death remained the one unsolved mystery in Ronnie's life. It was his disappearance that had kept her awake more nights than she could remember as she went over all the possible things that could have happened. The most palatable one, and therefore the one she would settle on if she wanted a chance of falling back to sleep, was ironically the most violent. She found it almost easier to imagine he had been murdered than to think that he'd had some sort of accident, or worse still, taken his own life. He had made plenty of enemies over the years, and there was a kind of logic in the idea that one of his gambling acquaintances might have decided to wreak revenge. The boat set adrift was the perfect decoy, and with no body or weapon, there was no murder. It made sense. She only hoped he hadn't seen it coming, hadn't experienced fear. The alternative explanation, that he had gone out to sea with a bottle of vodka and pockets full of rocks, to take the easy way out and escape financial ruin, filled her with horror.

The thought of going back to Waterman Lane that evening was weighing on her mind. Alice Delmar wasn't often lost for words. What she had to say must be something significant, and Ronnie wasn't sure she even wanted to hear it.

It was as she stood up to get her coat from the stand that Connolly appeared in the doorway again. Her face was grim.

'Jen?'

'A call just came in from the hospital.'

Ronnie held her breath, trying to stop time. The implications of what she was about to hear were already playing out in her mind. 'And?'

But she didn't need to listen to the answer. There could be only one reason for the call.

'Hannah Lloyd is dead.'

CHAPTER EIGHTEEN

Ronnie let the air out slowly, pulling it from every corner of her lungs until she was on the cusp of two worlds, the in-breath and the out, the focal point of meditation. Perhaps this was where the answers lay, if you could only stay there long enough to download them from the universe.

'So a murder enquiry begins.'

Mike Overton appeared, slightly out of breath. 'You've heard the news, I take it.'

'Indeed. Just digesting the implications.'

'Lydia knows. And DCI Preedy is on his way to mastermind the investigation with a whole bevvy of minions from major crimes.'

'Preedy?' Ronnie took another deep breath and held it for a second before exhaling slowly. She had first met DCI Matt Preedy on a manslaughter case some ten years earlier. In her head she assumed there would be a conviction for murder and saw no other way out for the accused who had a history of wife beating and coercive control, but the jury had taken a different view. It wasn't hard for the defence to discredit a dead witness. It was afterwards, in the bar after sentencing that Preedy had said something that stuck in her mind – something that made the hairs rise on her neck even now.

'Best not to get emotional about these things, DS Delmar.'

It wasn't unusual to hear those words from a male police officer, but he should have known better than to say it to her face. The male officers kept most comments of that sort for their private WhatsApp groups which languished undiscovered, until one careless one shared the material too far. In the heat of the moment, Ronnie had done what she'd have advised any other female officer to do – *let it go, never think of it again, water off a duck's back.* But her reaction to the mention of his name today suggested it hadn't entirely worked. The scene was still painted on her mind in Technicolor, his narrowed eyes, the hint of a smile on his lips.

'Not a fan, I take it?' Overton shifted awkwardly, watching her face.

'No, it's not that...' Ronnie scrabbled around for an alternative explanation. 'I was just thinking what this is going to involve. I was counting on her waking up. I didn't realise just how much.'

Jen looked concerned. 'It was touch and go, but they never let on quite how precarious the situation was, I guess. It wouldn't be the first time the doctors haven't given us the full picture, but we can only deal with what we have now.'

'Which isn't a whole lot,' Ronnie responded, uselessly.

'We don't have our key witness, sure, but we have other information. We haven't got to the bottom of the Delilah and Adam story, for one thing,' Overton offered.

She tried to smile. 'Of course. There's still a lot of work to do there, and elsewhere. Thanks for all your enthusiasm on this. God knows we need all the help we can get.'

'No worries, sarge, and if there's anything else I can do, apart from...' He glanced around. Jen Connolly had moved away to speak to the DI who seemed to be checking the tidiness of desks in some sort of panic that the headmaster was paying a visit. 'You know, the thing you asked about. I'm on it. Should have something soon.'

Overton was keen, intelligent, discreet. Just the kind of officer she'd need on her team once the DCI was looking over her shoulder. 'There will be. Let's talk in the morning.'

Frank's voicemail flashed up on her home screen as Overton walked away. 'It would be a pleasure to go with you, Ronnie. Can I collect you and drive you down? Helen's got a friend visiting for the evening and the carers come to settle her after that for the night. Perfect timing.'

Frank arrived five minutes earlier than planned, dressed in a quirky checked waistcoat under his trademark Barbour. He was a careful but efficient driver and as it turned out, the kind of conversationalist that made you feel like you were relaxing in a warm bath. He asked questions as much as he shared his own stories, laughed at hers about the antics of the twins, seemingly impressed at how she managed to balance career and single motherhood.

'How do you and the ex get on these days?'

It was a big question with a long answer that she didn't feel inclined to embark on. 'It's not too bad, especially since the divorce was finalised. He's got a girlfriend, the kids go over there pretty much when they want these days.'

'What about you? Anyone new on the scene?'

'Nobody... of note.'

Frank laughed. 'Good for you. Stay fussy until you meet the one who really deserves you.'

After that they sat for a while in silence as the countryside flashed past in the low light of sunset, until the trees met over the road and pavements gave way to brambly hedgerows. Ronnie closed her eyes and tried to remember what it was to be a child growing up on the borders of Kent and rural Sussex – the freedom to roam the high weald at the mercy of the elements, soaked with rain, drenched in sunshine, buffeted by the wind as you emerged from forest into open farmland. Her father had been determined that his daughters should appreciate their surroundings, understand the cycles of the seasons, distinguish the oak from the ash, a mushroom from a toadstool and look up, look down, observe. It was by his side that she had learnt her detective skills, and that the balance of man and nature was a delicate one.

They pulled into the drive at a quarter past seven. Alice Delmar was on the doorstep, her face a mixture of emotion, distress and delight, fear and joy. She was easy to read, and Frank's arrival had clearly done something to alleviate whatever pain she was going through. Ronnie felt the tension lift from her shoulders as she watched them reconnect, the longest hug, his arm around her as they stepped into the house, the hum of their voices as they skimmed the surface of ten years of news.

The smell of home cooking made her feel instantly at ease. Then there were the trinkets on the hall table, the family photographs on the mantlepiece, the hotchpotch of holiday souvenirs that clustered on the shelves her father had painstakingly put together in the alcoves around it. This was her life, their life as a family, living as if there would be no bad tomorrows, no future where one of them was missing, where a quarter of their number was removed, suddenly, with no reason and no answers.

And this was the room where she'd found her little sister, that evening more than two decades ago, crouched and terrified in the corner after being attacked by an intruder she had let into the house thinking it was Ronnie back from a party. Serena had insisted nobody must know, that their parents, away for the weekend at their seaside cottage, should never be told. She would deal with it herself. Ronnie had protested, had tried to call the police herself but Serena had shut it down with a promise to never speak to her again if she made her go through the nightmare of a court case. Ronnie had eventually acquiesced, riddled with guilt and resolved to find some other route to vengeance. Therein lay her lifelong commitment to the female cause, her determination to take the side of women against men when it came down to the wire. But it was a side of her that needed to be tempered, had to learn to adapt to the situation and get out of the way when required. That was something she needed to bear in mind, with Baz, with Preedy, maybe with Adam Lloyd. This wasn't a war she needed to fight every day.

When Alice brought a steaming shepherd's pie to the table, with peas, crusty bread and a bottle of Rioja from the cellar they tucked in as if they had never seen food before, and Frank said it was just like the old days, which brought a tear to Alice's eye.

Ronnie was checking the time on her phone by the time the reason for her visit was touched on. Alice took the dishes to the sink and cleared her throat, obviously needing all distractions to be removed for her announcement. Ronnie sat back with her arms folded, unsure if she wanted to hear it. The wine had gone to her head and her emotions were on stand-by, ready to flood out at the flick of a switch. Frank leaned forward, elbows on the table, his face suddenly serious, concerned.

'So, Alice, I understand from Ronnie there's something you need to tell us. Something about Fred, God rest his soul.'

It was an anachronistic expression, but her mother would have appreciated it, and Frank knew that. Ronnie smiled inwardly. Alice's face relaxed and her eyes rested on his, giving Ronnie the chance to watch them and take in what was going on between them as well as what her mother was saying.

'I'm still in shock. I didn't know what to do with the information when they came to tell me,' she began, suddenly flailing around for her words as the enormity of them engulfed her. 'They've found – a trawler boat found – a part of his skull.'

The tears came and she pulled out a tissue from the box next to her. 'I'm sorry. It was such a shock.'

Frank reached out to take her hand in his. Ronnie felt an instinct to pull it away and replace it with hers but stopped herself.

'When was this?'

'Two days ago. Tuesday. They took it to the police, who must have run tests and missing persons and they came to me this morning. Like the death knock all over again.'

Ronnie felt her insides turn over in shock as she replayed the news in her head. Frank asked more questions but she didn't hear the answers – just odd words that found their way through the mental barriers that were springing up as the information came in – jawbone, dental records, identification. Her job was to solve other people's mysteries, not her own. Finding your own family at the centre of an unexplained death was a different thing entirely from investigating the murder of a stranger.

Frank was running through the technical details of identifying a missing person from bone remains, which for some strange reason appeared to lift the mood slightly. The focus on the practical rather than emotional gave them something different to look at, and Ronnie found herself listening again, with strange gratitude.

'It's one of the clearer areas of forensic investigation, and with today's methods there are way fewer mispers in the back catalogue than there used to be. You don't need much to go on.' He hesitated for a second. 'Did they give you any details, as to the state of the remains, I mean? Was the bone intact? No trauma, blunt force? Bullet?'

Alice caught her breath and looked at Ronnie who had flinched in shock at the words, despite herself. 'No, why? Would that be something they would share with me at this stage?'

Frank let out a sigh. 'Not necessarily. You sometimes have to ask the right questions to get the answers you need. It shouldn't be like that, I know, but with the cutbacks and belt-tightening some of the cold cases get left on the sidelines, in my experience...' He drifted off. 'Let me look into it for you.'

'How do you mean – look into it? Check they're telling me everything?'

Frank hesitated, then smiled. 'Yes, just that. If there's anything else to know, I can find out.'

'Are you thinking there's a chance it could be...' Alice stopped herself saying the words. It might make it all true. Frank read her mind.

'Not necessarily. But whatever the case, you need answers. We all do.'

'And how are you planning on getting those

answers, Frank?' She gave him a look Ronnie remembered from childhood – the one that got the truth out of you every time.

'Well, if there is any suggestion of foul play, let's just say I've got a couple of contacts that owe me a few favours, if you know what I mean.' He threw Ronnie a wink.

Ronnie smiled uncertainly. 'I won't ask. I'm sure it's all above board.'

Alice was still holding his hand. 'It's just, it's so final. I suppose I was always thinking he'd come home, that maybe he'd run off to South America to escape from his gambling debts.'

Or his family, thought Ronnie. Things hadn't been plain sailing for the Delmars in Fred's last years with them. She had overheard the threats her mother had made to leave him unless he cleaned up his act, her dismissal of his efforts to rescue his failing business, her father's verbally violent responses to all that. It wasn't out of the question that he might want to find a way out, and stay there, however hard that was for her to accept.

When a pause allowed her to interject, she reached out for her mother's other hand. 'I'm so sorry, Mum. I feel the same shock. It's so hard to process. Have you told Seena?'

'An hour or so ago, when I knew you were on your way. She was up to her eyes in cooking so I'm sure it wasn't the best time, but I needed you both to know. It needed to come from me.' She had regained some of her composure and pulled her hands back to take hold of her wine glass with one and the tissue with the other. 'Thank you for coming. It meant a lot to me.' Her eyes drifted to Frank again, and his softened in response.

'It was a pleasure, despite the circumstances. Please let's not leave it so long next time.'

'You can come back anytime. I'll be here for another week, at least, sorting stuff out.'

'Well, let me make arrangements at home and on my next day off I will come and lend a hand. It's the least I can do.'

Alice beamed, and waved them off radiating a new aura of joy and warmth that Ronnie hadn't seen in a long time.

Their journey home seemed longer, as if they were weighed down by the heavy news. The silence in the car contrasted starkly with the rage of noise in Ronnie's head, picturing her father on his boat, imagining all the scenarios which might have led to his falling overboard. Were his debts so enormous that he took his own life, or was his death the work of an unpaid creditor who'd had enough of his prevarication? The thought of either made her feel sick. Now the very real possibility of murder had raised its head, perhaps it would be better to stick with the theory that he'd had a heart attack or a stroke, fallen overboard and been unaware of anything more than a twinge in his chest.

'Whatcha thinking?' Frank's words sliced through her misery and brought her back to earth. 'Or can I guess? And when I have, you've to stop it and change direction. There's no point dwelling on the past. You know that.'

He was right, but the pull of the mystery was stronger than her sense of self-preservation. 'I can't let go, Frank. Something inside me won't give up wondering.'

'I know. Believe me, and that's why I want to get involved and help if I possibly can. Sometimes I wish for something like this for me, some sort of closure about Jess, but I know it wouldn't be enough. There'd be more questions, more self-torture, thinking of all the ways I could have stopped it happening. At least you don't have that.'

'You're right, and I don't want to compare losing a father to losing a child, but the guilt still rankles. I'm full of guilt. I was seventeen when I let my own sister down. I wasn't there when she needed me. I'll never forgive myself for that.'

'For what?' He threw her an anxious glance. 'I don't think I know this story.'

'It's nothing.' She couldn't believe she'd nearly shared the secret she had sworn to keep. What was happening to her? Some kind of death-wish? 'Another time.'

'Guilt is like an uninvited guest. Turn them away at the door, or they'll take over in the kitchen, burn the dinner and spoil your evening.'

'Nice image. You mean I need to accept things and face them head on.'

'Yes, if you put it like that. What's done is done. Anything else is just self-sabotage.'

'I know.' Ronnie stared out of the windscreen at the black night. The countryside did darkness so much better than the suburbs, where it was almost impossible to escape the acid glow of streetlamps, but at least the light brought a certain comfort. It must have been hard for her mother in the months just after Fred disappeared – with no children at home and nothing but the bleak closing in of winter to look forward to. Thinking about it produced a stab of physical pain somewhere deep in her heart. 'And then there's the guilt about Dad. I can't get past that either now. He played poker to win money to help me and Serena through university. If it wasn't for us, he might not have got himself into debt and he'd still be alive now.'

'No.' With a swift turn of the steering wheel, Frank pulled into a rest area on the side of the road and killed the engine. He turned to face Ronnie, his expression more serious than she remembered ever seeing it. 'His death was not your fault. His gambling was not your responsibility. Will you promise me you will accept that as truth? Tell yourself that every day until you believe it. Whatever it takes. Anything else is a waste of emotion. A waste of life.'

Ronnie closed her eyes and exhaled. 'I promise, but only if you do too. We both go forward guilt-free and live our lives the way they'd have wanted us to.'

Frank started the engine. 'Agreed. But don't live yours like he did, Ronnie. There are limits.'

She laughed, and they fell into an easy silence until they were almost home.

'How's the investigation going?' Frank turned to her as they pulled up at the traffic lights outside Latchworth. 'Any progress with the neighbour?'

'Not much. Not enough,' said Ronnie, her shoulders slumping with the weight of the case back on her mind. 'There was a suggestion of something implicating her, and I've got someone looking into it but I suspect it's a false alarm. I'll find out tomorrow.'

'No other leads?'

'It's not an easy one. As long as Adam's in the clear, Baz is happy to pin it on just about anybody.'

'Defending his fellow alpha male?'

Ronnie looked at Frank quizzically. 'Have you met Baz? The two of them are in rather different categories when it comes to the Greek alphabet. But maybe there's something in that. I'm a bit suspicious of the patriarchy at the moment.'

'That's understandable. I'd feel uncomfortable being a woman in the police force. Ganged up on, at least. The bullying sends a lot of women away, puts a lot more off joining up in the first place. You don't think...?' He winced as if a sudden unpleasant thought had caught him by surprise.

Ronnie looked at him, alarmed. 'You think he might be one of them?'

'I have no idea, and I hope he isn't. I rather thought we'd seen the back of the whole sorry mess. I think that's what everybody hoped.' The lights went green and they pulled away. 'I don't know much about the psychology of it. I just know that there are layers to people, reasons for behaviour they'd rather we didn't know.'

'Not Baz Munro. He'd never be one of those, what do you call them, *bad apples*. He's one of the good ones.'

'Fair enough. I don't envy you Ronnie. SOCO is a much easier job. Go in, collect evidence that can't lie, job done. I don't miss having the job of going through literally every single person possible, running through every hypothesis. So much wasted time for a start.'

'It is, but there's no choice in this case, with everyone's prints on the knife and all the phones wiped clean of anything that might indicate a motive for murder.'

'Murder? I thought...'

'She died this morning. Sorry. I just assumed word had got around.'

'I'm so sorry. Although I can't say I'm surprised. It was a long way to fall.'

'The worst thing about it is we now get a visit from the DCI, obviously on the assumption that suburban cops can't handle the big stuff.'

'Who did you get?'

'Preedy.' She glanced at Frank, whose concentration was back on the road. 'I know. Totally the last person I need in my life right now.'

'He was a bit of a dick, if I remember rightly.'

'Yep. I'm going to have to dig deep and give myself a talking to so I can deal with all the "did you flutter your little eyelids at him" and "I'm not surprised you got a promotion, wearing that skirt," and — well. I won't go on.'

Frank glanced at her. 'I hope you complained to HR.'

'I wish I'd had the guts, but you know, when the reins of your career progression are held by your jailer, you kind of go along with it, almost conspire with the whole process.'

'You shouldn't be so hard on yourself. You were afraid to speak out.'

'People speak out nowadays, though don't they? Things are changing.'

Frank exhaled deeply as they swung into the estate. 'They are, slowly. But yes.'

When he pulled up outside Ronnie's flat and killed the engine, she leaned over and kissed him on the cheek, catching the scent of clean linen and springtime. 'I am so grateful you came with me,' she murmured. 'You have no idea.'

He gave her arm a squeeze. 'It has been an honour and a privilege to be of service. But I need to get home pretty sharpish. Helen will be suspecting all sorts.'

Ronnie watched the taillights disappear with a new-found sense of safety. The ground was no longer being pulled from under her. She had an ally. She could do this.

CHAPTER NINETEEN

Mike Overton was waiting at her office door at eight thirty the next morning clutching a water bottle in one hand, laptop in the other.

'Mike, you beat me to it. How did you get on with the cyber-stalking?' Ronnie pulled off her jacket and hung it on the back of her chair before gesturing to him to take a seat opposite her. 'Your face says you're not sure.'

He glanced over his shoulder. The office was filling up slowly with a new team from major crimes, some of whom Ronnie recognised from previous cases, but aside from the whirr of the printer and muted water-cooler chat, it was still quiet. He leaned over and spoke in a tone approaching a whisper. 'I found her.' He flipped open his laptop and placed it on the desk between them.

'Show me.' Ronnie pulled her chair in and leaned over to look at the screen, where the silhouette of a figure resembling Giselle, but who could have been anyone, stood in a window, backlit by moonlight. Clicking on the tabs revealed a list of 'discreet' services followed by a page of testimonials from happy clients.

'You're sure this is her?'

'Well, from the information you gave me...'

Ronnie zoomed in on the photograph. Generic. A

silhouette. 'I couldn't ID her from this, I don't think.'

Overton sat back and folded his arms. 'Fair enough. It was a match with her name, that's all, and it's pretty much advertising exactly what we expected.'

Ronnie turned the screen back to Overton and put her chin in her hands. 'Can you find out where the site is hosted, when it was set up and by whom?'

'We'd need a good reason to get the information on the source, sarge. They won't hand it over without a court order.'

'How about testing it out?' Ronnie looked him in the eye to gauge his response which was immediate, and verging on horrified.

'What sarge, you mean...?' Overton's eyes widened. 'You want me to try and book a session with a prostitute?'

'It sounds bad when you say it like that, but just test the form, see if it generates a response. Set up a fake account, obviously we don't want it being traced.'

'But, sarge, what if the boss finds out? Now we've got Preedy breathing down our necks, who knows what the penalties will be for stepping out of line? You heard about the latest round of sackings where he came from. Squeaky clean we've got to be, or we'll get the same treatment.'

Ronnie considered this. It wasn't the first time she had reached automatically for a line of investigation that wouldn't pass muster at a misconduct hearing, but most of the time it didn't come to that. She wasn't the only detective treading a fine line between lawful procedure and effective policing, and Overton would realise that, sooner or later, in his own time.

'I don't want you to do anything you're not comfortable with, but it just might draw a line under this line of investigation and clear her name. In any event...' She glanced at the time on her phone. 'Morning briefing with DCI Preedy. Brace yourself. This place has no idea what's about to hit it. And remember, I'm going to need you ready for our plan B.'

A handful of officers gathered around the whiteboard where Preedy stood in caricature manstance, legs apart, hands on hips, his gaze surveying the meagre turn-out. Ronnie observed him from the behind her coffee mug, willing herself to brush away the prejudices lodged in her mind. Their disagreement, for what it was worth, was far enough in the past to be forgotten, or at least overlooked, for now. She forced a smile, which Preedy caught and returned, his eyes meeting hers for a second with a look of curiosity. Whatever he wanted to know, she wasn't about to give anything away. Sensing her resolve, he turned back to the assembled audience.

'As you will know by now, I'll be overseeing the Lloyd case, following the death of Hannah Lloyd two days ago. I will be assisted by my very able team who will shortly be introducing themselves, and also by some of the local talent.' He gave cursory nods in the direction of Ronnie, Baz and Overton. 'With any luck we'll be bringing this unfortunate matter to its conclusion in short order.' He sought eye contact with as many officers as he could before continuing. 'And I applaud you all for your immense dedication to the job so far. Our current line of investigation, namely into Adam Lloyd, who appears to have reasonable motive and opportunity, has not as yet, despite the valiant efforts of Halesworth CID, yielded a case solid enough to warrant an arrest. My principal grounds for believing this are as follows.'

Ronnie held her breath and Preedy paused to let a rumble of dissent subside before continuing. 'He wasn't seen, by witnesses or cameras anywhere near the building at the estimated time of the attack, his extra-marital activity is just surmise, with nothing more than the theories of a bunch of gossiping women to substantiate it.' Another hum of disagreement washed across the room and Ronnie felt the hairs on her neck rise up in protest. 'I know this may not be a popular theory, but it's the one I want to go with. Adam Lloyd...' He paused for effect. 'Despite the statistics being against him, was in all likelihood not responsible for the death of his wife.'

Ronnie raised her eyebrows at Baz who mirrored her expression.

'Giselle Gaillard, however, the rumbunctious neighbour with a key to Hannah's flat, is much more interesting to me, especially given the allegations that have emerged relating to her side hustle, which Hannah seems to have been aware of, and was about to blow out of the water.'

Ronnie frowned, partly at the unlikelihood of the

scenario he was describing and partly at herself, already re-labelling Preedy as a sexist monster unable to have the finger of the law pointing at a white, middle-class Tory politician. She pushed the thought to the back of her mind. For now she needed to take him at face value.

'As I think we have established, emails can be programmed to be sent at a future date, so the timing of the message from Hannah's account is not the mystery it would appear to be.' Preedy and Baz exchanged a glance that made Ronnie furious with herself. She hadn't even considered the possibility of a delayed send option. 'And as for prints on the knife,' he continued. 'Well, just balance up the possibilities here – it's considerably more likely that Giselle Gaillard used her key and wore *gloves* than Adam Lloyd killed his wife to avoid his affair getting into the press.'

'What about the other witnesses, sir?' A voice from the back. 'Surely the brother...?'

'I was coming to that, but before we focus on James, let's take a look at Delilah Byrne. She's a practising solicitor with no previous history of misbehaviour of any sort. Then we come to the Garretts. There is some evidence that Hannah's brother and possibly therefore his wife resented the inheritance. James' alibi needs testing – so let's talk to the neighbour, get detail from them both on how the afternoon went, see if they trip up. Talk to his friends, colleagues, see what they knew about him, find out if he shared anything on social media that interests us. He's not off my radar yet.' There was nodding and scribbling from the cluster of officers before him. He looked back at his notebook. 'Ali Tremaine, the clinical psychologist swanning around Mauritius is of no interest to us. She left for the airport some time before the others departed and has no motive whatsoever. Lastly, we still have the issue of the unidentified figure entering Hannah's block at around four-twenty pm. Let's look at fire exits, CCTV on those and along any routes someone might take escaping that way. Take prints off the doors. If there's even a sniff of a chance they've been used in the last week I want to know about it.' He leant forward on the chair in front of him, grasping its back tightly with white knuckles. 'Any questions?'

The room fell silent for a few seconds before Ronnie spoke up.

'Actually, sir, if I might have a word when you're done. I think there's something you might be interested to hear. It's about Adam Lloyd.'

Preedy surprised her with a smile. 'Of course, DS Delmar. Now if there's nothing else, I want you to go back to your desks, you've all got a job to do building a case against Giselle Gaillard and James Garrett. Let's get this mess cleared up once and for all.'

With a clap of hands, the gathering was dismissed. Preedy led Ronnie into Lydia's, now his, office and leant on the desk, arms folded for battle.

'DS Delmar, I thought I made myself clear enough at the briefing. The case against Adam Lloyd simply doesn't hold water. The CPS won't touch it. I think I've been in this job long enough to know that.'

He was mansplaining, but she could womansplain back to him. 'Absolutely clear, sir and I don't dispute your reasoning either, but I just had one more avenue to explore. It involves an experiment, but it should prove something that in turn will suggest there may be more to this.'

'You've got it in for Mr Lloyd haven't you, Veronica?' His eyes made Ronnie feel instantly uncomfortable, but with a supreme effort she ignored it, and felt an unfamiliar rush of satisfaction just for having made the mental leap to remaining untriggered.

'If you mean do I want to find our killer, and turn over every stone to do so, then yes, you may be right there.' She faced him with a half-smile. 'But if you mean am I targeting him to the exclusion of all other suspects, then it's a definite no. Whoever was behind the attack on Hannah Lloyd, I want them found.'

'I'm glad we understand each other.' Preedy's mouth was smiling, but his eyes stayed cold and expressionless. Ronnie forged ahead. The sooner this was over, the better for all of them. 'There's something that I want you to witness, sir, before you make a final decision. It concerns Adam Lloyd, and may have a bearing on motive.'

Preedy motioned for her to go on.

'Adam Lloyd said in his statement that he phoned Hannah around one-thirty pm on the day in question, to confirm their arrangements. He was very definite about the fact that there was no background noise during the call, and Hannah didn't tell him she had friends round.'

'What does this have to do with anything? Parents make plans. I'm sure you speak to your ex from time to time about what's happening with the kids?'

Ronnie flinched. She couldn't remember ever having talked to him about the twins, and was momentarily puzzled not just how he knew, but why he had just chosen to bring it up. 'Of course,' she stammered. 'But that's not the point. The thing is, I believe he may have overheard something during that short call that might have alarmed him, given him a reason to at least visit Hannah to establish what was going on, what information she was sharing, and perhaps to remind her that that might be an unwise decision. There's a possibility, and I'm stressing the word possibility...' Ronnie paused to make sure she had his full attention. 'That one thing led to another. I'm not saying he meant to kill her, but he has a quick temper, by his own admission.'

'And the timings?'

'It just about works, if he's the mysterious figure coming into the building and took the fire exit, he could have made it to collect Max and back again.'

'Didn't he go on about the roadworks?'

'No cameras to prove or disprove that, but he could have taken a back route to avoid them. I think seven to eight minutes at speed each way. It's tight, but possible.'

Preedy looked at her with new interest, as if a switch had been flicked. 'Okay, I like the detail. You've done the sums. So what did he overhear? I'm all ears.'

'Ali Tremaine was leaving just when the call took place. She remembers Hannah going into another room to take the call, and she called goodbye through the closed door.'

'And?' Preedy was looking at his buzzing phone. Ronnie gritted her teeth for a second to gather her composure.

'She called out to Hannah that she was looking forward to hearing all the gossip later when she was at the airport.'

'And this is relevant because...?'

'Because if Adam is about to be outed as a philandering bastard, just before the bi-election which makes or breaks his political career, I think he might have something to say about it.'

'Something to say, maybe, but firstly it's a pretty vague word, even if he did overhear it, and secondly, murder? Really?'

'I know you have dropped the affair scandal idea as a viable motive, and I agree, it's probably not a credible motive for murder, even when the stakes are high. It's not worth the risk, or it shouldn't be, But firstly we don't know he intended to kill her, maybe it was just a threat. Like I said, he's got a proper temper. His little boy said the same. And secondly...' She paused for breath, now she was sure he wasn't going to interrupt. 'A sex scandal, or at least the kind of sex scandal we're envisaging here, isn't the only 'gossip' Ali might have been referring to. If there's something else he's involved in, something worse, something we haven't even thought of yet, then maybe that would be worth the risk.'

Preedy chewed the inside of his cheek and looked around his office. 'Right, so what's this experiment of yours?'

CHAPTER TWENTY

The phone rang four long rings before Adam Lloyd answered.

Ronnie sat down in Lydia's swivel chair to calm her nerves. The DI's office provided the perfect conditions for the call; a quiet room, a closed door. Now she just needed Overton to do his bit.

'Adam Lloyd speaking.'

His voice was jittery and Ronnie was momentarily flustered, before remembering that this was a man whose wife had only died two days earlier, and however difficult his relationship with her had become, she was still Max's mother. Looking after a child whose mother had died must bring its own challenges, even if you had committed the act yourself. She focused her eyes on the leather trim of Preedy's briefcase and cleared her throat. She needed to banish her presumptions about this man once and for all and focus on the evidence, a piece of which she was sure was just about to emerge.

'Adam. Sorry to bother you again so soon. And at such a dreadful time for you and Max.'

'It's not the best time, no. But you lot don't seem to give a fuck about that, if you'll pardon my French.' There was an echo. He was on speaker again, trying to get the power back. He was welcome to it if she got what she wanted out of the call.

'I just need to clear up a discrepancy between your statement and the evidence of another witness.'

'Again?'

'Again, yes I'm afraid so. It shouldn't take too long.'

There was a long sigh at the other end of the line. 'Go ahead then.'

'It's about the last call you made to Hannah about the arrangements for Max.'

Another sigh. 'Don't expect me to remember it word for word. A lot's happened since then.'

'Can you do your best for me?'

Ronnie signalled to Overton through the office window and he gave her a thumbs up before calling out the words, 'Briefing in three minutes sarge.' Ronnie gave him a thumbs up back.

Adam ran through the content of his conversation with Hannah. It had been little more than a reminder that he'd be bringing Max back around five, that he didn't have a key, that he needed to get straight off to meet the Home Secretary for drinks and dinner at his club. Hannah didn't need to know what he was getting up to, or so she told him, and reminded him he still had plenty of clothes at the flat that he might like to pick up. Then she hung up on him.

'So you really had moved out, permanently?' He'd never made it clear, but then again how clear were separations anyway? There were usually a good few months, even years, of to-ing and fro-ing involved in the break-up of a marriage.

'Yes, I suppose I had. Not through my choice.'

'And you still maintain that this was nothing to do with a relationship between you and Delilah Byrne.'

'Yes I fucking do. Not that it's relevant. But you're never going to believe me.'

'And she didn't say anything more to you on that call?'

'Nothing.'

'And there was no background noise to indicate she had guests. No voices?'

There was a sharp intake of breath on the line, Ronnie was sure of it, but Adam Lloyd wasn't giving anything away just yet. He answered her in a voice that betrayed nothing of his nerves, if he had any.

'I'm sure I've told you this before. I don't remember hearing anything. First I knew of any gathering was the mess when I arrived at the flat with Max. She kept her private life pretty private. Didn't give me any details.'

'Did Hannah want a divorce?'

'I don't know. I suppose that was where we were headed. Irrelevant now, though.'

Ronnie hesitated for a second, with 'irrelevant now' ringing in her head. Of course it was irrelevant, but then it sounded odd, the words coming from the man she thought had killed his own wife. Was she missing something? The flash of thought was cut off before it could develop. Adam's next words brought him right back into her line of fire.

'Anyway, detective, you'd better be getting to your

briefing rather than flogging this dead horse.'

As Ronnie ended the call, Overton pushed open the door and glanced at Preedy with a nod. 'Did you get what you wanted?'

Ronnie sank back on the plush leather and relished her moment of triumph. 'There's nothing wrong with Adam Lloyd's hearing. He's lying through his teeth. And there's definitely something he didn't want Hannah and Ali discussing.'

It took a few seconds for Preedy to absorb her words. 'I'm not sure how much it proves, but I agree that there may be more to uncover here. The interesting question is – why is he denying that he overheard something if it was innocent?'

'Exactly, sir.'

'And I saw from the transcript of your interview with Ali Tremaine that Hannah said she had some information to share with her?'

'Yes, although Hannah hadn't specified at any point, and neither did she bring it up during the lunch, so that rather confuses me.'

'Something for Ms Tremaine's ears only.'

Ronnie pondered the idea. With no Hannah to elaborate it was going to be a hard task finding out what this something was. Her mind was struggling to join the dots when Preedy interrupted with a series of instructions.

'Let's go back over Hannah's movements through the whole of the previous twenty-four hours. I want to know exactly where she went, who she saw, what she said, how she seemed. I want to know word for word what she said to Ali in terms of what she had found out. If there was something she knew, I want to know what it was.'

'Yes, sir.' Overton had already pulled out a notepad and was scribbling to catch up.

'And Ali mentioned that there had been some kind of text exchange between them? Did you find this on Hannah's phone?'

Ronnie felt a wave of heat pass over her. They hadn't gone looking for gossipy texts between girlfriends. They'd been too busy looking for accusations of infidelity. How could she have missed that?

'We have the phone. I'll get on that straightaway, sir.'

'And when is Ali Tremaine home from this holiday of hers? Can we bring her in?'

He was on board. She needed to dig deep and get it right this time. 'She's due back tomorrow night. Leave it with me.'

On her way home, she reflected that something had changed in Preedy's attitude towards her. His eyes lingered on hers a fraction of a second longer than was necessary, and not in a predatory way, but more as if the scales had been pulled from his eyes. Something in his mind had registered that she was more than another girl in the office. She had measurable value as a detective.

It wasn't till she was turning the key in the front door of her flat that her phone pinged with a text from him.

I think I have some apologising to do.
Then:
How are you fixed to meet up for a chat on Sunday?

CHAPTER TWENTY-ONE

Ronnie decided to take a cab to Serena's, in some sort of attempt to convince herself that she was (a) a free spirit without responsibility and (b) living the dream, where being chauffeured to a dinner party was just the norm. The truth was, she wanted to have a few cocktails and take her mind off the case for a few hours. Coming back to it after a break might make all the difference to her clarity of thinking, unless it was disguised by thick hangover. It was worth the risk though. She ran a bath and poured herself a glass of prosecco for an extra touch of luxury. It was so rare that she took a bath rather than a shower these days, and yet it was infinitely more relaxing. Like going to the theatre or going away for the weekend, it was an activity that went hand in hand with the question *why don't I do this more often?*

As she sank into the bubbles, the alcohol did its work, loosening her thinking and allowing her mind to wander. The events of the last week had left her grappling for certainty about anything at all and they needed unpicking and restacking if she had any chance of making some sense of it.

Hannah Lloyd had been murdered, or at least attacked with the intention of causing serious harm. That was an easy presumption to make, but like all presumptions, it needed to be challenged. Did whoever attacked Hannah actually intend to harm her? Or was it a fight that went wrong? Could it even have been a fight initiated by Hannah, where the murderer lashed out in self-defence? Or was it perhaps a botched attempt to frighten her or scare her off. Had she seen something? Did she know something she shouldn't have? Adam lying about what he had heard or hadn't heard was strong evidence for that, but they needed to keep their options open. What she had wanted to discuss with Ali T, and what Ali shouted through the door could both be unrelated to the actual attack. If Hannah knew something, they were still no closer to finding out what it was. Her diary delivered nothing more than a schedule of anodyne appointments which, with the exception of the mysterious *FC?* could be validated and explained.

The next question was the identity of her assailant, but to establish that, or hand in hand with that, was their motive. Revenge? Jealousy? Money? Love? They had dug deep into the Adam and Delilah angle, and neither that nor the family inheritance drama had yielded any concrete leads. It felt as if they were going round in circles, all the while looking for a chink in the armour of one of their witnesses that might lead to the final unravelling of the truth. Today they had come nearer than they ever had to that chink – another hole in Adam Lloyd's story. In Ronnie's experience, once one hole was found, more would follow, and after his mis-recollection of football pick-up time and his failing to mention taking the knife off Max, claiming not to have heard the voice in the background of his phone call with Hannah was his biggest mistake yet. She was certain they were getting close. Now it was just a matter of maintaining focus to the end, however long it took.

Yet the question of Adam being triggered into action by what he overheard was still a tenuous link in the chain of events and might just have led them down another dead-end street of investigation.

Pulling on a dressing gown over her bath towel, and pouring herself another glass of fizz to calm her agitated brain, she sat on the edge of the bed to send a text to Ali who would be boarding a plane at some point in the next twelve hours. It was worth one more go.

Give me a call when you're back. I have a theory I want to run by you.

As the message went, a voice note landed from Overton. She waited until the full minute had downloaded, then pressed play, hoping against hope it wasn't an office emergency, just when she'd decided to let her hair down.

'Hi, Ronnie, sorry, sarge, it's me, Mike. Just to say I did what you asked. I tried to make an... errr... appointment, on the online form, set up on a private browser, VPN and so on, and anyway the message came back undeliverable. I think whoever set this up didn't imagine we'd test it. And as you said, it wasn't a big deal. Sorry for being so squeamish about it.' There was a clearing of the throat, a shuffling of something, then, 'So that's it basically. Have a good weekend, and yeah I think we can conclude it's not our Giselle. She's not a hooker, I mean, sex-worker. Sorry, bye.'

Ronnie laughed, flopped back on the bed, stared at the ceiling and imagined Mike Overton composing his email to Giselle. It must have felt even more awkward than recording the voice note, which was clearly way out of his comfort zone. He was a real trooper, that was for sure.

***

By the time she knocked on her sister's door an hour later, the details of the case and her week in the office had faded from her mind and a haze of happiness had taken its place. She was ready to party.

Serena wasn't famous for her parties, but she had transformed the new extension into a sparkling grotto. A trail of fairy lights around the indoor plants, weaving amongst the ivy along the edge of the roof lights gave the new room a cosiness that was permanently missing from Ronnie's flat. A fire glowed in the hearth and the smell of melted cheese wafted from the oven as Serena closed it with a flourish. In the background, Bob Marley's dulcet tones reminded her not to worry about a thing. Ronnie felt a pang of envy at her sister's knack of turning a house into a home.

Frank Reilly was standing warming his hands by the fire and chatting animatedly to psychotherapist and ex-detective Susie Marshall. Spotting her best friend and former colleague in the doorway, Susie ran up to Ronnie and threw her arms round her.

'Ron! So good to see you!'

'And you, Suze, looks like Serena's gathered all my favourite people together tonight.'

Serena gave a little whoop of delight in response. 'And always invite the neighbours if you don't want complaints about the noise, isn't that what they say?'

George and Joel were at the island mixing drinks with movie-star gusto. George put down his cocktail shaker and planted a dramatic kiss on both of Ronnie's cheeks. 'Welcome *chica*. You're just in time to try our famous Negroni.'

Joel handed Ronnie a cocktail glass. 'We're going to have to behave ourselves with two police officers in the room. You're not on call or anything are you?'

'Absolutely not, but I'll be keeping an eye on the behaviour obviously, so maybe save the class A drugs for another occasion.'

George opened his mouth in mock horror. 'But I was about to invite you into the loos for a cheeky line.' He turned to shout over his shoulder. 'Joel, you'll need to put the smack away. Plod's here.'

Serena threw her arms around George's waist from behind and rolled her eyes at Ronnie. 'God, he doesn't know when to stop, does he?' She accepted a Negroni and called Frank over, reaching to turn down the record player. Frank sauntered over, raising his glass to Ronnie and mouthing *good to see you*. Ronnie raised hers back and smiled a smile that said *thank you for everything*.

Serena was clinking a spoon on her glass. 'Now

that you're all here,' she began, her bright gaze sweeping over her guests, 'I'd like to propose a toast. In this room tonight we are friends for so many different reasons: because we grew up together—' She gave Ronnie a nod. 'Because we live next door, worked together or played an important role in each other's lives, however long ago that was.' Her eyes rested on Frank until he acknowledged her with an embarrassed bow of the head. 'There are so many places in life where we meet people that make a difference to us, that support us, help us through the dark times. We're lucky to have each other. So here's a toast to friendship!' She raised her glass and her words echoed around the room. She was right, Ronnie thought, suddenly very glad she had made the effort to come. Without friendship, everything was pointless.

After the starter, where Serena stunned them with individual cheese soufflés that stifled all attempts at conversation, Joel asked the question Ronnie had been expecting, the one someone always asked her at a social event. The general public had a morbid fascination with detective work, clearly unsatisfied by the wall-to-wall screenings of police dramas on every streaming platform. A real-life detective, or in this case three of them, was too great an opportunity to pass up.

'What do you actually do all day, when there's no crime going on?' He wiped a piece of bread around his soufflé dish to catch the last traces of the starter.

Ronnie shook her head, smiling at her empty plate. 'If only people were as well-behaved as you believe them to be. In my almost two decades of policing, I can't remember a day when there was nothing going on. Doesn't mean we're arresting people the whole time, far from it. It's looking into things that takes the time. Plenty of investigations end up with no solution – sometimes it turns out there was nothing to investigate. The family jewels were under the bed the whole time. The husband hasn't taken his own life, he's run off with his mistress, or charges for assault are dropped by the complainant, often when they shouldn't be. There are all sorts of reasons why things don't go anywhere, and yes it can be frustrating, disappointing, a waste of time even.'

Joel looked disappointed.

'Next question?' Perhaps talking shop wouldn't be so bad after all. George was waving from across the table.

'Me, I've got a question. So what's the best way to get away with murder?' He leaned forwards, elbows together on the table, chin in his hands.

Joel threw his head back and laughed. 'I knew I should have put the lid back on the toothpaste. I promise not to do it again. Please spare me!'

Ronnie sat back and pretended to think about it. The strange thing was that the answer lay in solved murder cases where the murderer had been caught and therefore hadn't got away with it at all. In most cases it was the complexity of the investigation that had resulted in the drawing up of lists of dos and don'ts for would-be assassins.

'Frank will correct me I'm sure, as a scene of crime officer himself, but I'd say death by ice sculpture is always a winner.'

'Or a leg of lamb that you go on to cook and eat,' added Susie. 'Sorry Serena, but it probably doesn't work with tofu.'

Serena gave her a nudge. 'But what about the other stuff? Apart from the weapon, what are your top tips for murderers who don't want to be caught? I mean, wear gloves and dodge the cameras obviously.'

'I actually love this question,' Frank broke in. 'Right up my street. If you want to defeat us SOCOs, my advice is: Beware the DNA trail, which means you have to wear protective gear, not just gloves but hood, boot covers, the lot. We can find traces of you from practically anything these days, but a hair or a fibre from a piece of clothing can go a long way to identifying a suspect. So *that* means, if you want to make absolutely sure there's no link back to you, don't touch the body.'

Joel's expression was serious. 'Why do so many bodies get moved then? Happens all the time, doesn't it?'

'A whole bunch of reasons. Mainly to hide the evidence that a crime has been committed at all, or so they can make it look as if someone else did it, framing them by taking the body to another place, and then there's the old trick of making the body disappear by chucking it in a lake or an incinerator. By the time you find the ashes or dredge the lake there won't be much to tie the crime to you.'

'So lakes and incinerators are exceptions to the moving the body rule?'

'Joel! Stop with the gross questions!' George put his hands over his ears.

Ronnie was grateful. Frank was a fount of knowledge, for sure, but this was getting too close to home for comfort. All she could think of was her father. Susie caught her eye and mouthed, 'You OK?' She forced the thought away and nodded.

Frank was already answering Joel. 'Maybe, but then how do you transport it? Bound to be evidence you've moved it, traces of their blood in your car boot, a witness seeing you carrying a heavier than usual sack out of the building, DNA, a random phone in a pocket you've forgotten to check with a signal bouncing off masts everywhere.'

Joel's eyes widened. 'Christ, I'd never thought about it like that. What else do the best murderers do to avoid getting caught?'

Frank exchanged glances with Ronnie. 'Your turn, Veronica. What advice have you got for these young reprobates?'

Ronnie sat up straighter in her chair. She placed her cutlery on her plate and paused for effect. 'Let me see. Make a plan, well in advance if you want to get it right. Buy your murder tools and equipment out of town, a few weeks before the murder – unless it's an ice sculpture of course – in disguise, driving a hire car booked under a false name and destroy all the receipts. Create an alibi by booking yourself into something that they can't prove you weren't at.'

Susie put her head in her hands. 'I'm just remembering why I left the police.'

Ronnie was grateful for the chance to pass the baton. 'Go on, Suze, give these trainee criminals your top tips.'

'Well, I only have one piece of advice, and it's the hardest thing to do in real life. When they catch you, which they will, because in reality most killers get caught, don't speak at the interview.'

'Ah, the no comment thing.' George leant back in his chair and frowned. 'How does that work exactly? I mean, wouldn't you want to get your story out there, practise it before you get into court? Doesn't *no comment* make you look guilty? When you stand up in court and suddenly come up with a story you weren't prepared to give when they arrested you?'

'Juries are used to the no comment interview backstory. Despite the reminder they get from the judge to take it into consideration, they don't tend to view it as a sign of guilt. And if you get arrested for something you didn't do, and have no idea about, it's your best option. Come up with a statement with your solicitor, tell that to the detectives and the rest is no comment because it's like saying "*I'm not going to even join in with this ridiculous discussion.*"'

Ronnie laughed. 'Susie's got a point, and it's more likely to make the police incredibly frustrated, and bearing in mind they only have twenty-four hours in which to charge you or release you, it's one way of not finding yourself in front of the magistrates in the morning.'

'And most importantly you don't risk implicating yourself, or giving something away accidentally, something the police didn't know, or that they can dig into to make your story collapse.'

Ronnie pointed at Susie. 'I remember you being a dab hand at interviews. They'd be all "no comment" with a smug grin on their face and then you'd drop something in about their girlfriend or their mother and trigger some sort of automatic response that would have the whole story pouring out unabridged.'

Susie smiled. 'Once or twice maybe. But it definitely wasn't my favourite thing, interviewing a suspect.'

'What was your favourite thing?' Frank asked.

'Sitting back and spotting the bullshit. I'm fascinated by the psychology of lying.'

'How does that work again?' Frank asked with a chuckle. 'Averting the eyes, fidgeting, sweating...'

'If that was all there was to it, we'd be a lot more confident charging them.' Susie laughed. 'The problem is, liars often have a practised story they have perfected – and they've learnt to cover up all the tell-tale nervousness signals. By the same token, you can be a nervous person telling the truth. They've done studies on it, and relying on visual clues only gives you a fifty-fifty chance of detecting a liar.'

'So how do you tell? Ronnie, you do this all the time. What's the secret?'

Ronnie shrugged. 'Hard to put your finger on. There are verbal clues, like overdoing description, or missing out one key sensory element of a scene. Say, if you were describing being at a party and you don't mention the music. But most of all it's gut feeling. You just get a nose for it. Each individual is different. To a certain extent you can work out the tells, by letting them tell you things you know to be true, then something you know not to be. But it's not failsafe. Hence the gut thing.'

'What was it about policing that made you switch careers, Susie?' Frank asked.

'The toxic patriarchy?' Joel again.

'Strangely nothing to do with that,' Susie began, thoughtfully. 'I didn't come up against much sexism personally, or if I did it went over my head.' Ronnie gave her a look. The truth of it was that Susie could give the men as good as she got, and wasn't above overt workplace flirtation if the situation required it. She was one of the guys when it came to sexual politics.

'My problem in the police was that I was all about what motivates a person to commit a crime, and there isn't the time or resources for that in the police. It's catch them and hand them over to the CPS, then go and catch more. I was always more curious about what had gone on in their childhood, what early life influences had turned them into a person that breaks the law, risks their own life and freedom by taking away someone else's.'

'So it's not their fault. It's their parents?' George's

expression was more mischievous than serious, Ronnie was relieved to see. She dreaded the thought of being solely responsible for her children's future crimes, but it was something she had thought about on more than one occasion when she saw the homes some gang members came from. Family background and the environment you grew up in played a part without a doubt.

'To a certain extent, maybe yes.' Susie took a sip of her wine and wiped her mouth with a napkin. 'And that way of thinking didn't endear me to CID, but it's a compulsory requirement for the job I do now, so there you go. We need to play to our strengths.'

'Here's to that.' Frank poured everyone a top-up of wine. 'And cooking a fabulous meal is clearly one of Serena's. To our hostess!' They clinked glasses across the table. 'And now, Veronica and I shall clear the plates and she shall not lift a finger.'

'Well, this has been a welcome change from my usual Friday night in front of the telly,' said Frank, pulling open the dishwasher. 'And Helen had her book club coming round, so I wouldn't even have been allowed downstairs.'

'How is she doing? I keep meaning to invite the two of you over. It's accessible at the flat, lifts and ramps everywhere.'

'That's kind of you Ronnie. I'd love to take you up on it. It's been such a pleasure reconnecting with your family. I'm just so sorry about what your poor mother's going through at the moment. Must be so difficult for her.'

'She'll get through it.' The words sounded more callous than she had intended.

'I meant what I said by the way,' he added, lowering his voice. 'About following up on a couple of contacts.'

'What kind of contacts?' Ronnie had an image of Frank banging on doors looking for trouble in the name of some sort of misplaced loyalty.

'After we went to see your mother, I did a bit of digging. Pretended I was getting in touch for old times' sake, suggested we go for a beer and reminisce. Didn't mention a thing about, you know, the discovery.'

Ronnie frowned. It unsettled her to think of him embarking on some sort of solo investigation into her father's death. As much as she wanted closure, she dreaded finding out the truth, in case she couldn't handle it. It had once seemed a more palatable outcome than suicide, but now, the thought that he might have been murdered in cold blood, or worse still, out of revenge for something he'd done, so therefore in the murderer's eyes, he *deserved* it, suddenly filled her with impossible horror.

'I think we should let sleeping dogs lie.' Straight out of Baz Munro's portfolio of idioms. She held on to the thought of her DC as a distraction from the place her mind had just taken her to and wondered how the hospital tests had gone. It occurred to her that worrying over a child not yet born was strangely parallel to worrying about a death that was in the past. Only the baby still had a chance at life whereas her father wasn't coming back. 'Can we do that?'

Frank gave her arm a squeeze. 'I'll be careful. I promise not to go stirring up trouble, just finding answers, getting justice for your dad.'

'OK, if you must. I just don't want to...'

'Wake up the dogs?' He shut the dishwasher and dusted off his hands. 'I promise. Anyway, what's been happening with the Lloyd case? Any progress?'

'Going round in circles, the way it does when someone's hiding something and you can't quite get to it. Trying to keep Adam sweet, not scare him off too much in case we need to interview him again, but not quite enough evidence to arrest him with a prospect of a charge. We think he overheard something that Ali Tremaine said on her way out.'

'Aha, so there's some information he might have picked up on, maybe acted upon, you're thinking?'

'Possibly something that scared him enough to confront Hannah. Along with goodbye, Ali shouted out that she wanted to talk to Hannah later from the airport.'

'So she had some information?'

'Maybe, or thought that Hannah did, which is more likely we think, given what happened next. I've spoken to her on Zoom a couple of times, but didn't get the impression she was in possession of any state secrets.'

'Best to cover all bases. When's she back? That line definitely needs following up, if you ask me.'

'She's flying into Gatwick from Mauritius

tomorrow at half-five so we might be able to clear it up then. If this new line of enquiry works, we're almost there, but not quite.'

'Almost might be good enough, if you get the CPS on a good day.'

'Thanks, Frank, but your optimism is not shared by my DCI, who has been helicoptered in to run the case now it's a murder enquiry.'

He frowned. 'I'm sorry to hear that. Could have been your big chance to prove yourself, and now you've got a babysitter. Any more on the drug trafficking neighbour? It sounded as if there was a chance she was going down for it a few days ago.'

'Funnily enough that's who DCI Preedy wanted for the murder, along with the brother, until one of our officers went undercover to try to procure her services and discovered the whole thing was a sham. She may have been set up, but there are no resources for that investigation so we're just trying to seal the deal on Adam.'

'Hang on, did you say DCI Preedy?' Frank stopped, saucepan halfway to sink, and turned to her with a furrowed brow.

'Yep, the very same.'

'You need to watch out for him, my girl. He's got his own agenda, more than likely.'

'You're preaching to the converted, Frank. I'm wary as hell.' A wave of confusion crossed her mind. She had been on her guard with Preedy, but since receiving his text message earlier some of that wariness had abated. Perhaps it had happened even earlier than that, when he had willingly gone along with her experiment on the phone to Adam. That must have been the moment at which the tension between them had dissipated. And *that* was the reason she hadn't replied with an immediate no to his suggestion of meeting up. 'He wasn't exactly a walking advert for equal opportunities when I last knew him.' It was true enough. Frank didn't need to know her attitude had softened.

They took their seats back at the table to find that the conversation had taken a turn for the banal, as Joel, George and Serena, with no anecdotes of involvement in more serious crimes to share, swapped stories about their recent driving awareness courses.

'I couldn't believe they did me for literally doing twenty-four miles an hour,' Joel protested.

'Twenty is plenty, don't they say?' George admonished him with a tap on the wrist. 'What was it that they kept telling you on that course, the thing you had to do to make your driving better?'

'*Say what you see. Say what you see.*' Joel mimicked the London accent of the course instructor. 'I whispered *what I see is a nutter running a driving course* to the girl next to me and I think he heard, so he picked on me for the rest of the morning.'

'What's "say what you see"?' Susie asked. 'Sounds a bit like primary school.'

'White van speeding towards me, traffic jam ahead – a running commentary on what's going on around you on the road.'

'Still sounds like primary school. And I thought all the solo drivers whose lips were moving were singing along to the radio or on the phone hands free. Now I know what they're all up to.'

'George likes to do all three at once, phones me on hands free, and sings what he can see.'

Laughter broke out at George's expense and he retaliated by fetching a set of shot glasses and producing a bottle of Sambuca. As the rest of them acquiesced to the pressure to have one for the road, Frank took his leave, patting Ronnie lightly on the arm as he passed.

'Cheerio, Ronnie, and let's hook up again soon. Good luck with the case.'

Ronnie held onto his sleeve for a second. 'I meant what I said about letting sleeping dogs lie.'

'I'll be careful.'

Susie was pulling her coat on too. 'Ronnie, you still good for Wednesday night? I finish early and we need to catch up on so many things.'

'Absolutely, barring emergencies. Come round seven-ish?'

George and Joel stayed a while longer, wanting updates on Ronnie's love life, which she steadfastly refused to provide, despite their begging. 'I bet there are some hot guys in the office you've got your eye on,' said Joel with a twinkle in his eye. 'And I bet there aren't any women as gorgeous as you in CID.' Ronnie promised they would be the first to know when it was time to buy a new hat, and they took their leave with a promise to hold her to that.

When she was finally alone with her sister, Ronnie sank into a bucket chair by the French doors and put her feet up on the footstool. 'You did so well tonight, See. Everyone loved it. Food was delicious. Now you can sit back and wait for the return invitations to roll in.'

'Do you think so? I didn't realise I'd invited so many police. I forget that's where you met Frank. And I can't even remember Susie working there. Feels like she's always been a therapist, but I guess that's just because it's her calling. It suits her.'

'Yes, they've definitely both moved on. I like George and Joel. Only met them a couple of times but they're good fun. George has an events business, if I remember.'

'And Joel – in huge contrast – works for the civil service in the modern slavery department. Quite traumatic apparently, some of the cases that come their way.'

'I can imagine,' Ronnie mused. 'It's not something that crosses my desk often thankfully. It used to be the standard defence for drug trafficking and illegal immigrants, sex workers, you name it – saying that someone else was pulling the strings, making them work for nothing, threatening them with torture.'

Serena did a double take. 'He didn't tell me about that side of it.'

Ronnie drained her wine glass. 'It's not a popular view, but there's always a flip side to any laws designed to protect. Plenty of people want to stand under the umbrella, and it just gives the criminals another loophole and makes my job harder.'

'Well, I guess it's got to be a well-guarded umbrella then.' Serena perched on a stool at the island, twisting her empty glass in her fingers. 'Call me a woolly liberal, but I think we need to have the rules in place first and foremost. Enforcing them was never going to be easy. It's the same in schools. Making the rules is just the start. Making kids stick to them is a full-time job.'

'Which is why the rules have to be carefully thought out. The tougher they are, the tougher you're going to have to work to uphold them. The broader the definition of whatever it is, let's say slavery in this context, the more claims you're going to have, and the more manpower you're going to have to put in to assess their validity.' Ronnie closed her eyes. 'I don't mean to be negative, it's just that it's been a long week.'

'I get it,' Serena smiled. 'And we need you in that job, Ron. When are the twins back?'

'Sunday afternoon. I can't believe how long it seems since I saw them. So much has happened.'

'Any closer to finding Hannah Lloyd's killer?'

Ronnie flinched inwardly at the word. At work, it was always 'attacker' or 'assailant' and they talked about witnesses, suspects, arrests and charges, but this was the brutal truth. 'I think we're getting warmer,' she ventured. 'I'm not jumping to any conclusions yet though.'

'And since Joel brought it up, I hope it's me rather than them that's the first to know of any new love interest.'

Ronnie eyed her suspiciously. 'Why is everyone so keen for me to settle down suddenly?'

'Not keen, just interested. How's it going with the DCI?'

Ronnie sighed and smiled. 'Actually, he's changed, or he's not the misogynist pig I remember from the old days anyway. He's asked me out for a drink, says he has some apologising to do, and I'm debating whether to say yes.'

'Oh my God, Ronnie, that's – well, exciting I suppose. You sure he's changed?'

'As sure as I can be, but don't worry, I will be carrying out further investigations before coming to any conclusions.'

Serena looked relieved. 'Well, I'm sure you're the best judge of whether he's turned over a new leaf.'

'And if I'm going to look the part...' Ronnie stood up and stretched, catching sight of the clock on the wall. 'It's way past my bedtime. I need to head off.'

CHAPTER TWENTY-TWO

It was a while before Ronnie could sleep that night. She tossed and turned on one side of the bed, then the other, finally settling somewhere in the middle. Her dreams were wild and confused and when she woke at nine, she struggled for a few seconds to distinguish the real from the imagined. Images of Joel rescuing children enslaved by drug lords battled with Susie Marshall treating all her patients with cheese soufflés. She pulled on her dressing gown and made herself a coffee. Her last hours of freedom before motherhood took over again. If there was anything she needed to do, now was the time.

But once the mountain of washing had been done and put back in the twins' rooms, their bedding changed and a shopping delivery ordered for their return, she found herself wandering around at a loss, strangely disappointed at the tidiness. Granite kitchen worktops gleamed pointlessly in the light of the pendant lamps, the polished wooden floors stretched from wall to wall free from stray trainers and sports bags, the shoe rack in the hall cupboard bore its contents proudly paired, with coats hanging smartly above. In the living room, plumped cushions stood like soldiers on the corner sofa Tilly had been so adamant they bought in the January sales. On the coffee table, a few books and magazines sat neatly piled in expectation of readers that never materialised. It was clean. It was spotless in fact. But it was undeniably and uncomfortably boring.

She picked up a framed photograph of the three of them on their last holiday, tanned and grinning into the camera held by a waiter who had managed to position a palm tree directly behind Eddie's head. It usually made her smile every time she looked at it, but today it left her cold. Her head felt like sludge. She poured a glass of prosecco from last night's open bottle and took a sip, pulling open the balcony doors to take a deep breath of the evening air, but the magic wasn't working tonight. She poured the wine back into the bottle and put a pan of water on to boil.

Television was background noise that didn't sink in, but it was better than nothing. She flopped onto the sofa with a bowl of pasta and flicked through the channels. It seemed that outside her bubble the world was a sea of creativity – knitting, cooking, building eco-homes, but the thought of making things was exhausting. Since her separation from Simon, she had barely opened a recipe book, let alone had a dinner party. Birthday and Christmas presents had been instantaneously purchased on Amazon and food shopping delivered via the Favourites list online. Where had all the energy gone that she used to have? Serena had suggested it was all hormonal, but this was too early for the menopause, wasn't it? There were some things that made her happy, and some people. Serena, Susie, and more recently Frank Reilly. His reappearance in her life had sparked something in her mind, some sort of reconnection with the past, and she was grateful for that.

In the advert break she googled her symptoms – fatigue, irritability, negative thoughts, and was directed to a myriad of pages each promising a more catastrophic diagnosis than the last. There was no point scaring herself if Serena was right, but even the thought of that made her feel on edge. What if she met someone new and wanted more children? She wasn't too old at forty-two to have a baby. Tilly and Eddie would be gone in a year and a baby might fill the empty nest.

The chimes of Big Ben had just given way to a stony-faced presenter when her phone pinged with a text from her mother. Was she free for a chat? On autopilot, she turned the TV to standby, abandoned her half-finished tortellini and found the number at the top of her favourites list. It had barely rung before Alice Delmar's voice quivered at the other end.

'Veronica? It's Frank. He's been in an accident.'

'What? When? How?'

The switch from standby to operational flicked in her head as Alice recited the facts as she knew them. He'd gone looking for one of Fred's cronies, on some kind of mission to get to the bottom of what they now knew to be his death at sea.

'I told him to stay away from all that. What did he think he was doing?'

'He was doing it for us, Veronica. He loved Fred. He wants justice for our family, and since the police aren't interested...'

It was a jab at her, but she ignored it. Once she had the name of the hospital and ward, she was out of the flat and taking the stairs to the lobby two at a time. Jumping into the driver's seat, she accelerated out of the carpark, while a voice inside her head shouted: *I knew something was wrong.*

The hospital was a twenty-minute drive from Glendale House, but she did it in less than fifteen. The main reception computers were down, but eventually she found Frank's location and within a few minutes she was at his bedside where he lay with his eyes closed, monitors beeping around him. A bruise was spreading across his left cheek, purple and yellow like an angry winter sunset.

'He must have nodded off.' The nurse who had directed her to him stated the obvious, her eyes scanning the numbers on the screens. 'But we need to keep him awake, with the concussion risk.' She gave his shoulder a gentle shake. 'Mr Reilly? You have a visitor.'

Ronnie hated hospitals. They were a reminder of human frailty and the pointlessness of everything. How many people could honestly say that their friend or relative had expected to be there that night, or that they had it coming to them? The vast majority of admissions were emergencies, blue-lighted into A&E with hours of waiting ahead of them, only to be told they'd be seen by the doctor 'soon' or that there were others in the queue ahead of them, in greater need. Hospitals were the proof that plans were futile, where fate made a mockery of human ambition.

'Ronnie?' Frank's eyes flicked open. 'What are you doing here?'

'Mum said you'd had an accident. What on earth happened?' She pulled a chair close to the bed and sat down.

'Oh, she needs to calm down, your mother. She phoned me while I was in the ambulance. The paramedics spoke to her.' He tried to smile, then thought better of it. 'Ouch, that hurt.'

'So, are you going to tell me?'

Frank heaved himself up onto his elbows, wincing with the pain. 'It's nothing. Honestly.'

'Doesn't look like nothing.'

'You should see the other guy.'

'Who was the other guy?'

Frank's eyes settled on hers for a second, then closed again. 'You know I said I'd do my best to find whoever was responsible for Fred's demise. I tried.'

'And how's that working out for you, being a vigilante?' Ronnie pulled a chair over and sat down, her eyes still fixed angrily on him. 'I told you to keep out of it. If there's any information you might have, give it to the police. They're much better equipped than...'

'You forget, young lady, it wasn't so long ago that I *was* the police.'

Ronnie sighed heavily. 'You know what I mean. The police aren't miracle workers. We both know that. But they have systems. They run operations. If there's a gang, if there's a risk to life, as there clearly was by the looks of you, they are just going to be a much better bet. What happens if you take the law into your own hands is they end up getting away. And I know you already know that.'

Frank had settled on the vaguest inkling of a smile, but it was clear he was amused. 'DS Delmar, since when have you been extolling the virtues of playing by the book? Last I heard you were maverick all day long, doing things your way and fuck the consequences, if you'll pardon my French.'

'Unfair. Or even if fair, don't forget I have backup. People know where I am.'

Frank raised an eyebrow. 'I bet that's not always the case.'

'OK, *most* of the time they do. But the fact remains, you can't go beating up gangsters on your own. Apart from anything else, look at where it's landed you, and who knows, if they press charges, you're the one going down for assault.'

Her last words seemed to hit home. Frank took a long and noisy breath before reaching for her hand. 'You're right. And I'm sorry. I shouldn't have gone raking over old ground and I admit – it was partly my own selfish search for justice. Fred was my mate. If anyone's hurt him, I want them behind bars.'

Ronnie sat back, feeling the anger drain from her momentarily. 'So, who was he?'

'Better you don't know. And turns out it wasn't him. I went in all guns blazing, but it wasn't him. I made an assumption. I was wrong. And he was bigger than me. I'm sorry.'

'OK. Apology accepted. But no more of this.'

'No more of this, I promise. Oh, and Veronica...'

Ronnie started at the sound of her full name. It wasn't often she heard it, except from her superiors and her mother: the mother superior.

'Call Helen for me, or text her. Let her know I'm alright.' He recited a number that Ronnie plugged straight into her phone.

'I will do that. Should I go round?'

'No need. She'll be in bed. I'll be home by morning. If not, I'll be sure to let you know.'

'Call me anytime. I'll be working tomorrow. Need to track down Ali Tremaine for a start.'

'She didn't get back to you?'

'Not yet. I don't imagine she'll be delighted at the prospect of another interview going over the same old ground.'

'But that's how you solve a crime.' Frank grimaced. 'The truth rarely comes out first time. You've just got to be careful how you get to it. Don't alienate the witness, make them feel you're fighting crime together, Batman and Robin. And play fair. As you've just reminded me, the rules are there for a reason.'

'I'm afraid visiting time is over. I'll be in trouble with Sister.' The young nurse looked at Ronnie apologetically, and she stood to leave.

'Oh, and Ronnie, don't forget to watch out. For yourself, I mean.'

She frowned. 'In what way?'

'Preedy. Just be on your guard.'

The walk back to the car felt heavy, with gratitude and anger battling for position in her soul. Only a day or two earlier she had welcomed the existence of someone who was truly on her side, and yet seeing him weakened and defeated tonight was like holding up a mirror. He was right. She was usually no stranger to going it alone, sticking two fingers up at procedure to get justice done. But the image of Frank diminished to basic human form by his hospital gown was a reminder that whether things went well or badly could be down to the smallest twist of fate. She'd been lucky so far that none of her professional transgressions had landed her in serious trouble, but it might only be a matter of time.

It occurred to her as she climbed into bed an hour later than she hadn't replied to Preedy's invitation. In the circumstances, she felt a sudden and unfamiliar need to conform to expectation. There was no reason not to meet him. She could put a bid in for a coffee instead of a drink, although she had been for drinks with other colleagues before, so why not Preedy? If Frank was right, and she needed to be wary, then wasn't there a saying that you should keep friends close and enemies closer? And anyway, who knew what he might have to say, what olive branches he might want to offer to draw a line under the past and start afresh? It would be churlish of her to reject the making of amends, however late in the day it might be. She typed a quick reply to his WhatsApp message.

I'm free lunchtime tomorrow. Kids back around 4pm.

Her message had a blue tick against it almost immediately and then Preedy was typing, then stopping, then typing again, grey dots dancing in the text box. She smiled at the thought of him trying to find the right words. It wasn't something he was famous for.

Meet you at Hemingways at 1?

She replied with a thumbs up, thinking for some reason what her mother would advise in the circumstances. *There's no need to give him any unnecessary encouragement.* Then she flicked back to her inbox. Ali's message remained unread. Perhaps her flight had been delayed, or the jet lag had kicked in. Whatever it was, it could wait till the morning. Then, she just might pay her a visit.

CHAPTER TWENTY-THREE

Ali Tremaine's address turned out to be less than a mile from Ronnie's flat. She contemplated walking there, but settled for the car on the basis that if Ali was out or asleep, it would lessen the frustration. Her WhatsApp message remained unticked and her calls had rung un-answered, but with no reported flight delays it seemed like a sensible second-best option to pay her a visit. At the back of her mind, there was the prospect of meeting Preedy for lunch with a job from the list already done, and she couldn't deny a flicker of anticipatory pleasure at seeing his reaction.

Samphire Avenue turned out not to be as exotic as it sounded – a string of thirties semis with postage stamp front gardens overshadowed by mature trees which made the place feel a lot darker than it should have been. Why was it that foliage and greenery were always either too sparse or too plentiful? The new estates springing up around West Dean and Wakehurst were famously devoid of plant life, whereas these older houses were almost strangled by the wisteria and ivy that splayed up the walls and snaked around the apple and pear trees that guarded them. Ronnie found a parking space a few doors down and switched off the engine. She tried Ali's phone again, not wanting to go banging on her door uninvited, and then tried a

WhatsApp call which went unanswered. She climbed out of the driver's seat and walked to the front door of the house, glancing over her shoulder at a neighbour trimming their wayward boxwood hedge. All was well in suburbia, it seemed.

She rang the bell three times in all, the first a tentative tap, followed by a more resolute press in case the first one hadn't sounded. A third time for luck. In the drive, Ali's silver Ford Focus looked as if it had come straight out of the car wash, except for a scattering of fallen leaves on the bonnet. Peering through the glass, she saw a suitcase and handbag lying at a jaunty angle on the floor by the stairs, as if they had been dropped or discarded in favour of something more pressing than unpacking. It was hard to see any further, no lights were on, but then it was a bright morning with no need for it.

It was puzzling, but not exactly mysterious. Ali was perfectly within her rights to ignore her phone and go straight out or straight to bed after getting home from a holiday. She was more than likely fed up with being asked the same questions again and again by the police and probably had nothing more to say. Added to that, her good friend had been murdered in her own flat, only a week earlier. The shock of that would take some getting used to, might make her wary of answering the door even. Ronnie should give the girl a break.

The neighbour with the hedge trimmer turned it off and waved.

'You looking for Alison?'

'I am, as it happens. Have you seen her?'

He frowned and rubbed his chin thoughtfully. 'I think she came back last night. She's been away for a week – I know that because she asked me to keep an eye on the house. It's a nice neighbourhood like that. Always someone to feed your cats and water your plants.'

'Did you see her come home last night?'

'I thought I heard a car. Must have been a cab from the airport that pulled into the drive. But as you can see, there's not much chance of spying on people round here.' He indicated the low-hanging branches of his apple tree. 'So I can't say for sure.'

'No worries. I'll come back later. Her phone's off, that's all.'

'Ah, she's probably having a detox. She was into all that. Always jogging down the road with a yoga mat under her arm. Gosh, look at me sounding like a nosy neighbour after all. But she was quite a character, tall, striking-looking, hard to miss I suppose.'

'A detox. Of course. Thanks for your help.'

Ronnie snapped a photo of the front of the house to get a record of the position of the curtains and blinds, then clicked open the car and sank back into the driver's seat with a twinge of discomfort. It didn't sit well with her that she couldn't get in touch with the key witness they needed to see. On the way back to her flat, she went over in her head the words Ali had used when relaying her conversation with Hannah through the closed door of the study.

'*Let's have a catch up on the gossip when I'm waiting with the girls at the airport.*' Were those the exact words? She might have said *call me* at the end. She should check her notes. Then something dawned on her that gave the story a whole new weight. Ali had said that Hannah had had something to tell her, but from what she shouted out, it could easily have sounded to anyone listening in as if it was Ali who had news for Hannah.

Or was she overthinking it? The answer came in the form of a loud hoot from behind reminding her that the traffic lights had changed. She should shelve the Ali Tremaine issue for now. After all, it was just when she decided to stop thinking about something that inspiration usually chose to strike.

***

Hemingways wouldn't have been Ronnie's choice, with its reputation as more of a hot night spot than a Sunday lunchtime venue, but she was surprised by its transformation when she stepped inside to find a live jazz band playing and a handful of couples scattered at the surrounding candlelit tables. Preedy was seated in one of the booths, menu in hand. He waved when he saw her.

'Is this OK?' He gestured to the room as a whole. 'Not exactly a pub, but still...'

'Sure. It's absolutely fine.' Ronnie hung her jacket on a hook and slid into the seat opposite him. 'Sorry I'm late. Crazy morning.'

'No problem. Thank you for coming. I know it's

209

an odd choice but I rather like the booths in here. A bit more private. You don't get overheard.'

Ronnie raised her eyebrows with a half-smile.

'Not just because of the confidentiality of the case. I also wanted to have a chat with you off the record, outside the office, away from all the distractions. Now what will you have to drink? And shall we order a bite to eat?'

All in all, Ronnie found the meeting with Matt Preedy a whole lot more pleasant than she had expected. For the best part of an hour they kept off the topic of their past contact, until he mentioned a tricky situation he'd had the previous year involving 'disciplinary issues'. Ronnie pricked up her ears.

'What sort of disciplinary issues?'

Preedy took a sip of his wine. 'You won't be surprised to know that there were issues coming up every day of the week around misogyny and racism, all sorts of bullying in the workplace. Once the dam broke, the allegations started pouring in. It was a mess.'

Ronnie twisted her glass left and right. 'I can imagine it must have been hell, trying to deal with all the claims coming in. How did you get any police work done?'

'With difficulty. The main problem was, we found out that all this went a lot further than we realised.'

Ronnie suddenly felt cold sobriety descend on her like a brick. 'How much further? Do you mean up the ladder in terms of hierarchy?'

Preedy drained his glass and poured another,

reaching to top up hers as well. She didn't refuse. It was a story that would be told and questioned more fluently with a bit of Dutch courage.

'The network was entrenched up the ranks and spread out over other forces and other law enforcement agencies. We ended up putting a spy in their midst, and eventually we had the names of all the members of the WhatsApp groups, screenshots of some of the material that was being shared around, you name it. Obscene, most of it. Some good coppers amongst them, but you can't make allowances in these situations, so within a few days, we lost twenty per cent of our staff. But that's water under the bridge now, Veronica.' His use of her name jarred, the way it always did, and brought Ronnie down to earth with a bang. 'The thing is...' He hesitated. 'It did make me realise a few things.'

Ronnie sipped her wine and picked at the last chips on her plate. Anything to lessen the tension. Preedy seemed to be about to apologise and she almost couldn't bear the stress of it. Luckily she didn't have to wait long.

'I wasn't perfect either. I think on balance none of us was. The worst of them probably ended up kicked out the door, but that doesn't mean to say the rest of us are saints. And I know that when we worked together I may have said some things to you and to others which I now regret.'

Ronnie let out the breath she was holding and met his gaze. Her words came out before she'd had time to consider them, and the relief was instant.

'Apology accepted.'

'Thank you.' His eyes met hers. She looked down at her hands, suddenly struggling for something to say, anything to change the subject, but still she wanted to find out everything, because there might not be another chance.

'About the sackings. Letting people go, whatever you call it – how do you know you got to the bottom of it?'

'How do you mean?' He tilted his head slightly. On the back foot, or genuinely not understanding, Ronnie wasn't sure.

'I mean did you pull it out by the roots, the infestation of bad behaviour?'

Preedy raised his eyebrows. 'I like the analogy. There is a certain amount of pleasure to be derived from digging deep enough to pull out a weed by its roots, but it's funny how they always come back. Maybe we can only do our best, but sometimes the rot runs deep.'

'Japanese Knotweed,' Ronnie thought aloud. 'You think you've got rid of it, then it ends up eating the foundations of your house.'

'That's dramatic, but I do see where you're coming from. And yes, we have put things in place – training, for a start, to make it one hundred per cent clear what is and what is not acceptable in the workplace.'

Ronnie nodded. 'I get it. You can only do so much.'

'You're right to ask though. It's not unlike taking out the drug trafficker and leaving a whole supply chain unfed, just waiting for a new one to step into the shoes of the previous. This time, more careful, less likely to be caught.'

'Sounds pretty depressing. I think I'd rather believe you'd zapped the problem out of existence.'

Preedy laughed. 'Let's pretend that's what happened then. The point is, we did everything we could at the time to tackle it, and are doing everything we can on a daily basis to make sure that remains the case. But now...' He pushed his plate away and leaned across the table, hands clasped in front of him. 'Tell me what you got up to this morning that was so crazy.'

Preedy listened with the kind of attention Ronnie wasn't used to. The workplace didn't cater for it and her colleagues were mostly too busy to do much more than nod vigorously and scribble things down for a few seconds before dashing off to respond to a call. When she had finished, he sat back and drummed his fingers on the table, his eyes scanning the room for an answer.

'Sounds like a lesson in patience,' he said eventually. 'When I was a DS, and especially when I was a DC and doing most of the hands-on investigating, I had a habit of getting ahead of myself, running with an assumption that wasn't ready, going in all guns blazing where there was nothing amiss. Somebody had forgotten to call someone back. The missing person I was after had moved out, he'd even told the wife he was leaving her. Like I said, it's taking someone's word for it when the real story might be very different.'

'So how does that apply here?'

'It may not apply, but in case it does, I'd say that it's very much a possibility that Adam overheard Ali and Hannah's plan to swap notes on something and got scared. It's also possible that Ali knows more than she's letting on about what that gossip was, and that she's even gone off-grid to regroup and work out what to do next.'

'So, either way, don't we have a duty to follow up?'

Preedy leaned back. 'Until we have reason to believe she's missing, she's not missing, and until we have more on Adam, he's free to go about his life. I'm not saying he's innocent. I'm saying slow down. It will come good. You'll see. You've got your theory which, if true, will be proved right. Give it time.'

Ronnie was still letting his words sink in as she arrived back at Glendale House. She wasn't sure she believed him, but the sentiment was genuine and in the context of his apology, and his explanation for the mass dismissals at the Met, it felt good. She could do with putting the brakes on from time to time. But her usual take on it was that slowing down meant losing out, giving someone the time to escape and make another plan, and she was far more worried about that than going in too fast.

***

She must have nodded off because it seemed like she'd barely flopped onto the sofa when there was the fumble of a key in the lock, then the slam of door

214

against wall as first Eddie then Tilly, each loaded with backpacks and wheelie cases exploded into the flat.

'Mum! We're back.' Tilly was first to clamber over the spilt luggage to embrace Ronnie, while Eddie grinned from behind her and waited his turn for the hug. Their faces were several shades darker and Tilly's hair streaked with blonde by the sun.

'Wow, suntans. Good weather then?'

'Boiling hot. And they've got a boat so we were on the sea every day, catching the rays.' Eddie turned round to show her the back of his neck. 'I kinda forgot to put cream on in some places.'

Tilly flopped onto the sofa, kicking her trainers off and putting her feet up on the cushions. 'The journey back was *so long*. Going through customs took literally hours, and we were in a massive people carrier like a minibus, so they made us all get out and lifted up the actual *floor*.'

Ronnie sat down opposite her in an armchair. 'Must have had a reason. Maybe they'd had a tip-off about a drugs haul or something. Drugs come into the country with all sorts of people, some of them just passengers with no knowledge of it.'

'I think they were looking for people.' Eddie's face was suddenly serious. He sat on the edge of the sofa, turning a cushion over in his hands.

'He thinks he overheard them talking about human cargo,' Tilly said, in a voice that said just how ridiculous she thought her brother was.

Eddie glared at her. 'Don't be like that. I heard

them say it. Something about it being standard procedure now.'

'He's just looking for drama where there isn't any. What's for dinner by the way, Mum? We're starving. The food on the boat was rank.'

Having the twins home was a mixed blessing. On the one hand they were her pride and joy and reason for living. On the other they had a habit of sucking the life out of her within seconds of arriving. Questions, viewpoints, washing, mess and hunger. They were constantly going on about food in the way that she couldn't remember doing as a child. Perhaps today's children were more physically active than she and Serena had been. Maybe being on your phone used up more calories than reading a book or whatever it was they used to do to pass the time. Either way, it was expensive and exhausting. But given the choice, between that and the oppressive emptiness of the place without them, she wouldn't have it any other way.

CHAPTER TWENTY-FOUR

Roadworks and an overturned lorry on the flyover meant Ronnie had to take an unexpected detour on her way to the office the next day. She called in ahead to let Baz know she'd be late and he laughed.

'I thought something was up. You're never a second past eight. I can set my watch by you. The half-termers are trickling in, but they'll be a while showing off their tans and Insta photos so I wouldn't hurry if I were you.'

'Well if anyone asks, I'm taking the scenic route. Not sure I've ever even been down here before.' She swung left to avoid a tractor coming out of a side road. 'It's practically the countryside. I just had a near miss with a farm vehicle. I think I might even be lost.' The tractor took the next turning into a field and Ronnie pulled in to the side to look up directions on her phone. 'It says I'm on Fayre Court Lane. You still there, DC Munro? I might need you to talk me down.'

'You're way off course, sarge.' She could hear him chuckling into his coffee as he spoke. 'If you're up that way you've definitely missed a turning.'

'That's not helpful. Where am I then?'

'Isn't Fayre Court Hall the new hotel they're converting up by Beddingly Forest? Have a look as you go past. It's supposed to be a proper five-star luxury spa place with golf courses and weddings and everything. You never know. Might come in useful.'

'You can hold your horses on the wedding front,' Ronnie said as she pulled out into the lane again. 'I've spent the weekend with two gay men, my sister, a vigilante with two black eyes, Susie the detective turned psychotherapist and yesterday none other than DCI Preedy.'

'Not a date?'

'No!' Ronnie said, aghast at her own indiscretion. 'A catch up on the case.'

'That's how he lured you in, was it?'

'Shut up, Baz. Nobody was lured anywhere.'

'So he didn't propose then?' Baz was on good form. 'He promised he was going to.'

'Haha, no, but he did apologise, which was almost as unexpected as a proposal. Clean slate. New day, new week.'

'Good stuff. See you when you've run the gauntlet of the home counties countryside.'

'Wait. Baz? You still there?' A thought flashed across her mind, making her brake and pull over, hazard lights on. 'Something's just occurred to me.'

'Yes, what's up?'

'Fayre Court. Could that be the "FC" in Hannah's diary? Could she have had an appointment to go there looking for a new venue?'

'I doubt it. The place is a building site. It's possible they're leasing out parts of it to fund the work, but I doubt the income from a yoga class would make much difference to the kind of figures they'd be talking.'

'Still, worth asking, maybe.'

'Well, since you're in the area, why not?'

Ronnie ended the call, just as she passed a dirt track signposted Works Traffic Only and *Fayre Court* painted in capitals on a board beneath. She must have missed it as she drove past the first time, concentrating too hard on her GPS. She glanced in her rear-view mirror and almost jumped with the shock. There it was, a monstrous Gothic tower clad in scaffolding several metres higher than itself, cutting a harsh outline against the leaden sky. She stopped and reversed a few metres to get a better look, then turned into the entrance to make space for a passing lorry. As she did so, a bearded, unsmiling man in hi-vis leaned out of a portacabin and waved her in. She hesitated. At this rate she'd be arriving even later at work, but perhaps with Preedy's newly bestowed approval she had nothing to worry about on that front. A few more minutes wouldn't matter.

The hi-vis gatekeeper lifted a makeshift barrier and a few seconds later she found herself navigating the sweeping drive that would soon be welcoming wedding guests and weekend golfers. A gentle curve to the left swept her around the back, where the imposing stone façade gave onto a rolling expanse of untended gardens framed by pine trees to one side, and wasteland to the other. In the distance, a buzzard hovered above ploughed fields, then swooped low and fast, rising instantly a second later with its prey in its beak.

Climbing out of the car, she clicked the door shut

and was met by the sudden crunch of a transit van swinging round the corner too fast and skidding to a halt in front of her, making her stomach leap in shock. The driver leaned out of the window. 'Sorry, lady. Wasn't expecting pedestrians. It's closed for a refurb you know.'

'I know.' Ronnie gathered herself. It wasn't even a near miss, not really. She was fine. 'Just making an enquiry.'

He nodded and pulled away, parking up at the far side of the gravel frontage on the other side of a leylandii hedge.

'Can I help you?' The commotion had brought a figure to the front door. She was slight, dark-haired, maybe East European from her accent, which sounded not unlike Baz Munro doing an impression of his countrymen. She hovered in the entrance, waiting for Ronnie to explain herself.

'I live locally and have never seen this place before. It's very impressive,' she lied.

'Yes,' the girl answered, seemingly inviting her to continue. Momentarily, she toyed with her badge in her jacket pocket, then decided against it. Sometimes you could find out more as a civilian. This girl looked suspicious enough already.

'Anyway, I was just passing by and thought I'd pop in to find out what's happening here. Looks like there's some great work being done on the refurb. Will it take long? My daughter's getting married next year and it looks like the most perfect location.' She wasn't sure where that came from. The thought of Tilly getting hitched at eighteen filled her with horror, but she kept the smile plastered on her face.

'It supposed to finish six months ago. Never ending work. We hope soon though.' The accent was coming together for Ronnie now. The woman spoke exactly like one of her neighbours in Glendale House. It was the same rolled rs, the same guttural h. It was worth a guess.

'I don't suppose you're from Ukraine, by any chance?'

The girl frowned. 'No Ukraine.' Then her face softened as if she'd forgotten then suddenly remembered her lines. 'Georgia.'

'Ah. My apologies. And none of my business. I just thought you sounded like someone I knew.'

'Lots of people say that. I think many East European people sound similar. It is normal.' She offered a tentative smile and Ronnie remembered the question she had come to ask.

'I don't suppose you're leasing out space in the building at all? A friend of mine is looking for a venue for her yoga classes. So much demand and not enough venues. She's running out of ideas.'

'Nothing for now, only for after one month. Maybe three. Boss will decide.'

'She might have already called you. Her name's Hannah.'

'Yoga?' She laughed. 'Nobody come asking for yoga.'

It wasn't the most useful of chats so far. Time to wind things up. 'So, after three months you think everything will be ready? Fully open?'

The girl rolled her eyes. 'I think no ready, but boss say ready, so who can argue?'

Ronnie had thanked her and was halfway through the door when she turned and asked her last question. 'Who's the boss? Are they here?'

The girl hesitated, filled the gap with an even bigger smile and a fluttery laugh that spelled nervousness. 'Not here today. Maybe tomorrow.'

'Oh and just one more thing.' She'd started, so she had to finish, but she was regretting it already. 'I don't suppose the name Adam Lloyd rings a bell?' The girl's face clouded with incomprehension. 'Sorry, I mean have you heard of the name Adam Lloyd? Does it sound familiar?'

The girl shook her head. 'I don't know. English man, yes?'

'Yes. English.'

She shrugged her shoulders. 'Maybe he come here and I don't introduce to him. All English look the same. I don't know all names.'

'Of course.' Ronnie gave her a thumbs up. 'I'll come and see how it's all going in a few weeks then.'

Ronnie sat in the car for a second before restarting the engine, trying to recapture something that had been lingering on the periphery of her mind. Something that made her ask about Adam. One second it had been there, front and centre of her thinking, then as soon as the words had escaped her lips, the thought had vanished, chased away by the mockery of logic. Still, she had no reason to think the girl was lying, in which case there was nothing to pursue. She turned the key in the ignition and checked her mirrors before reversing and pulling out into the drive.

In the window, the girl's pale face watched her leave.

CHAPTER TWENTY-FIVE

'Ah, I know where you mean.' Overton was following her down the corridor with a case file in one hand and a coffee in the other. 'The roadworks – they're the same ones Adam Lloyd was complaining about, I think you'll find...'

His words slowed to a halt as Ronnie stopped to open the office door with a heave of her shoulder, allowing him to pass. 'You said that as if those roadworks were the missing link. Perhaps Hannah's murderer is hiding in the gas mains, or whatever they're fixing.'

Overton paused to unload his cargo at his desk and looked at her, wide-eyed. 'I hadn't thought of that, but it's as good an idea as any we've had yet.'

Ronnie wondered for a moment whether he meant it, and decided to assume not. It was a sad reflection on their performance if he was serious. 'I hope not, for all our sakes. I'm still running with the lead we established on Friday.'

Overton smiled. 'Glad that little game wasn't a waste of time. Any progress over the weekend? Did you get hold of Tremaine?'

In a few short sentences Ronnie summarised the story of her visit to the house, and Preedy's verdict on Ali not being 'missing'.

'So when is she *missing*, officially I mean?'

'You know the drill. Nobody's reported her missing. She's not a high risk.'

'Yes, but she's also not home when she said she'd be.'

'She could be out. Anyone can go out. Anyone can leave their phone at home, or just have a day off comms.' Overton was shifting uncomfortably. 'What's wrong? What are you thinking?'

'It just doesn't make sense, sarge, that the neighbour saw her come back, that you can't get through on the phone, that she's not answering.'

'Look, Mike, I know what you mean, but the neighbour only *thought* he saw her, or heard the cab come back. The trees would have obscured his view. And even if she did, as I said, her movements over the past day...'

'More than a day. Getting on for two days now.'

Ronnie sighed and brought her hands up to her face. Something about shutting out the surroundings and the warmth of skin on skin gave her the reassurance she needed to stick with the plan she'd been given. 'With the DCI here my hands are tied. Better to have him on board than be working against each other, so I'm happy, for now, to go at his pace. But I promise that as soon as we have good reason to suspect that Ali Tremaine is a misper we will be out there looking for her. In the meantime, we need to be examining Hannah's phone for conversations with girlfriends, particularly with Ali, that refer to anything that might be classed as 'gossip' or 'news' with a view to working out what conclusion Adam might have jumped to. There could be a whole other story out there we haven't stumbled on yet.'

'We've been through the phone, sarge. That's what I was coming to tell you.'

Ronnie wanted to shout *Why didn't you say something?* He was infuriating her now, but by the looks of his face she was having the same effect on him. She took a deep breath, tried to focus on the outcome rather than the immediate frustrations. 'Shall we sit down in my office?'

The move to a new setting did something to break the tension between them, but Overton was clearly still on edge. Flipping open his laptop, he showed her a series of screenshots of messages sent by Hannah to various people, each mentioning the word 'gossip' or 'news'.

For the most part they appeared to be harmless invitations to share the latest on a new boyfriend. One text, sent almost a year earlier to a group called Friday Drinks Club had the word NEWS in capitals followed by a dozen exclamation marks, and a link to an article in the *Guardian* online about more misdemeanours in the police force. Ronnie and Overton exchanged glances.

'It's all out there,' he said glumly.

'But nothing of interest to the case.'

'Not a sausage.'

'No result maybe, but we can cross off another avenue of investigation. Good work, Mike.'

Overton turned to leave, glancing out of the window as he did so. 'Nice view from here, sarge. I hadn't clocked that before.'

Ronnie followed his gaze. 'It's a good one. Helps work things out, looking down at Nico's café and the people coming and going. They're still sitting outside as well, with blankets this year. That's a new addition.'

'Softies, the lot of them.' Overton stepped away from the window and picked up his laptop from the desk, but Ronnie's attention had been caught by something and she reached out a hand towards him as she spoke.

'Mike, look. Sitting in the corner with her back to us. She just turned round. I'm sure it's her. Over there.'

'Isn't that Hannah Lloyd's friend? The one who was there at her birthday?'

'Delilah Byrne. It's definitely her. I'm going to pop out for a coffee. Want one?'

Without waiting for an answer Ronnie pulled on her jacket, pulled open the office door and took the stairs two at a time. There had been no new information to warrant getting either Adam or Delilah back in for questioning, but she had a feeling they weren't done with either of them. Delilah was on her own, might not mind a casual chat about how things were going. It was worth a try.

Delilah had already spotted her by the time she reached the traffic lights and waved. Ronnie waved back. This was turning out to be ridiculously easy so far. As she got closer, she saw an open laptop on the table next to a coffee and a plate of pastries. Delilah jumped up and reached out her hand to shake Ronnie's.

'Detective Delmar – fancy seeing you here! Do come and join me.'

'Thanks. I didn't want to presume.'

'Not at all. Presume away. I'll be glad of the company.'

'Nice office you've got here.' Ronnie raised her eyebrows at the cosy set-up. 'I might follow your example. Give myself some thinking space.'

Delilah laughed. 'Well, I can recommend it. I'd forgotten you were across the road, as I discovered the other day. I suppose that's where you want to be if you're the police. Central but subtle.'

When Ronnie returned with her coffee, the laptop was shut and refreshments had taken centre stage. It was almost as if she'd been lying in wait for her.

'So how's the investigation going? Any news?'

Ronnie shrugged. 'Nothing to write home about. We're following up a few leads but I can't reveal the details obviously.'

Delilah took a bite out of something covered in icing sugar and made a face that said it was heavenly, before proffering the rest of the plate to Ronnie. 'Go on. They're delicious.'

Ronnie waved it away. 'I've got a sandwich upstairs. Don't want to spoil my appetite.'

'So, did you talk to Meghan? Is she in the clear?'

It was a brutally straightforward question which made Ronnie smile inwardly. She'd have taken the same attitude herself in Delilah's position, straight to the point, get to the facts, no messing about, but she had no choice but to shut it down. 'It's best if you don't ask for details on the case. I won't be able to answer many questions, but I can tell you that Meghan Garrett is not under arrest.'

'What? Even with the family feud? I wouldn't put it past her.' She took another mouthful. The carbs were giving her a burst of vocal energy that was almost unsettling.

'What makes you say that?' Ronnie sat back in her seat, doing her best to play the role of polite friend rather than working detective. 'I wouldn't say she comes across like that at all.'

'You know what they say. The quiet ones are the worst.' Delilah popped the last of the pain au chocolat into her mouth and dusted off her hands.

'It's a pretty grave accusation, imagining someone could kill their sister-in-law in cold blood.'

'Injure, not kill. The killing could have been accidental, unplanned at least.'

'The law doesn't distinguish, as long as the intent was to cause serious harm.'

'Whatever.' Delilah slumped back, defeated. 'I'm sure you have to give everything a fair go. I mean you had me in the frame for a while, didn't you, thinking Adam and I were in a plot to elope and run off with her money or something?' Her eyes were fixed on Ronnie's now, completely unafraid of the challenge. Ronnie held her gaze.

'As you say, we have to give everything and everyone a fair go, as you put it.'

'Even Ali Tremaine? She's got the physique for it. Scarpered off on holiday pretty quickly afterwards. I guess you must have checked she got on the flight?'

Ronnie counted to five before replying. It wouldn't do to lose her cool just now, with Delilah in such a talkative mood. 'She left before the incident, and now she's back.'

Delilah looked interested. 'Really? She's not answering my calls. I thought she seemed like fun, and now we have a shared experience to bond over.'

Ronnie warmed her hands on her mug. 'I'm sure she'll be in touch. I thought you found her a bit over-enthusiastic.'

Delilah frowned. 'I was being harsh. It's an admirable quality, and fun people are hard to come by these days, which is why I asked her for her number. Looks like she doesn't feel the same way though.'

Ronnie took a sip of her drink. 'We can't be everyone's cup of tea.'

Delilah looked genuinely confused. 'It's just that most people want to be friends with me. I'm one of those people. I was almost offended when she didn't reply.'

Ronnie suppressed a smile. It was rare to find someone with this extraordinary level of self-confidence. She wondered what Susie would make of it. Was there a clinical label for being almost ridiculously self-possessed? 'Well, who knows what's going on in people's lives?'

'You've ruled me out though, I presume, or you'd have arrested me by now.'

'It's true, you need decent evidence to arrest someone, or it's a waste of time. We usually like to make sure we've got all that sorted out before we go in all guns blazing.'

Delilah nodded and smiled at a customer coming out of the shop, or maybe that was what she wanted Ronnie to think she was doing. It was a clever way of diffusing the situation, especially if she had understood what Ronnie had wanted her to understand, that it was by no means over.

Ronnie tried a new tack. 'How's work? I'm imagining you have a lot on, with everything that's going on in the news, prison breakouts, police scandals, migrants crossing the channel in dinghies every day trying to get across before winter really hits.'

Delilah ran her hands through her thick hair, holding it up in a pony tail before letting it fall back around her shoulders. 'Something like that. The Border Force are the worst. The Home Office isn't the most cushy number if I'm honest. So much red tape, and it changes the whole time, new minister, new systems, new typeface, new house style. What you gain in work life balance you lose in sanity.'

'I can imagine,' sympathised Ronnie, willing her to talk more, to take the focus off the intricacies of the investigation. 'Do you have a good team of lawyers around you?'

Delilah's hands went up in despair. 'If only. Bunch of wasters, most of them. Came to the civil service for an easy life and they do the minimum. Nobody thinks outside the box. It's all about putting up barriers, saying why it won't work rather than thinking about how it could.'

'How do you mean "think outside the box"? Surely the law is the law. That's what I tell the people I arrest anyway.' Ronnie allowed herself a smile. She wanted Delilah onside, relaxed, because there was something else behind what she was saying that needed to be brought into the open.

Delilah hesitated and picked up her coffee cup to drain what was left, then placed one hand protectively on her closed laptop. 'The law is the law. I'm not saying it's not. It's just that there are ways of making things work, legally, if you use a bit of creativity.'

'Like tax avoidance, as opposed to tax evasion?'

'Just like that.' She looked up now, with a serious lawyer face.

'And how does this manifest itself in the workplace? How do you get around red tape, legally?'

Delilah's eyes narrowed slightly. 'However I'm told to.' She looked at her watch. 'And I'll be told to pack my bags if I don't get back online soon. I'm supposed to be working from home, not from the High Street.'

Ronnie pushed her chair back from the table. She'd clearly been given her marching orders, but perhaps Delilah would agree to dropping one more titbit before they parted company.

'And I guess Adam shares your way of thinking.'

'Adam *invented* thinking outside the box.'

'He wouldn't ask you to do anything you were uncomfortable with, I presume.' A statement rather than a question. Delilah could ignore it if she wanted to. But she didn't. She gave Ronnie the biggest grin as if she'd just put her hand up with the answer to a difficult maths problem.

'Never presume. Isn't that what you said?' And with that, she picked up her phone with one hand and dismissed her companion with a little wave.

CHAPTER TWENTY-SIX

Baz was standing by her desk when she got back, writing a note. He stood up and grinned as she came in.

'Ah, sarge. I was just on my way to see Preedy for a de-brief. You got a minute?'

Ronnie felt the heat rise to her face. 'Sure. I'll pop over there with you. How's Amber doing?'

He pushed through the door and held it for her. 'Not been great over the weekend actually. We were back in hospital again yesterday with a little scare. She's home now, but still worrying a fair bit. I'm going to duck out for the afternoon if that's OK, just to be on the safe side. How's the case going?'

As they walked, Ronnie gave him a summary, skirting over her lunch at Hemingways with the boss. Baz didn't need every detail. She finished with an account of her 'accidental' coffee with Delilah. 'And now she's really got me thinking about what's going on behind the scenes at work.'

Baz stopped in front of the DCI's office door, fist poised to knock. 'You mean what shortcuts they're taking? They're lawyers. Put a foot out of line and they'll be disbarred. The press would have a field day.'

'Same goes for the police and all those officers who got fired. Didn't stop them taking the risk, did it?'

'Won't happen again.' Baz shook his head.

'Everyone's learned a lesson.'

'Well, Adam's her boss and from what she said I'd say he's sailing close to the wind.'

Baz smiled in appreciation of the expression. She could almost see his lips move as he silently repeated it to himself.

Through the window, Preedy was holding up one finger, asking them to wait as he finished his meeting. Someone was in there with him but she couldn't tell who it was from the back. They were sitting down facing him, then the figure leaned forward to look at something Preedy was indicating on his computer screen, showing a head of hair cut in a neat dark bob. Jen Connolly. What was she doing with Preedy? Ronnie felt a wave of heat pass through her – a sensation she didn't recognise until Preedy and Jen both threw their heads back and laughed at a shared joke. A second later, the door opened and Jen slipped out with a smile of greeting Ronnie didn't return. Preedy beckoned them in.

He was in a good mood, in peculiar contrast with the news he had to deliver.

'I've just spoken to Ali Tremaine's employer – her supervisor at the Mind Clinic. It seems she didn't turn up for work this morning.'

Ronnie nodded, resisting the temptation to say *I told you so.*

'And uniform's been to the house. There's no answer, and at this point I don't think we can justify going in with force.'

'Understood.' Baz was quick to agree where Ronnie's instinct was to challenge.

'That's on the basis of a risk assessment?' she asked.

'That's right. What are your thoughts?' He looked from one of them to the other.

'I'd say we give it to the end of the day. If she hasn't told her employer she's not able to come in, then the likelihood is she isn't well enough to use a phone, which makes it more reasonable to go in.'

Preedy nodded. 'DC Munro?'

'Low risk as a fit and healthy adult who hasn't been reported missing by friends or family, I'd say, sir. And even despite the overheard phone call theory, I'm struggling to establish a valid connection with our investigation, which has to take priority.'

Preedy raised one eyebrow. 'Thanks DC Munro. I appreciate your focus on the task in hand. It's a tough call. The overheard phone call may have been a trigger for Adam Lloyd, and if there is anything more to it, if Ali Tremaine has found something out since we spoke to her, and is unsure about coming forward, then I'm interested. But we have nothing to go on. DS Delmar, I think we'll go with your plan. Give her to the end of the day to get out from under her duvet and face the post-holiday blues.' He glanced up at her and she felt the same heat rising inside her as before, unwelcome and unexplained. She turned to go. 'Wait, DS Delmar, if you could stay behind – DC Munro, give us a minute?' Baz took his leave, obedient and oblivious, and Preedy gestured to a chair.

'No thanks, if that's OK. I'd rather stand.' It sounded aggressive. She hadn't meant it to, she just didn't want to be there for too long. Something was making her uncomfortable. Searching around for a compromise, she perched on the edge of the desk as he pushed the door shut.

'As you like, Ronnie.' He gave her a warm smile. 'I just wanted to say how much I enjoyed lunch yesterday.' His eyes pierced hers. She felt seen, and suddenly didn't want to be. She should have taken the chair, let him do the same and at least have the barrier of a desk between them.

'It was good. I enjoyed it too.' Her words came out stilted and unnatural. Why couldn't she behave normally in his presence? There was something inside her still resisting everything that he represented, and yet his behaviour was exemplary. She couldn't rationalise why she felt so on edge.

He seemed to read her mind. 'I don't need an answer now, but if you'd like to do it again sometime...'

Ronnie felt her stomach turn over in shock. Through her mind flashed images of the two of them fifteen years earlier in a London bar, where the then DI had made her feel objectified and insignificant. Was this really the same man she remembered? Had he changed, or was he putting on a show? She fiddled with the notebook and pen she was holding, grateful for the distraction, as Preedy went on.

'I just thought maybe a drink or dinner next week

if you're free one night.'

'That would be nice. I just need to check the diary. Can I get back to you?' Enthusiastic but not confirmatory. Polite but not formal. Preedy opened the door again, touching her arm as she went through.

'Oh, and by the way, I'm going to make sure Lydia is aware of what a good job you're doing on this case.'

Ronnie floated back to her desk and through the rest of the day in what felt like a parallel universe, where her life wasn't constrained and defined by her role as mother, daughter, sister, detective. It was a feeling which, however much she tried to deny it, was not altogether unpleasant. Then back came the memories of the old Preedy, and into that jumped a mental screenshot of Preedy and Jen Connolly sharing a secret joke behind his closed door. Her insides curdled and fizzed with the alarm bells it set off. It was complicated. She should be careful. She should.

She took the same route home that evening, passing the faded sign for the hotel an hour after sunset. The lights in some of the rooms were on, which struck her as odd. If it was still closed, then why waste the electricity? They couldn't be working on the building at night, unless they were falling behind on the work, but it was unlikely any builders would be happy to do that kind of overtime. As she turned back onto the main road beyond the watermain repairs, her phone pinged with a text from Alice. She sat at the traffic lights smiling at the message which the previous day she might have found to be a trigger for resentment, for thinking *why don't you ever ask how I am instead of talking about yourself?* But today, impatience and exasperation had been replaced by the rosy glow of something else.

Frank came over today the text said simply, then, *He's helping me sort out your dad's things.*

You could do worse :) Ronnie texted back.

Alice Delmar replied with a shocked face followed by a laughing face, then in case Ronnie hadn't understood, *cheeky – he's closer to your age than mine*

I may have my eye on someone else she texted back as the lights changed.

CHAPTER TWENTY-SEVEN

Ronnie woke early, her heart pounding as if she'd been dreaming about being chased, as was often the case. But this time, however hard she tried to recapture it, she couldn't recall the dream. Pulling on a dressing gown she went to the kitchen to make herself a coffee, and while the machine hissed and gurgled into life, she stood at the French windows looking down at the green space below. The first dog walkers were clustered in the middle of the grass which, after the recent rain, was looking decidedly waterlogged. What was it they talked about as they stood around in the drizzle each morning while their charges wandered around sniffing each other? Perhaps pet ownership was a lot less onerous than she had imagined.

Full of unanswered questions, her thoughts turned to her mother and she typed a quick text asking if she was free for a chat. The first thing on her mind was whether Frank had elaborated any further on his encounter with the reprobate that had put him in hospital. Alice was more likely to be understanding, even encouraging of any act of revenge for her husband's death, whereas Ronnie was more circumspect. With no evidence of foul play, the last thing anyone should be doing was scaring off a witness. But there was nothing she could do about it now. He was just another civilian bent on wreaking vengeance, and some would say (including her own mother) that the police only had themselves to blame for the public taking the law into their own hands.

She checked her phone again. No reply. It was too early to call. Alice would have forgiven Frank for whatever he'd done. She'd have welcomed him with open arms, and he'd have felt quite the knight in shining armour. It occurred to her that Frank kept his home life very much to himself, and she had no idea how his wife felt about him spending time away from home, often with other women. While it was almost appealing to imagine the possibility of a romance between him and her mother, it was easy to forget that in the background there was a wife. Perhaps she should give his home number a call later. If he was at work, she might even get to speak to the mysterious Helen. Perhaps she and Frank had an understanding of some sort when it came to how he spent his time. Anything was possible – in her experience, relationships were as individual and unique as people, and what for one person would be intolerable, could be perfectly acceptable for another. In the early days of her own marriage, Simon had struggled with her need to build a career and would have cited her long work hours as grounds for divorce if she hadn't persuaded him to wait two years and do it by consent. Even then, he had only agreed because of the children. Whatever he thought of her priorities, even he could see it would have been unfair to tell the twins their mother didn't love them enough to look after them.

Relationships had been few and far between since her split with Simon. A few dates that led nowhere, a guilty kiss in a pub carpark with a man who turned out to be living two lives. It hadn't been the greatest advert for post-divorce happiness. Swiping left and right on middle-aged bald men holding large fish had yielded very little. She allowed herself to imagine Preedy in her life. Properly in her life. It wasn't something that was encouraged in the force as a rule, to prevent conflicts of interest and protect professionalism, or what was left of it, but once he was back at his London base, none of that would be relevant. What would the kids think of him? Serena would be a whole other issue. Would she be forever reminding her of his past behaviour and that leopards never changed their spots?

The ping of the coffee machine drew a line under her wondering. There was movement from the children's bedrooms and a bathroom door slammed shut. She sipped her coffee as she flicked through the news on her phone. Sure enough, migrant crossings had made the headlines again, with a record number of dinghies being intercepted the previous day. Others were still coming through in lorries and vans with false walls and floors. There was one case of a Border Force officer being alerted to a cargo of people by the smell of one of their bodies rotting in the cavity space. Ronnie retched at the thought of it. Tilly emerged and poured herself a coffee before coming to look over her shoulder at the article.

'That's so gross. How bad must their lives be to

take that kind of risk coming here?'

'Pretty horrific, you have to assume,' said Ronnie, stirring milk into her mug.

'Is it the same as people trafficking?'

'Not always. Plenty of migrants come here of their own accord and work things out for themselves when they get here. Others are lured here with false promises, then exploited and forced to work for nothing. That's trafficking.'

'I thought slavery was over.'

'It is, legally. But this still goes on, and while people can get away with it, they'll carry on trying to do it.'

'Oh, Mum, it's awful. I hate it. All of it.' Tilly leant against the kitchen worktop and stared over her coffee mug at the wall opposite. Ronnie put an arm around her shoulders.

'So do I. So do we all. But fighting this, as well as other things, is why I do what I do. It's why I won't give up. And half the battle is having you, the young people, on board and aware of what's going on out there.'

'Has someone died?' Eddie appeared in the doorway. 'What's all the drama about?'

'We're talking about human trafficking,' said Tilly, freeing herself and topping up her coffee from the machine.

'But now we're going to talk about parents' evening.' Ronnie reached for the proforma and pulled up the calendar on her phone. 'I need to book slots to see your teachers. And don't tell me you don't need to come along. I'm not falling for that again.'

Once the twins had left for school, on time for once and without leaving any of their books behind, Ronnie set off to work with a heavy heart. As she pulled onto the A-road that ran between Wakehurst and West Dean, her thoughts turned to what lay ahead of her that day. Ali Tremaine still hadn't made contact. Her messages remained unanswered and WhatsApps didn't appear to have been read. Preedy had agreed to a revisit of the situation after a day, and a day had passed. Moreover, Ali's house was on the way to the station. It wouldn't take her more than ten minutes to do the detour via Samphire Avenue and try her doorbell again. She was about to phone Preedy to tell him she'd be late when she realised firstly that she wouldn't be late, even after the detour and secondly it might be a more satisfying turn of events if she arrived having already accomplished something. If he was serious about putting in a good word to Lydia then using her initiative could only be a good thing.

It was shortly before eight when she knocked and then rang the bell of Ali Tremaine's house. Stepping back after getting no answer, she surveyed the windows above the front door and compared them to the photo she had taken two days earlier. No change. The same half drawn curtains on the top floor, the lopsided roman blind in the small window. Another slow drizzle had begun, rainclouds darkening the sky foretelling worse to come. She pulled up the hood of her jacket and rang again, then knocked again, and was about to leave when a thought occurred to her. Preedy had been reluctant for them to use force to enter, but perhaps there was another option. She glanced up at the tree-pruning neighbour's house which was sitting in similar darkness to Ali's. She walked around the front gate and rang the bell but there was no answer either, then she tried the neighbour on the other side but with no luck. *Someone* must have a spare key. She went back to her car and stood leaning on the door, staring up at the house. It was only a few seconds before inspiration struck.

'I wonder,' she said aloud, walking into the hedge-trimmer neighbour's drive and fumbling under his plant pot. 'I wonder who had the idea first – you... or Hannah.' A second later she was holding a silver yale key with a blue tag. The key slotted happily into Ali's front door and in another second she was inside.

Stepping across the threshold, she took a moment to gather herself, in anticipation of explaining her way out of it later. She imagined Preedy's expression, transformed from infatuated to disappointed. Without a warrant or a danger to life, she was on rocky ground already, even without actually breaking in. The key was irrelevant in the eyes of the law. The front door could have been wide open and she would still be in the wrong to walk straight in. Her finger hovered over her phone keypad as she deliberated whether to call someone, or at least send a message to say where she was. But then if she found nothing, she could replace the key without it ever being known that she'd been there. She pushed her phone back into her pocket. First things first.

'Hello! Anyone home?'

No answer. Ronnie did a quick sweep of the downstairs to assess whether anyone had been home. Apart from the bags that were in the same place as she'd seen them two days earlier, nothing looked lived in or recently disturbed.

'Ali, are you okay? It's DS Delmar, Halesworth CID.'

Her words echoed in the empty hall and up the staircase that wound up to one floor after another. The house was an estate agent's dream, deceptively spacious and full of original features that would merit a few decent close-up photos on Rightmove – black and white floor tiles, freshly painted picture rails and the original Victorian cornicing. The stained-glass window above the front door refracted the sun's rays across the hallway, throwing coloured shafts of light into the kitchen where the hum of the fridge and the tweet of a bluetit clinging to a bird feeder outside the window performed an incongruous duet.

She pushed open the sitting room door and a black cat jumped down from the sofa, making her jump. It rubbed against her legs, miaowing, then wandered into the kitchen, tail high, inviting her to follow. Sitting down next to an empty food bowl just inside the doorway, it gazed up at her forlornly. Another miaow, in case she hadn't understood the first one.

In the kitchen, the woody smell of the hallway gave way to the lemony freshness of floor-cleaner. The fridge was empty apart from a few vegetables in the lower drawer and jars on the top shelf. Nothing imminently perishable. The kettle was cold and empty. A lonely basil plant flopped over the sink, unwatered, while an orchid bloomed on the sill, in no need of any sustenance. The surfaces stood gleaming in the early light, not a crumb or a smear in sight. She walked back into the hall, where a pile of unopened post caught her eye, spread across the doormat and into the corner. She didn't remember the door meeting any resistance as she opened it. The pile of envelopes must have already been disturbed before she arrived.

'Ali?' she called again, feeling the thump of blood in her ears now as her mind raced to explain away the nightmare that was unfolding in her imagination.

She had one hand on the banister and was about to investigate upstairs, when something stopped her. Whether it was her gut instinct throwing her a well-timed clue, or whether she had unconsciously registered a human cry, she couldn't say, but something made her turn back. There was another door she hadn't tried. It was the kind of door you might assume led to a broom cupboard, stuffed to bursting with vacuum cleaners, mops and buckets, or just coats and boots, bags of hats and gloves that went unworn year on year, the kind of door behind which a potential purchaser might hope to find a downstairs loo or utility room.

Ronnie turned the handle and pulled, at first with no result. It must be locked. From the other side there was a sound like a muffled howl – another cat? She tried again, harder this time, and there was a fraction of movement. One more heave, and it was open – far heavier than it looked and sprung like a fire door, made to fall shut immediately on release. She held it with her foot as her eyes grew accustomed enough to the darkness inside to find a light switch.

As the light flickered on, Ronnie took in the flight of stone steps that turned left and disappeared into the black. A smell of damp rose to meet her nostrils, and a rush of colder air made her shiver.

'Ali?' she called.

She heard something. Movement below. A mouse perhaps, the scuffling of an animal or a bird trapped in an air vent. She went down three steps, using the walls on each side for support, and there it was again – a muffled moan from somewhere below. She felt her heartbeat move up a gear as the adrenaline surged, preparing her body for fight or flight. Pulling out her phone torch to see ahead of her she identified a box of Christmas decorations, a clutter of paint tins and a jumble of cardboard boxes that once contained household items and heard her mother's voice – *you never know if you're going to need the packaging to send it back*. It was only when the light landed on the recess behind the staircase that she caught her breath in shock. At first it looked like a pile of dust sheets, but now she could see movement, a kick from underneath the covers, then a white trainer.

She got down on her knees and pulled the sheets away. Underneath, tied with duct tape by the wrists, ankles and around her mouth, was the unmistakeable lanky, tanned figure of Ali Tremaine. Ronnie tore clumsily at the tape, making her cry out as it grazed her face, and again as her hands were released from captivity.

'Oh my God, who did this to you?' Ronnie pulled her gently into a sitting position and shone the torch over her to check for injuries. 'Your face looks like someone gave you a bit of a beating.'

Ali's head lolled sideways. Her lips parted, tried to speak, then closed again. Ronnie pulled out her water bottle and shook her gently by the shoulder. 'Try to drink. You're dehydrated. I'm going back upstairs to call for help. There's no signal down here.'

Jumping to her feet she headed back to the steps and made her way up them carefully. It wouldn't do for both of them to be stuck in a cellar unable to move. Reaching the top, she grabbed the door handle and turned it right and left, pulled, pushed, shook it but it refused to budge.

'For fuck's sake!' Ronnie screamed with the full force of her lungs. Why had she not left it propped open? Then again, who would put an internal door in that you could only open from one side? She gave the door one last shove with her shoulder, which just sent her ricocheting back down the stairs into the pile of empty boxes. At least it was a soft landing. Picking herself up, she made her way back to Ali whose eyes were closed again, water bottle rolling across the concrete floor at her side. She touched her arm.

'Ali, the door's locked. How do I open it from the

inside?'

'There's a wedge attached to it so it doesn't shut.' Her voice wasn't much more than a whisper. Ronnie held the water bottle to her lips again.

'It's not there now. You mean it locks automatically when it closes?'

Ali sipped gratefully and tried to shift position, wincing in pain as she did so. 'From the inside, yes, never thought it was that much of a risk. Only been in the house six months.'

Ronnie slumped down next to her, switched her phone off and on again but still no signal.

'What do we do now?' Ali murmured, touching her left wrist which was red and raw from the tape. 'Does anyone know you're here?'

'Not as such, but they'll work it out.'

'What does that mean?' She blinked, her eyes hollow, disbelieving.

'You were reported absent from work. I guess they know you deal with a lot of complicated clients, so there's a certain amount of concern for your personal safety.'

'I hardly think...' She paused, sipped more water, closed her eyes again. 'Actually I'd believe anything now. Someone did this, so why not a psychologically disturbed therapy patient? Probably top of the suspect list.'

'Well, let's not jump to any conclusions just yet, but they said it was their standard protocol in these situations.' She glanced at the time on her phone. It wouldn't be long before someone would put the pieces of the puzzle together, surely? But then Baz was off, so it was really down to Overton and Preedy. She willed Overton to harness his eye for detail and register that she would normally be in the office by this time. In the meantime, she might as well find out everything she could from Ali while they were stuck there together. 'So, the obvious question is – can you remember what happened to you?'

'I'm trying to piece it together, but it's a blur. Jet lag for a start, and then – oh my God. The taxi driver who collected me at the airport...' Her eyes sprang open.

'*He* did this to you?'

She blinked hard again. 'He took me to the car. I got in, he drove me home.'

'He had your address? Or did you have to give it to him?'

'He knew where I lived. But I expected that. It was the same firm that took me to the airport last Sunday. They would have known the address.'

Ronnie rubbed her temples to stem a burgeoning headache. Her fall down the stairs had seemed painless at the time, but as the adrenaline wore off, pain was sliding in to take its place. 'So, when you got home, what happened?'

'I had just unlocked the front door when I felt a shove from behind and then I was on the floor. After that, it's a blur. He was asking lots of questions, wanted to know what I knew, what she'd told me. I didn't know who he meant, I told him I didn't know, I think I kicked and screamed until he silenced me.'

'Take your time. It will come back.'

Ali pulled the paint-stained sheets around her. 'I'm cold. I feel wet. Oh God, I've wet myself.'

Ronnie took off her jacket and put it around her shoulders. 'Don't worry about that. They'll be here soon and we'll get you cleaned up, checked over. Tell me about the driver. Anything you can remember.' In her head she had an image of Adam Lloyd – chiselled features, salt and pepper hair that seemed to have a life of its own. It was the only feature that might distinguish him in a line-up. Otherwise he looked not dissimilar to any other man his age.

'Middle-aged, about my height, so five ten. It was quick. He was wearing a beanie hat and holding a sign up so I didn't really get a look at his face, then the next minute we were facing forwards, walking towards the car. He was pulling my suitcase. I got in the back, might have fallen asleep. My phone was in my hand luggage in the boot. I remember wishing I'd kept it on me. I think I had a funny feeling.'

Ronnie's heart sank at the mention of the beanie hat. Hats disguised hair, forehead, eyebrows, half the elements that went into an e-fit. They might come up with some sort of image, but it didn't sound promising so far. 'Anything else? Can you remember what gave you the funny feeling?'

'I remember thinking he didn't look like a cab driver. Too, I don't know, professional. Like he was covering it up, trying to look young and cool, and in a hurry. Drove fast, pulling away from other cars at the lights faster than I would.'

'What about his voice? Did he have an accent? Was he British?'

'British – yes. No accent that I remember, but I don't remember. I don't *fucking* remember.' Tears formed in the corner of her eyes and she thumped the floor with her fist.

'It's OK. Stay calm. It will come back.' Ronnie took Ali's hands in hers and tried not to react to how cold they were. She didn't want her worrying any more than necessary until she was safely out of the cellar. 'CID know you're missing. We were going to break into your house today if you hadn't shown up, so they will know that's where I went. As soon as we get out of here, we'll get you somewhere safe and work out who did this to you.'

Ali turned her head to Ronnie, eyes pleading. 'I can't stay here. He must have the key – if he was planning on letting me go, or feeding me at some point.'

'Ali, I need to ask you something. I know it's a foggy memory and you've been through the mill. You may not know the answer to this but I need to ask.'

Ali nodded and wiped her face with her sleeve. 'Go on, what?'

'Do you think there's a chance your taxi driver was Adam Lloyd?'

Ali let her eyes fall shut again. 'I only met Adam once. He collected Hannah from a restaurant in town. I came out to say goodbye and was introduced through the car window. I couldn't say. He looked like any other bloke to me. What makes you think it was him?'

'We'll show you a picture when you're out of here. There's just a chance he might have overheard you and Hannah when she was on the phone to him, and what he overheard – I think it may have spooked him.'

'Into killing Hannah?'

Ronnie shrugged. 'We have no evidence. At the moment it's somewhere between a hunch and a theory, and we can't get any further until we work out what it was he thought he heard. You mentioned gossip or news and going to the airport, but that's not giving us much to go on. If there was a link, we'd be up and running.'

'He thought that Hannah knew something and was going to tell me when we next spoke?'

'Or that you were the one who knew something. It's just that, in either case we have no idea what it was.'

A tear escaped from one eye and ran down her cheek, unchecked. 'So it's my fault she's dead.'

'It absolutely is not your fault, Ali.' Ronnie felt her voice rise to a panic. She should never have let the conversation take this turn, and now she had to steer it back. 'There is only one person whose fault it is, and we're going to find them.'

The water bottle was almost empty. Ronnie checked the time again. Everyone would be in the office by now. Overton, maybe even Preedy would be clocking her absence and raising the alarm. The cogs would be turning. They'd realise, they *must* realise why she wasn't there. They'd be trying her phone and not getting through, and things would start adding up. She had enough of a reputation for spontaneous action, going it alone where it might have been wiser to bring a colleague along. Lydia had reminded her often enough how close she was to a disciplinary hearing. It was less than an hour ago that she had been feeling smugly distant from the bad apples and now here she was, bending the rules on her own whim. It was hardly setting an example.

She stood up and looked around for inspiration.

'Right, how are we going to fill the time until we get rescued?'

'How long do you reckon we've got?' came Ali's feeble reply. She had less faith than Ronnie did in the team at Halesworth. 'Enough time for Monopoly, or were you thinking more hide and seek?'

'How about we swap life stories? I bet we don't get further than toddlerhood.' Finally spotting what she was looking for, Ronnie reached behind the pile of boxes and pulled out an old stripy deckchair, dusted off the cobwebs and sank into it. 'You start.'

CHAPTER TWENTY-EIGHT

It was one hour and forty-five long minutes later that the door at the top of the cellar steps opened and a torch shone down on them from above.

'Sarge, you gave us a proper fright there.' Overton's first words were surprisingly restrained. He ran back up a few steps and shouted, 'They're here, sir, both of them.'

'DS Delmar. You have your strict time-keeping to thank for this early rescue.' Preedy was trotting down the stairs and helping them both to their feet. 'The second we saw you weren't at your desk bang on eight and that your phone was out of range...'

'What took you so long?' Ronnie accepted a bottle of water from Overton and handed it to Ali who glugged gratefully.

After getting Ali up the stairs and filling her rescuers in on the backstory, Ronnie was impatient to put her plan in place. Ali was in the bathroom and, having called the paramedics, she took the opportunity to make her case for the next steps.

'It's not like I haven't had time to think about it. Once we've got Ali checked for concussion and moved her somewhere safe we need to watch the house in case he comes back.'

'How long for? We don't have the resources to run

an endless stake-out.' Preedy's tone was stern. All traces of the relief at finding his DS alive and well had clearly evaporated.

'As long as it takes. This is the closest we've come yet. What she's just been through, dreadful though it was, is the biggest development we've had in the case and I'm not going to just let it go.'

Preedy waited a beat, his steely eyes on hers. 'I'm not sure that's your call.'

Ronnie looked to Overton for support. He shifted nervously, unsure which way to jump. 'Shouldn't we start by getting the young lady checked over in hospital?'

'My car's here.' She met Preedy's gaze, undaunted. 'Sir, come with me. Once Ali's been taken care of, we go back to the station and Mike—' She fixed him with her best please-do-this-one-thing-for-me stare, 'can keep watch.' She turned back to Preedy. 'If he's interested in keeping her alive, he'll be back today.'

Preedy took a second to reply. Behind his eyes, Ronnie saw a whole raft of possibilities unfolding. It should have been an easy point to win. Overton wasn't objecting and if they could catch their kidnapper red-handed, they'd be another major step closer to finding Hannah Lloyd's killer. She was sure of it.

'OK.' He spoke just as Ali emerged from the bathroom.

'What's happening?' She seemed suddenly much shorter than her five feet ten as she looked from one of them to the other. 'Are we done here?'

'Yes, but not in the way you think. We need to get

you checked over by a doctor for dehydration amongst other things and that bruise on your forehead doesn't look too good to me either. We need to do things by the book.' He gave Ronnie a half-smile, which sent a wave of relief through her.

***

After the paramedics had given her the all-clear, Ali opted to go to her sister's house for a few days. 'Now I've proved myself to be supernanny on our holiday, I'm sure she won't mind a bit more help around the house for a bit. I'll get the neighbours to feed the cat for a few more days.'

'Don't overdo it,' Ronnie said automatically. 'I mean, you've been through a trauma. You might find you go into delayed shock. Sometimes it can manifest itself in strange ways, like sleeping longer than usual. Take whatever time you need.'

'I will. Don't worry, and no spilling the beans about my cheating at snakes and ladders when I was five.'

Ronnie gave her a wink. 'I'm sure they won't press charges. I'm just glad we didn't get to my turn in that autobiography game.'

Preedy was quiet for a while on the way back to the station. Ronnie filled the gaps with comments on the news, trying to stimulate a conversation that didn't stray into the personal sphere. The traffic was heavy, a combination of the roadworks, the rain and the end of half-term, and the journey took twice as long as it should have done. At the crossroads on the edge of town, he cleared his throat.

'So, we're a man down without DC Munro.'

'Yes, he's had some issues with the pregnancy, or his girlfriend has. They've been having some tests I think.'

'Hmmm.' Preedy braked again as the traffic slowed to walking pace and turned to look at her. 'You've met her, this Amber?'

Ronnie thought about it. She'd met her once, working in Hemingways some years earlier, but hadn't ever seen them together as a couple. She wondered how much of that to share with Preedy and decided on a simple answer that might discourage the line of questioning.

'Once, I think.'

'A shame to lose him, just when things are heating up.'

Ronnie looked at him. His eyes were back on the road now the bottleneck had eased so it was hard to gauge his expression. Was he suggesting Baz was bunking off? She decided not to comment. He could read into it what he liked.

'So, what did you learn about each other?' A minute later, out of nowhere. Ronnie had no idea what he was referring to until he explained. 'You and Tremaine. You said something about an autobiography game. I'm guessing you shared some stories.'

It was a roundabout way of getting her to talk

about her childhood, but if that was what he wanted, then at least it showed genuine interest in her as a person, which said something for his humanity.

'OK, what do you want to know?' She forced a smile. 'We're trapped in a car together for another ten minutes at least, at this rate. Where shall I start?'

Preedy laughed. 'Rumbled. I was always curious about you, Ronnie. I knew a bit about what happened to your father and I always wondered if there had been any closure. Was it ever resolved?'

Ronnie hesitated, pretending to be checking for traffic coming from the right at the junction. It wasn't exactly an odd question. It was thoughtful of him to remember and to ask after so many years, but she didn't feel the sincerity she wanted to feel. When it came to discussing the tragedies in her family, she was more guarded as time went by, preferring to keep her cards close to her chest rather than risk the judgement of even the most well-meaning of friends. In her experience, behind every murder and even suicide lay a whole layer of shadowy doubt as to the moral status of the victim, and her father was the very definition of shadowy. His gambling debts had landed him and the whole family in financial trouble on plenty of occasions, and it wasn't unusual for the bailiffs to come knocking on the door of the house in Waterman Lane. If it hadn't been for the life insurance money, it would have been sold a long time ago.

That was the problem. The question mark that hung over Fred Delmar's disappearance at sea had been a legal minefield. It was only with the expert testimony of their family GP that the insurance company had finally agreed to pay out. Unbeknown to the rest of the family, Fred had reported symptoms of coronary heart disease three months before he was last seen heading out of Rye harbour, and was on the waiting list for angioplasty surgery which could have saved his life. As things stood, the build-up of atherosclerosis and a record of high blood pressure all pointed to the eventual prospect of a heart attack.

None of that was anything to be discussed with her DCI in a traffic jam, especially when their relationship was hovering between professional and personal, at least in his eyes. He would find out everything as and when the time came, on a need-to-know basis.

'Not properly resolved because we'll never know what happened on that boat. But we got a certificate of presumed death and we had a memorial ceremony last year, ten years after the event.'

Preedy exhaled with a whistling sound. 'Must have been tough. I guess she was always waiting for that knock on the door.'

'Yep. *"I'm back, what's for dinner?"* That would have been so typically him as well.'

'Did your mum ever meet anyone else?'

'Not yet.' She remembered her resolution to try Frank's home number. They were just pulling into the parking lot. It was the perfect time. 'Actually if you don't mind I just need to make a quick call before I follow you upstairs.'

'No problem. Take your time, Ronnie. You've had a bit of a morning after all.' He waved over his shoulder as he disappeared through the swing doors.

It was a strange urge she felt as the phone number connected. An urge to check him out, get to the truth behind his marriage before allowing him to spend any more time with her mother. Alice was a wealthy enough woman, and good-looking for her seventy years. It wasn't out of the question that Frank had designs on her, whether they were primarily romantic or financial. He must be in his early sixties, but what was an age gap these days? Women would do well to pair up with younger men on the basis of life expectancy, and today's aesthetic treatments could take a good twenty years off your real age, as Lydia could testify. So it was perfectly natural that before letting her mother get involved with Frank, she would want to know about the mysterious Mrs Reilly. Calling their home on the pretext of discussing a case was one way of finding out more, or at least if she really existed.

It rang four times before going to voicemail. There was a click and a whirr before the recorded message started. Ronnie listened once, then called the number twice more to hear it again. She could explain away her repeated calls if she had to later, but for now she needed to concentrate on the voice, which reassured her, disappointed her and fascinated her all at once.

'This is Helen and Frank's place. Leave a message after the tone and we'll call you back.'

It wasn't much to go on, a dozen or so hurried words conveying a standard message that in itself gave her no clues to go on. Helen was real. This was her, or that's what she could assume for now. Then there was the twinge of disappointment. At some level Ronnie wanted Frank to be free. Having supported her as she navigated her early career in the police, and having propped her mother up so tirelessly after her father went missing, he deserved his place in the fairy tale ending. And he was still earning it, or trying to, in his attempts to avenge his friend's death. Perhaps he had no designs whatsoever on any of her family and her imagination was running away with her. Perhaps she should stop digging and get on with her own workload which, with Baz away from the office and leads sending them racing in all directions, was not inconsiderable.

She pushed open the doors to the station and nodded hello to the front desk staff. As she climbed the stairs her limbs felt heavy and drained. Preedy was right in saying she'd had a bit of a morning.

'Sarge, you're back. Heard you got trapped in a dungeon.' Jen Connolly held the office door wide for her to pass. Ronnie wondered fleetingly about the sincerity of the smile.

'Thanks, yes, something like that.' She hung her coat on the peg and filled up her water bottle. A day off syrupy coffee was in order. 'I'm thinking we need to get SOCO down there, soon as, to look for fingerprints, fibres, DNA. Whoever it was that picked her up must have left some sort of trail.' There was another reason to contact Frank. It might even merit a visit to his house if she couldn't get hold of him.

'On it, sarge. They're on their way. Overton is under instruction to shout as soon as there's any sign of the kidnapper returning. We don't want him scared off by the men in white suits dusting down the front door.'

'Good thinking.' Ronnie glanced through the messages on her phone. 'Can I leave that with you?' A message from her mother saying Frank was coming for tea.

He's on a job in the next village.'

Below it was a photo of a Victoria sponge she'd made in his honour.

Don't say anything, darling. It's tea with an old friend, that's all!

She forced her mind out of suspicious mode. She'd been a detective too long, always trying to investigate things that didn't need investigating. What her mother needed now was a cup of tea and piece of cake with an old friend that had shared some happy times.

Lucky boy! Enjoy.

She flipped her phone shut just as it buzzed with another message. This time from Overton.

He's back. Get SOCO to hold off a bit longer.
Who is it????

Ronnie was bursting with impatience. Why he had to draw things out that could be said straightaway was beyond her.

You were right sarge

Then, a second later:
It's Adam Lloyd

CHAPTER TWENTY-NINE

Adam was less than delighted to be back in the station for a third time. But this time Ronnie detected an edge to him she hadn't seen before. Some of his earlier bravado had been replaced by something else, something almost childlike, as if he was running out of energy and was beginning to give up. He'd even allowed them to call the duty solicitor, who had obviously failed to convince him to say 'no comment' to everything.

'What can I tell you, apart from what I've already told you? I was going to collect the suitcase she'd borrowed from Hannah. My suitcase to be exact.'

Ronnie tapped her pen, looked at him and waited for him to say more.

'The day Hannah was attacked, last Sunday, I called her, as you know to talk about Max and she said that Ali was just leaving, and that she was borrowing a suitcase. I said 'not my suitcase I hope' and she said I'd lost all my rights to anything I'd left behind long ago, or something like that.'

Ronnie nodded, unwilling to interrupt the flow.

'It's been on my mind. I know it sounds mad to you, but when you lose someone...' His face clouded, eyes suddenly glassy with tears. 'You can get kind of obsessed with all the other things. Unimportant things. It's like everything's slipping away.' He took a sip of water from the plastic cup in front of him and blinked hard. 'I'm sure someone here knows what I mean.' He looked at Ronnie and Baz, even threw a glance his solicitor's way in desperation.

'The suitcase.' Ronnie raised her eyebrows at him. 'You didn't mention it last time we discussed your phone call with Hannah.'

'It wasn't relevant then. I wasn't thinking. For Christ's sake, I'd just found out she was dead.'

Ronnie waited a beat for him to calm down. He had a point, but she was reluctant to let it carry any weight. 'Can you describe the suitcase?'

'Navy blue, hard plastic shell. You know the ones. Big, pull-out handle, nice smooth wheels.' He was looking around at them all now, wanting validation.

'And just to clarify, Ali borrowed it from Hannah, but it was actually yours and you wanted it back. So today you were just on your way to pick it up when DC Overton stopped you.'

'Correct.' His head went into his hands.

'How did you find out where she lived?'

Slowly, his fingers parted and slid half-way down his face. 'I dropped Hannah at her house once when I was taking Max to a friend's in the same road.'

It was a decent answer. It was still possible that Ali hadn't met him properly. Ronnie paused before her next question. She needed to see his face. The moment his hands sank back to his lap, she began.

'Where were you last Saturday night?'

'At home with my son. You can check, can't you? Phone signals?'

'We found Ali Tremaine tied up in her own cellar, dehydrated and confused. Someone posing as a taxi driver collected her from the airport and imprisoned her in her own home. We assumed whoever put her there would be back to either get information from her, feed her, release her or all three. Which one was it?'

Adam gripped the edge of the table, his knuckles turning white. 'That is *nothing* to do with me. Can't you find some way of finding out where I was and rule me out?' Ronnie considered her next move, but he made it easy for her. 'I need to get back to work.'

'Ah, now talking of work.' She exchanged glances with Overton. 'I hear your department has its hands full at the moment. All this stuff in the news about asylum seekers doing anything they can to cross the channel, dead bodies behind false walls in the back of trucks. Must be tough.'

'I'm leaving the department next month. Going into politics.'

'So I hear, and soon it will all be somebody else's problem but in the meantime, how are you bearing up, especially with everything else going on in your life? It's a lot to manage.'

He sat up straight and refocussed. 'I'm not sure what you're getting at.'

Ronnie paused a second before rephrasing it. 'I'm just wondering if you've ever been tempted to cut corners. You know, rubber stamp an application, turn a blind eye to a missing document. I'm sure it goes on, and the lawyers are the ones to sign off on such things, I imagine?'

The solicitor leaned forward to object but Adam's fist came down on the table first. 'Are you questioning my professional ethics, Detective *Delmar*?' He pronounced her name with a snort of derision that said he wasn't going down alone. 'And that coming from *you*, a member of the hotbed of corruption that calls itself the police force?'

She let him speak without showing any reaction. He wasn't going to get a rise out of her by bringing her down to his level. She was more in control than that. Overton threw her a glance that said they should be ready for more. They didn't have to wait long.

'Before you come knocking on my door, you need to look around your own house. Take the blinkers off and look a little more closely at what's going on right under your noses. The public haven't heard the half of it, believe me.'

'I don't remember asking what your opinion is of the police, Mr Lloyd.' Ronnie fixed him with an expressionless stare. 'But it is common knowledge in your department that you are not averse to cutting a few corners, breaking the odd rule by – let's draw a parallel with tax avoidance rather than evasion. I'm sure you're managing to stay the right side of the law, you're clever enough to cover your tracks, and the workings of the Home Office legal team are not under investigation here, but I want you to know it's been noticed.'

Overton stole a look at her and she gave him the slightest of nods to reassure him it was all going according to plan. She didn't take her eyes off Adam, whose forehead was beginning to glisten with sweat. He reached for the cup of water and brought it, shaking, to his lips. His solicitor leant over and whispered something about taking a break but he shook his head. Then, crushing the empty cup in his fingers, he leaned across the table, narrowed eyes on Ronnie.

'Maybe I haven't been the golden boy civil servant. We work under pressure. We have to deliver outcomes with limited resources and most of the department work for peanuts with no prospects. The workload doubles in a week but we don't get extra hands on deck to do it and there are no excuses. Applications for asylum go up every day, allegations of slavery and trafficking are going through the roof. It's not physically possible for human beings to deal with this level of work without losing their shit. If I've lost my shit occasionally it was so I could survive. Literally survive. And now I'm a widowed single parent in a police station under suspicion of murdering my wife and kidnapping her friend. And you wonder why I'm losing my shit again?'

His voice had reached a crescendo. The solicitor's hand was on his raised arm and even Overton had pushed his chair back, ready to call for back up. Ronnie was imagining him in the car with Ali, just managing to get her into the house before 'losing his shit' and locking her in the cellar. It occurred to her that a man as volatile as this must have left a whole trail of DNA at the scene, and unlike the flat at Mulberry Court, Ali Tremaine's house had no reason to contain any traces of Adam Lloyd.

It was like a still from a movie, as if the director had said *freeze* and he'd stopped mid-way through throwing a punch. His fist was still in the air. Then suddenly his arm was down. His hand unclenched. He blinked, like a sleepwalker disturbed mid-ramble.

Ronnie looked at Mike. 'DC Overton do you have any questions?'

'Mr Lloyd, I've been listening to everything you've said with great interest, and as my colleague here said a few moments ago, it sounds like a lot to deal with. But last I heard, it was the Home Secretary the buck stopped with. You're not the buffer at the end of the line. He is. And HR. Where do they come in? Aren't they supposed to manage the health and well-being of the staff? I'd be paying them a visit if things were as bad for me as they are clearly are for you.' He sat back in his chair and folded his arms. Ronnie was impressed. She had underestimated him.

'Try telling that to NHS nurses. Our job isn't that different.' Adam clasped his hands together to stop them from shaking. 'I think I need a break now.' He pushed back his chair and the solicitor shuffled some papers together before following him out of the room, where a uniformed officer took charge.

Overton stopped the tape and shook his head. 'What do you think?'

Ronnie inhaled deeply and let the breath out in stages, waiting for inspiration to land. 'I don't know. I thought I had an instinct for these things but right now it's failing me. I think his professional ethics are in jeopardy, but how relevant that is to us now I don't know. It feels more like a symptom of something much bigger. It feels to me that he's falling apart on so many levels. He can't even lie convincingly. The suitcase in Ali's hallway, the one she took on holiday, was red.'

'You didn't tell him you knew he was lying about that.'

'I don't know he was lying. Maybe Hannah really had told him that, and either Ali changed her mind about the suitcase or Hannah was just saying it to wind him up – *we're using all your stuff and there's nothing you can do about it – serves you right.*'

'So there's no way of proving he's lying about it?'

'Not without waking the dead. Even if Ali says she knew nothing about it, we've still got the possibility of Hannah playing games. Pointless exercise digging any deeper.'

Overton looked crestfallen. 'Shouldn't we be looking into the work thing though, on a separate issue, alert the Home Secretary to trouble in the ranks?'

Ronnie pondered a second. 'It's a completely separate matter, and a tenuous link to what we're doing here, but it wouldn't do any harm to set the ball rolling. Only thing is, we'd have to get decent witnesses to come forward if we were going to make any kind of case at all. Delilah may have put us onto him but I'm not convinced she'd go any further when it came to incriminating her boss, her godson's father, and goodness knows what else they have going on together.'

'Fair enough. I'll wait for your shout on that one.'

'There was one other thing.' Ronnie bit her lip. Sometimes vocalising something helped assess its importance. It might be nothing, but it had bothered her somehow. 'He was vehement about the police. What was all that about?'

'The usual. It's all over the press, all the resignations and sackings. It's like the whole force is being overhauled on a zero-tolerance basis.'

'Which you'd think was a good thing.'

'Sometimes people like to stick with the bad news long after there have been measures in place to fix what's wrong,' Overton said, stroking his chin. 'But I agree he sounded very bitter, as if it was personal somehow.'

'Exactly what I was thinking.'

The door opened and Adam came back in looking slightly more together, although his hands remained out of sight for the rest of the interview. He answered the next few questions with emotionless brevity until Ronnie brought up the phone call again.

'So, Mr Lloyd if I may take you back to that conversation about the suitcase.'

'Yes, go ahead.' His flat smile said he knew they were never going to get him on whether the story was a lie or not. 'What about it?'

'Ali was leaving the house, while you were on the phone, taking your suitcase with her.'

'That's right.'

Ronnie smiled. 'How do you know that's right?'

'Because I heard Hannah say goodbye to her.'

'And how do you know it was her?'

Adam looked flustered for a second, then found his answer. 'She used her name, of course. How else?'

Ronnie nodded. 'And remind me where you were at the time?'

'In my flat, where you found me when you came looking for my laptop.'

'Phone in your hand? On a table?'

'Phone was on the table, on speaker.'

'OK. And you were on your own?'

'Yes, of course I bloody was. Thrown out by my wife, living on ready meals, life of riley.'

Ronnie paused for a second before making a note on her pad for later. Thoughts were coming to her faster than she could ask her questions, and she didn't want any of them to slip away. 'And during the phone call, can you confirm that nothing else was audible, from the others in the kitchen, from Ali on her way out – nothing at all?'

'Nothing. How many fucking times...'

***

When she was left alone with Overton again a few minutes later and they were packing their paperwork away, she smiled the first proper smile of the day. 'I got it back.'

'You got what back?' Overton looked confused.

'My instinct for this.'

He sank down in his seat again. 'You mean the lying thing?'

'Yep. Exactly that.'

'So what's his tell? What does he do that gives him away?'

'Anger, swearing, hiding his face.'

'Pretty standard stuff then?'

Ronnie gave him a look. 'If it's so basic, you tell me what was lies and what was truth.'

Overton made a face. 'OK, maybe if I re-listen to the tape, now I know what I'm looking for.'

'The thing is...' Ronnie packed her file and notebook in her bag and slung it over her shoulder. 'I think we might have just hit the tip of the iceberg.'

CHAPTER THIRTY

Ronnie swivelled her office chair to face the window. The sight of normal life going on around her usually gave her the sense of equilibrium she needed to organize her thoughts, but it was gone five o'clock and the café where she had sat with Delilah only the previous day stood empty, its windows in darkness. The traffic was heavier than usual – rush hour compounded by the incessant drizzle which had turned to a downpour, and the sky was a leaden grey. If she was looking for inspiration, she needed to focus her attention elsewhere.

She ran over the events of the day in her head to see if she could reach a narrative that made sense. Ali was kidnapped by a man she didn't know for reasons which remained a mystery. Nothing had been stolen, there had been no sexual assault and no attempt to get information out of her. Adam's story about the suitcase was at best half-lie half-truth. He may well have been told his suitcase was being borrowed but it was beyond unlikely he was on his way to retrieve it when they intercepted him. He was more than likely not a squeaky-clean civil service lawyer, but quick to challenge the system and claim he had no choice, even quicker to point the finger back at the police. What was driving that?

She took herself back to her last conversation with Preedy at the Tremaine house. She'd got a feeling from him that had set her on edge when she'd suggested Overton stay behind and watch the house. He'd been uncharacteristically quiet in the car, and when they brought Adam into the station later, he'd been determined that she and Overton do the interview. Individually those observations meant nothing special, but together they added up to more than a sum of the parts. Or did they? Was she reading too much into it?

She checked her messages for an update on Ali Tremaine. Confusion... post-traumatic amnesia... uncertain whether those memories will be recovered... medically fit for discharge.

She ought to be pleased that Ali had made some sort of recovery. She could have died of thirst and hunger in there, but the amnesia was a worry. What had happened in those hours she couldn't remember? What did her kidnapper want and did he get what he wanted?

A text pinged in from her mother asking if she was free to chat. It would be a welcome distraction from the labyrinth she was currently navigating in her mind. Sometimes a complete change and revisit was all you needed to see what was staring you in the face the whole time. She scrolled down her recent calls to find *Mum mobile* and her finger hovered over the number. On the screen a few numbers later were three calls to a landline. Frank and Helen Reilly. There was another piece of unfinished business, but it could wait until later, and maybe what her mother had to say would throw some light on the situation.

Frank's visit had been a great success by all accounts and he had earned his cake. Together they had filled the boot of Alice's car with Fred's belongings that had spent the best part of ten years in boxes in the loft. Frank had driven it to the tip and come back to raise a glass to his old friend. He had indeed mentioned his encounter with Fred's former poker companions and Alice had echoed Ronnie's insistence that he stay well away from administering any kind of retribution. Whatever was in the past was in the past and she had no interest in pursuing random acts of revenge so long after the event. If there was foul play involved, she could imagine Fred had played no small part in it himself.

Ronnie listened and alongside relief at being part of an anti-vigilante united front, felt a sudden wave of emptiness. Her father had gone. He wasn't going to magically reappear one day. He had died, either through natural causes or at the hands of a would-be gangster, a disgruntled creditor – who knew? And more than likely they would never know. Living with not knowing was the challenge. It was against her nature, against her job description. Alice could draw a line under it but for her it was just different.

She sat with her hands on the steering wheel for a minute, contemplating what would be next. There were moments in life where you could make choices, take one turn or another and change the course of fate. What was it that led to those choices? Was it predestined by character and genes? Were human beings pre-programmed to take each decision they faced in a certain way or was free will a random roll of the dice? So many questions and so few answers. Her body tensed in response, fight or flight as a reaction to the unknown. She started the engine and fastened her seatbelt. First things first. Put one foot in front of the other – wasn't that what they said to people suffering from anxiety and depression? She pulled out of the car park and indicated not right for home, but left heading for Latchworth. There was one more thing to do before she could finish for the day.

Latchworth had a reputation as the genteel, more sedate alternative to West Dean which had over the past few years become the centre of suburban cool full of gin bars, gastropubs and vintage clothes shops. A good three miles from the nearest station, it was home to multi-car families living in gated private estates with more money than they knew what to do with. Outside every second house there was a builder's sign advertising extensions or loft conversions, vans bearing the insignia of swimming pool installation companies. Living half-way between the two neighbourhoods, Ronnie enjoyed being part of neither one nor the other, but the outward serenity of Latchworth's perfect exterior held a peculiar fascination for her. She'd been in the area long enough to know that what lay behind the electric gates was not always what you'd been led to believe.

Darkness had fallen by the time she reached

Orchard Lane, which led to a building site where they were converting an old hospital into accessible flats. About half the road had been completed and the remaining section was fenced off. An artist's impression of the finished product announced the imminent arrival of state-of-the-art eco-homes – *sustainable living at its finest*. Ronnie drove as far as the road allowed before turning back as far as the car she recognised as Frank Reilly's. Switching off the engine, she took a deep breath and climbed out of the driver's seat. She still didn't know exactly what had drawn her there, but she needed to see him on his own turf, with his own wife. Once she'd done that, she could relax and forget all about it, give the case her full attention again. Her excuse was prepped and ready. Ali Tremaine's house needed dusting for prints. She wanted to know if the job had been assigned to him. Continuity and all that. It was a decent reason to drop by. Meeting the mysterious wife would be a bonus.

Frank's Volvo was parked just outside a door fitted with a ramp and a railing – which seemed to be one of many entrances to the flats. The ground floor units had individual access, while the other floors were reached via the main front doors in the centre of the block. Ronnie hesitated before ringing the bell. How would he react to her just turning up like that? Would he find it intrusive? Rude? Before she could talk herself out of it, the door opened wide and Frank was standing before her, beaming smile and open arms.

Her eyes flicked over the background that framed

him. A wide hallway with open doors into three rooms. The floors were smooth wood, no rugs. It looked bare, as if they'd just moved in.

'Veronica! What a lovely surprise. Come in, come in.' He stood back and motioned for her to cross the threshold. 'To what do I owe this pleasure? I've only just got back from seeing your mother.'

Ronnie bristled at the use of her name. It sounded defensive and aggressive at the same time. She forced a smile. 'I heard you were very helpful, sorting out Dad's things and going to the tip. Above and beyond the call of duty I'd say.' She followed him into the sitting room, where a folded wheelchair leant against a high-backed armchair opposite a wall-mounted television. A walking frame stood in the corner by the window as if banished in favour of its more useful replacement. The place smelt of medicine, and she felt a sudden urge to open a window. Reading her mind, Frank did just that.

'Sorry, gets a bit fuggy in here. We keep the heating on quite high. You get cold if you can't move around much.'

'I can imagine.' Everywhere Ronnie looked there was evidence of illness and disability – a walking stick, a tray of medication, a packet of latex gloves. It explained the lack of rugs on the floor for a start.

'Sorry, Frank, I didn't realise...'

His smile was flat in response. He sighed and pushed the door closed. 'Of course you didn't. Don't worry. Helen has motor neurone. Diagnosed two years ago and a swift decline since then. It's not something I tend to bring up in conversation.'

'Of course. Poor Helen. Poor both of you. It must be so hard, with your job as well as caring for her.'

'I manage.' There was a beat of silence as Ronnie floundered for something to say.

'Look, I don't want to disturb you if you're busy. Just wanted a catch up on the case. Have you been pulled in to look at the house on Samphire Avenue? We had a break-in – well more of a kidnapping actually, and there's a good chance it's connected.'

Frank shook his head. 'I didn't hear about that, but then I've had a few days off.' He pointed down the hall. 'First my little hospital visit, then it was new carers starting and I wanted to make sure they got off to a good start.'

As if on cue, a call came from another room. 'Frankie?'

'Coming. One sec,' Frank called back, then turned to Ronnie. 'It's that time of the evening. I'm needed in the bathroom, but if you'd like to wait, I'll be back in a few minutes. I just need to show them how to work the hoist.'

'No, don't worry at all. It's a bad time. I'll pop in again another day perhaps. You get on with your evening.' She sidled towards the door, burning with embarrassment at having found herself there on his doorstep ready to challenge him for not having a wife, or for running some kind of double life. This set-up was exactly as he had described. If he was spending some of his time elsewhere then who could blame him? At no point should she have suspected romantic intentions towards her mother. In fact, the idea now seemed completely ridiculous. He'd been her father's friend and his involvement with the family had been purely for the purposes of finding out the truth about his disappearance. It would have been strange if he *hadn't* wanted to be involved. She had obviously spent too much time in CID. At least today she had seen the truth with her own eyes – that Frank Reilly was a dutiful husband who spent half his time caring for the sick and the other half fighting crime.

CHAPTER THIRTY-ONE

'Veronica? It's me, Matt.'

Ronnie twiddled the wine glass that sat on the island in front of her. Of course she knew it was him. His name was on the screen, but she'd decided for some reason to answer just with a questioning *hello?* The pick-up line designed to throw friends off balance, or to show a new love interest you hadn't saved their number yet.

'I know. Sorry, I was just in the middle of something.' She was in the middle of drinking wine, so it wasn't exactly untrue.

'How was the rest of your day? I can't believe you're still up and about.'

'I'm not.' She couldn't find the warmth, not tonight. She pulled her dressing gown more tightly around her.

'Sorry, I thought you said...'

Ronnie let out a long sigh which did better than words at conveying how she really felt. 'I mean I'm not exactly firing on all cylinders. More like in some kind of purgatory between asleep and awake. I tried going to bed but tossed and turned for an hour and now here I am back up again.'

'Ah.' It was a hesitant, awkward response, the kind she expected from a man if she overshared anything to do with emotions, which now clearly included sleeping trouble. 'Anything in particular keeping you awake? I mean, apart from the obvious unsolved mystery of Hannah Lloyd's murder and Ali Tremaine's kidnapping? Or were you just excited about our next date?'

Ronnie made a stab at a laugh which came out as more of a *hmmph*. She should give him a little more leeway, but the seeds planted in her mind about the police by Adam Lloyd earlier that day had taken root and she couldn't shake the thought that was going round and round in her head. There had been something about his manner that had thrown her back into uncertainty about Preedy, and if she was right about Adam's unconscious lying behaviours then she needed to take what he'd said seriously.

'It was Adam Lloyd on my mind actually.'

'Anything in particular? I shouldn't have let you do that interview today, Veronica, I'm sorry if it was too much after the morning's ordeal. I know the rules, the mental health of the officers in my charge comes first.'

'No, wait.' Ronnie found her voice, and the reason for her coldness, in one flash of understanding. 'That was just it. Why didn't you do the interview? You were there. He's been in twice before. It would have made sense for a more senior officer to take over given that we pretty much caught him in the act. Textbook SIO job I'd say.'

There was a long pause. Then his voice was calmer, quieter. No trace of the joviality of a minute ago.

'I'm not trying to pull rank here, but shouldn't I be the judge of that?'

It was Ronnie's turn to hesitate. She glanced at the wine bottle. She'd only had one glass, but it had warmed up her honesty. She should stifle it before she said too much.

'I don't know. You know how these things are. Maybe I'm overthinking it. As you said, it was a difficult morning. I knew we'd be rescued, but there was a chance that it might be too late for Ali.'

'I know, and those things take their toll on us, mentally.' He was being good cop now. But sympathy was less effort than talking openly. He was taking the easy way out. She should find the bravery to confront him on the issues that were bothering her. He wasn't going to come out with anything unprompted. This was her chance to talk to him, unrestrained by the chains of the workplace or the eyes and ears of the public, and she owed it to herself, to Hannah, Ali, maybe all women, to make the most of it.

'If you must know, it was what he said about the police. Got me thinking, got me questioning, I suppose, what goes on behind the scenes in the force, the stuff I don't know about that gets brushed under the carpet.' It was hard to go on, not being able to see his face but he wasn't interrupting. 'He threw a few harsh accusations which I wouldn't have taken any more seriously than usual, but...'

'Everyone's got it in for us, Veronica, since all the stuff in the press about the misogyny, the racism, you name it, we've been accused of it, and they're not far wrong. The whole system was due an overhaul, and believe me it's getting one.'

'I know, and like I say, it's not something that would keep me awake at night normally.' She ran her finger around the rim of her wine glass, wishing for more time to plan her words. It was bound to come out wrong. 'It's just that I'm thinking... Maybe I'm in the wrong job.'

Preedy let out a noisy sigh. 'Is that what this is about? One bad day and you're losing your nerve? That's not the DS Delmar we all know and – like.' He drifted off uncertainly, one foot dipping tentatively in the sea of humour that could ease the tension between them. 'You are a capable, accomplished, highly respected detective. You know that, don't you?'

'Thank you. But it doesn't make it any easier to be part of an organisation that is, at the moment at least, so heavily scrutinised, criticised, disrespected. It's demoralising. I suppose when Adam said what he said—'

'Which was what?' The interruption was harsh, sudden. Ronnie was momentarily thrown by it but gathered herself enough to answer.

'Listen to the recording. You'll see what I mean.'

'I will.' His tone was serious now, a teacher telling a pupil that the slate had been wiped, no action would be taken as long as they didn't do it again. 'But I need you to know that when all that stuff started coming out, we did everything to stamp on it. Literally everything.'

'You believe that. You think it's been wiped out? How did you manage that? Isn't it a culture that's become totally ingrained?'

'Well short of sacking every single officer and starting back at zero, I think we did a good job.'

'How did you do it? I mean, how did you infiltrate?'

Another sigh. 'Look, Veronica, one day, I'll tell you the whole story. But not now. It's not the time, and it's still too recent, too fresh to discuss. Some of the cases against our officers are still ongoing, and there will be more, at all levels, and geographically widespread as well. I've already told you more than I should have.'

Ronnie let the words sink in. 'You're right. I shouldn't be going on about it. Too much in one day. It must have got to me.'

'It's obviously affected you a lot.' The harshness was gone again, replaced by therapist-like gentleness. 'If you need to take some time...'

'No. I'll be fine. Get back on the horse and all that. There's some other family stuff going on I didn't tell you about before.'

'Go on.'

'They found a part of my father's body out at sea. I didn't tell you because it seemed irrelevant.' She closed her eyes tightly, partly to stem the tears and partly in anticipation of what Preedy might say next.

'That's hardly irrelevant. What do they think happened to him?'

'A trawler boat dredged up part of his skull.

Doesn't give us any clues about how he died, but we know he's dead. No pretending anymore.'

'Oh Veronica, I'm so sorry.' His shock seemed genuine. She allowed a tear to escape. Just one.

'Thank you. It was a shock.' She wiped her face on her sleeve and glanced at the time on the oven clock. 'Now, if you don't mind, I'm going to try again to get to sleep and put today behind me.'

CHAPTER THIRTY-TWO

Overton was working on one of his famous spreadsheets when Ronnie went up to his desk and leaned over his shoulder.

'May I disturb the genius at work? Lydia wants to see me but I just thought I'd pop by in case you had any news.'

'Sarge, great timing. I was just going through the evidence listing the issues that haven't been resolved.' He looked up and a flash of worry passed across his face. 'It helps me organize my thoughts. Sorry if it seems weird to you.'

'Not at all.' Ronnie smiled. Overton was one of the good guys. Probably the last man in the world you'd find on an incel WhatsApp group, and a good reason to still have faith in her profession. 'What's on your list?'

'I was going through the files they pulled off Adam's phone and laptop to try to establish what needed further investigation, especially the contacts, frequently used numbers and what have you.' He spun his computer to face her. A multitude of minimised documents filled the screen, illegible until he zoomed in on one.

'Looking for anything in particular?' Ronnie peered at the list of numbers, dates and times. 'Short of ringing them all ourselves, we're not going to get much from that.'

'On Adam's phone history there are plenty of calls and messages to Hannah, a few to Delilah but no contact with Giselle, hardly any with Meghan Garrett or her husband, Hannah's brother. And it seems to be true that he didn't know Ali Tremaine. Her number isn't in his contacts.'

'What about other numbers we don't have on our books?'

'That's where it gets interesting.' Overton zoomed in on a mobile number, then scrolled down to show it repeating several times over the course of each day, for what looked like most of a week. 'I've looked further back and it goes on for weeks, calls and messages to this number, the calls being always at the same time of day. It may be nothing of course, but I thought I'd flag it up.'

Ronnie frowned. Leaving no stone unturned was always admirable, but unveiling a whole new mystery was the downside. The number didn't look familiar, but then numbers never did anymore, with phone storage being what it was. 'It's a burner I presume.'

'What kind of messages are they sending?' she asked.

'That's the weird thing. Giving nothing away, just a few brief words, and every few days a series of numbers in the messages.'

'What kind of numbers?'

'Reference numbers of some sort. I've put them together here to see if I can make any sense of it all.' He pulled up a document showing a series of letters and numbers separated by dashes, dots and slashes.

Ronnie looked at the time on her phone. Lydia was expecting her any minute but this new information needed a closer look. 'Can you print it off for me?'

'Sure.' Overton's face lit up with the joy of a job well done.

***

Lydia was beaming when she opened the door of the meeting room, which threw Ronnie off kilter for a second. Had she had some good news? Was there a development in the case she was about to share?

'DS Delmar, it feels like an eternity since we touched base. Please have a seat.' She gestured to the room, where several uninviting plastic chairs encircled a Formica table. 'No office for the moment so we'll have to slum it in here.' She pulled out a chair and sank into it. 'They're not as uncomfortable as they look actually. Can I get you a glass of water?' She reached for the jug and poured one for herself. Ronnie held up her hand.

'Thanks, ma'am, I'm fine for now.' Ronnie sat down and opened her notebook. If Lydia wasn't anxious to begin then it was up to her to get the ball rolling. 'A lot's happened since we last spoke. I'm assuming DCI Preedy has been keeping you in the loop.'

'Oh yes, and there has been mention of your excellent work on the case. I think you've made quite an impression.'

So Preedy had meant it when he said he'd put in a good word. Ronnie felt her cheeks redden. 'Thank you, ma'am, but I don't think I'm approaching this case any differently from usual.'

Lydia smiled conspiratorially. 'I'm sure. But it's nice to be appreciated.'

'Yes, ma'am.'

'And how are you managing, generally?'

'How do you mean?' Ronnie's mind flicked back to her chat with Preedy the previous night. Surely he hadn't gone straight back to the DI with what she'd confided in him.

'What with the Lloyd murder, the Tremaine kidnapping, and then with your own personal issues...' She raised an eyebrow at Ronnie, who kept her gaze firmly on Lydia's face. 'You've been through a lot. DCI Preedy was genuinely concerned for your emotional welfare.'

Ronnie did a double take. 'What are you saying, ma'am, that I'm not coping?'

'Not at all. Not at all.' Lydia's head was cocked, eyes full of worry. 'It's just a question. I'm here to listen, if there is anything you need to talk about.'

'So this isn't about the case?' Ronnie flipped her notebook shut.

'If you want it to be, if there's anything about the case you want to discuss, get off your chest, then please don't hold back, or if there's anything else...'

'There's nothing else.' Ronnie forced a smile. 'I'm absolutely fine. I'm sorry the DCI worried you. There was no reason to.'

'I'm glad, and believe me, it was all in good faith, coming from a good place. The police force has learnt its lessons over recent years. We look after each other, and we don't put up with transgressions.'

Ronnie nodded. 'That's good to hear.'

'I understand you had your concerns on that issue as well, DS Delmar, but I hope you are satisfied that everything has been done to oust the bad apples in the force. Squeaky clean is our motto from now on.'

Bad apples – those words again. Ronnie smiled once more and pushed her chair back from the table. 'If that's all, I should be getting on.'

'That's all, but please take the offer seriously. A few days off could do you the world of good, and we'll manage in your absence, just about.' Ronnie didn't reciprocate the offered smile this time. The red mist was descending faster than she could brush it away.

'Thank you, ma'am. Much appreciated, but it won't be necessary.'

As the door clicked shut behind her, she took a few deep breaths. Preedy must have gone behind her back as some sort of punishment for not accepting his offer to go for another drink, unless he was trying to get her out of the way for some reason? Had Adam Lloyd been about to reveal something about police misconduct that wasn't already in the public domain? If that was it, everything suddenly made complete sense. Adam was trying to tell the truth when he mentioned the police. She'd been right about that, about the anger and swearing being a sign of lies. His comments about the police had been calm, measured, honest. She'd shared her concerns with Preedy and he'd shut it down before it came to anything. The tone of his voice on the phone the previous night had said it all.

She pushed open the heavy office door and made her way through the desks. Overton looked up as she passed, a frown of concern on his face. 'Everything OK, sarge? I printed off the pages and left them on your desk.'

She nodded. 'All good. Thanks, Mike.'

She rarely pulled the partition across that divided her workspace from the rest of the office. It not only went against the open-door policy but against everything she believed about her role as a mentor, a supervisor, a team player. When she'd been a new DC back in the day, the lack of access to senior officers was part of the job. Nobody had expected anything different, but it had its repercussions. Information wasn't shared where it should have been, and officers thought twice before asking key questions of their superiors which might have influenced the progress of a case. The culture of fear had put the brakes on when it came to solving crime, and Ronnie had sworn that when her turn came, she'd make sure to ring the changes. And so she had, until today. But right now she needed to be alone, take her mind off the minutiae and let the bigger chunks of thinking fall into place. She was on the edge of something.

The scene on the street below was livelier than it

had been the previous day. With the milder temperatures and a break in the rainfall, Nico's Café was buzzing with activity. No sign of Delilah, but a few other working-from-home types sat in the window, laptops open, heads bowed. Out on the terrace a middle-aged couple wrapped in scarves and jackets nursed hot drinks in their hands as they huddled over their table, deep in conversation. Ronnie thought about what it must be like to be in a relationship where neither of you worked on a Wednesday, where you were free to go for a coffee mid-morning and still had things to say to each other. For a brief moment on Sunday, and maybe Monday, she had dared to entertain the thought of having that kind of relationship with Matt Preedy. There might have been a few sharp words, a bit of disapproval from the shadows once the story broke at work, but it wouldn't have presented much of a problem for either of them in terms of protocol. Retirement was less than a decade away for him, longer for her, but they'd still have many years of freedom to have a Wednesday morning coffee together, and hopefully a lot more. They could travel the world, set up a stray dog charity in Romania, build a school in Mozambique, do good things in the world she didn't have the appetite for on her own.

Yet just in the last twelve hours, it was if a switch had been flicked and any dream she might have had about a future with Matt had evaporated into thin air. He had admonished her and gone over her head to Lydia. He had avoided the interview with Adam Lloyd, and dismissed Adam's allegations as baseless.

Meanwhile, Delilah had questioned Adam's professional morality, and his phone records indicated the existence of someone he was in regular contact with. Putting two and two together, especially given Adam's state of heightened stress when talking about work and the pressure he was under, it was an easy conclusion to draw that the messages and calls on his phone records had something to do with whatever was going on at work. Was there a connection between Border Force and the police? On the one hand she might be delving too far into speculation, but on the other, plenty of crimes were only solved by exactly that, by one detective running with a theory that appeared ludicrous to their colleagues. What was it that Baz always said? *There's no conviction without conviction.* It was a reassertion that gut feeling went a long way. The number on Adam's phone records had rung unanswered and was unregistered, a burner phone, and Preedy certainly knew all about those. The final straw was that Preedy had suggested to Lydia that she, Ronnie, needed to take some time out. He needed her away from the office until the business with Adam had blown over, she was sure of it.

She spun her chair back to face her desk. Preedy could make all the appeals he liked, but she wasn't about to be forced out of the office, and in the meantime she was going to take a look at the reference numbers on the texts sent to Adam's phone. That was where the answers lay.

CHAPTER THIRTY-THREE

'You'd forgotten I was coming over, hadn't you?'

Susie was sitting on the steps of Glendale House when Ronnie climbed out of the car.

'God, I'm so sorry. Completely slipped my mind.' She gathered her friend in for a hug and held her for a second. She smelt of soap and sandalwood. How was it that some people carried their fragrance around all day when her own seemed to wear off in seconds? She rummaged in her bag for her key. 'How long have you been waiting? The kids should have let you in.'

'Just arrived. Saw your car wasn't here so decided to wait rather than bother them. They're probably hard at work revising or something.'

'Of course. That's them all over.'

Tilly and Eddie were as excited as new puppies to see their favourite non-auntie Suze, and Ronnie took the opportunity to check the emails and messages on her phone. Preedy had sent her some sort of gif with a teddy bear holding out a bunch of flowers saying 'sorry'. So he *had* been talking to Lydia, and if he was apologising, he must feel he had something to apologise for. There was another message from Frank asking how things were and inviting her back to his house.

Come for dinner next time. Helen wants to meet you.

Ronnie tapped a quick reply.

Love to. Name the day!

There was a voicemail from her mother which could wait until later, and a long WhatsApp from Susie who always typed her messages on a laptop and managed to fill several more pages than the average correspondent. She clicked her phone off and dropped it on the sofa.

'Right, who's doing homework and who's cooking dinner with me?' The question had barely escaped her lips before the teenagers had vanished. Ronnie pulled a bottle of red from the wine rack and unscrewed it.

'Only joking about the cooking,' she whispered. 'There's a perfectly good delivery service I don't mind taking advantage of. Here you go.' She poured Susie a glass, and one for herself, savouring the glug glug sound with its promise of healing and warmth. 'Cheers.'

'How do you do it?' Susie took a sip, then set her glass on the table and looked up, smiling and wide-eyed.

'What do you mean? How do I do what?'

'Everything. Run your life, your job, your up family, your down family... I mean your original family and your children.'

'I know what you mean. I remember you saying up and down family once before and thinking it was the dead ones and the ones left alive.' Ronnie pointed upwards with one hand and downwards with the other. 'Both my families, up and down, are small but perfectly formed. My life is my life. It just carries on and I feel like I'm just a passenger, riding the waves, looking out for storms ahead and hoping we manage to avoid the rocks.'

'I love the boat analogy. Although I feel you are definitely the captain of your ship.'

'Thanks. I think. I suppose if I'm not the captain then I don't know who is. It just feels like a hell of a responsibility sometimes, when you think about it, which you've just made me do.'

'Well, I reckon you're acing it.'

'I feel like an imposter, or I'm in the wrong job. With everything that's going on with the police now, with the press all over us, I just feel I should have jumped ship when you did. It weighs on me every day, wondering if I'm part of the problem.'

'You're part of the solution, Ronnie. It's because of people like you that there *is* hope for the police force in this country.'

'Serena thinks I'm menopausal, or I need therapy, or both.'

Susie paused. 'That's a big jump to make. I'd say it's pretty normal to feel unsure about things in the currently climate. It would be weird if you didn't.'

'So you don't think I'm a headache?'

'No, and I'm sure she doesn't either. Nothing wrong with a bit of therapy though. It's somewhere to offload without worrying about what they want to hear, somewhere to work things out. You don't have to be in massive trouble to get therapy, it's like going to the gym for your mind.'

'And what about the hormones? Could I be perimenopausal?'

'I have no idea, but if you feel depressed, or your moods are affecting your ability to work, or you get hot flushes, then go to the doctor, but it's unlikely they'll get you a proper diagnosis, even with a blood test. Hormone levels go up and down all the time. There's no quick fix. I just think you need to accept that life in the police is hard at the moment. It's like being a traffic warden or a tax inspector. Nobody wants the job, everybody hates you, but it's got to be done, and in my opinion you're the best there is. There. I've said it.'

'Thanks. That's just what I needed to hear.'

'Now, are we allowed to talk shop? I'm desperate to hear how the case is going. Do you still think it was the husband that did it?'

Ronnie took a sip of her wine and let the warm feeling spread through her insides before replying. It had occurred to her in recent weeks that she was becoming dependent on it; not drinking excessively, but definitely enjoying a glass after work more than she'd like to admit.

'Yes and no. It's complicated.'

'How can killing someone be complicated? Either he did it or he didn't.'

She had a point, but Ronnie wasn't sure she could answer the question.

'I don't think he did it,' she said slowly. 'But I don't think he's squeaky clean.'

'An accomplice? He was in it with someone else?'

Ronnie tried to imagine Adam and Matt conspiring to commit murder but the picture refused to formulate in her mind. 'Possibly, or he asked someone, paid someone to do it, but we're still a long way from finding whoever that is.'

'What's the rest of his life like? Sounded pretty chaotic to me.'

Ronnie thought back to Delilah's commentary on Adam's working style. 'I think you're right there. He's all over the place. Makes you wonder how he got where he is, and why on earth he wants to go into politics, which is going to be a whole other ball game stress-wise.'

'Does he seem to feel any guilt at all?'

'Guilty of murder or of leaving her? If he was showing the signs, it could be either and we'd be none the wiser.'

'Fair point. The good thing about stress though, if that's what's controlling him, is it makes you slip up. Don't you think?'

Ronnie was half-way through her glass and Susie had barely touched hers. She set her own glass on the coffee table and sat back further into the sofa, hoping increasing the distance from temptation would have the desired effect.

'He hasn't slipped up yet. Not unless you count showing up at Ali Tremaine's place when to all intents and purposes she was tied up in the cellar. But he managed to talk himself out of that one. I didn't believe him for a minute, but it was impossible to prove he was lying.'

'That's tough.' Susie reached for her glass and

Ronnie felt a twinge of relief. 'If he's in league with someone, you'd expect him to be leaving some sort of traces, documents, messages, something, surely?'

Ronnie grabbed her work bag and pulled out the plastic folder Overton had given her earlier. 'There was one number he was calling and messaging a lot. And when I say a lot, more often than Mum calls me and Serena put together.'

'Did you ring it? Who's it registered to?'

'A burner phone. So no clues, and yes of course the DC tried it but it rings out. Whoever it is has been sending him what look like coded messages. Here.' She pulled a page out of the folder. Susie shuffled nearer and peered over her shoulder. 'Makes no sense to me at the moment, but I thought it would be one of those things that comes to you later on, when your brain has rifled through the filing cabinet in the back office. What do you reckon?'

'It looks like a code, but with slashes and dots as well as numbers I'm thinking morse code.'

'And while you and my subconscious work on solving that little mystery, I can work on our menu choices. I was thinking pad thai...'

Two hours later, after a delicious takeaway with two surprised and unusually grateful children, Ronnie switched on the news and snuggled back into the corner of the sofa with a warm, satisfied feeling inside. It was a rare thing, since the recent onset of her malaise, and she closed her eyes for a second, relishing the moment where all was well. Anxiety was a strange thing, an unwelcome visitor in anyone's life, but mostly for its inexplicability. Her life was, on the outside, perfect. She had her health, a good job with a decent salary, wonderful kids, a flat, a car, and no ties. Yet there was a nagging unease, something she couldn't put her finger on, that seemed to be stalking her night and day waiting for its chance to pounce, waiting for her to make a mistake, for a moment of weakness that she was struggling to keep at bay. A glass of wine or two in the evening did something to relieve her of it, and tonight was one of those nights. She drained her glass, her third that evening, but who was counting? It was less than a bottle, and she'd had a guest round. It didn't matter.

She turned her attention to the television, realising she hadn't heard a word the newsreader had said. On the screen, environmental protesters were blocking roads, waving banners and hurling debris from bridges. Motorways were gridlocked, cars turning back, unable to cross the Queen Elizabeth Bridge. Uniformed police were doing their best to control the traffic and keep the disturbance to a minimum. Ronnie didn't miss her days in uniform. Watching them now, the sworn enemy of protesters and drivers alike, it dawned on her that nobody was on your side in the police unless you moved over to CID, and even then your supporters were thin on the ground. Victims of crime were never avenged to their satisfaction, even if a perpetrator was convicted and jailed. The police would always have failed in the eyes of the public, for letting crime happen in the first place. She'd been lucky to have Frank holding her hand through the early years, and not so lucky to have men like Preedy dishing out the kind of comments that would slap down any burgeoning confidence a new recruit might be managing to gather. She had thought he'd changed. He'd shown a side of himself that had interested her, almost attracted her, but perhaps that was wishful thinking. Did people ever actually learn lessons and change for the better? The jury was still out.

A reporter was interviewing a tattooed, shaven-headed man who had chained himself to an iron railing on the Essex side of the bridge.

'We don't want to cause trouble, but we've run out of options. This way, people will listen.'

Behind them, cars hooted and flashed their lights. It was unclear what they were trying to achieve. There was no chance they were going anywhere anytime soon, but human nature had a habit of not admitting defeat.

Looking back, it was hard to say at what moment the penny dropped. One minute she was filled with relief at no longer having to patrol the public highways and the next she was staring at the number plate of the car flashing its lights. Within a second the camera switched back to the studio, but it was enough time to work out that right in front of her, there on the Queen Elizabeth bridge, was exactly the answer she'd been looking for.

CHAPTER THIRTY-FOUR

'How did you work that out?'

'Don't ask.' Ronnie was busy scanning the list of letters and numbers and lifting the vehicle registrations from amongst them.

'What's the rest of it about then?' Overton had an irritating habit of not picking up on signals sometimes. She was perfectly capable of managing this job by herself, and had no intention of delegating it, however much he hung around and leaned over her shoulder.

'The rest...' She was scribbling in her notebook now, setting out numbers in pairs and in threes, underlining the double zeros and circling the twelves. 'Look at this. What only goes up to twelve?'

'Days of Christmas? Apostles?'

'Not quite. Look again.'

He squinted at the screen and straightened, frowning into the distance. 'I'm not sure, sarge. Mind's gone blank.'

At least she wasn't the only one with brain fog. 'They're dates and times. Look.'

He shook his head and closed his eyes. 'Of course. I don't think I'd have spotted that if you hadn't said. Very impressive, sarge.' He looked as if he meant it. 'Have you told Preedy?'

'Not yet.'

'Worried he might close it down?'

Ronnie gave him a sidelong look, wondering how he had read her mind, but his eyes were back on the numbers.

'So the reg numbers relate to vehicles that will arrive at a certain place at a certain time. The question is, where?'

'And the answer to that lies in what Adam Lloyd does. He works at Border Force.'

There was a silence punctuated only by the whirr of the photocopier and the rattle of venetian blinds against the window frame. Harsh sounds for a harsh realisation, Ronnie thought. Overton sat down in the guest chair opposite her desk and looked at the ceiling.

'I can check the ferry times for those dates, check the reg numbers on the vehicle bookings.'

'And get down to the port to see who was on duty at those times.'

He pulled out his notebook and picked a pen from the pot on her desk. 'You're thinking there's another person in the chain?'

'Someone on the ground – got to be. I doubt Adam's making the journey himself each time, and there'd be a few raised eyebrows if the legal department kept popping down to Dover to wave a few lorries through.'

'Trucks?'

Ronnie shrugged. 'Not necessarily. Could be cars if it's drugs, vans if it's firearms.'

'Or people.'

The words hung in the air between them. Outside in the open plan office, a phone rang. Someone shouted for Overton, who got up and leaned around the doorway to indicate he'd be there in a minute.

'We need to trace those vehicles, find out who they belong to, where they went. ANPR footage around the port, see if we can at least get a direction of travel.'

'Of course. I'll get onto that. What about Preedy? He needs to know.'

Ronnie hesitated. She needed to think it through. 'Can we wait, just until we've done some preliminary investigation on this? In case we're wrong.'

'We can't be wrong. Or if we are, then it's a perfectly plausible story, makes absolute sense to follow it up. Is there something else you're thinking?' His eyes narrowed. 'You don't think Preedy...?'

'No, nothing like that.' She forced a smile. 'I'm just being cautious. It's like you said – I don't want him to close it down before it's started. He has a habit of shunning my suggestions out of hand, doesn't give them much of a chance, so I need all the evidence I can get that it's a good plan.'

CHAPTER THIRTY-FIVE

Alice Delmar was never one to beat around the bush, and came out with it straightaway.

'Frank said you'd been round checking up on him.'

'I did nothing of the sort. I was passing by and thought I'd pop in to say hello.' Ronnie felt her face heat up and was grateful that it wasn't a video chat. Her mother might also have had something to say about her sipping a flat white on the café terrace when she should have been chasing criminals. The idea of remote working was still a mystery to Alice, and Ronnie felt it best not to provoke her into another rant about pouring public money down the drain.

'And Serena tells me you're soft on your boss.'

'She what?' Surely Serena knew better than to deliver titbits of gossip to their mother. It would be in the national news before they knew it, or in the *Daily Mail* at least.

'She says it's the one who had a bit of a reputation as a ladies' man, from when you were working in London.'

Ronnie sighed. 'Look, I think she misunderstood.'

'So is it true or not? I mean, it's about time you started thinking about settling down. You and Simon have been apart for years.'

'Four years, Mum.' Ronnie closed her laptop. She

clearly wasn't going to get any more work done, and her lunch break was technically over anyway.

'Well, whatever. But it's time to get back on the horse.'

Ronnie wondered for a second what had possessed her mother to use that sort of imagery, and why she was suddenly so obsessed with her finding a new boyfriend. Where had the fiercely feminist campaigner gone? Then the penny dropped.

'This isn't about me, is it, Mum?'

'What do you mean? Of course it's about you. I worry about you and I want you to be happy. That's what it's about. That's what being a parent is about. I'm sure you feel the same about the twins.'

'No, I mean...' Ronnie waved thanks to a car that slowed to allow her to cross the road, then changed her mind about opening up to her mother completely. However she phrased it, Alice would take it as an accusation. She'd deny any interest in Frank and remind Ronnie that he was happily married. Better to backtrack and stay on message.

'Sorry, Mum, I'm just going into a meeting. Thanks for your concern. As soon as there is some news, I promise to keep you in the loop.' The words rang with untruth as she spoke them.

Preedy was in the lobby pulling his coat on as she stepped into the warmth of the station reception.

'DS Delmar, just the person I was looking for.'

Ronnie regarded him blankly. He didn't need to know her thoughts. He had waived that right when he went running to Lydia, spreading rumours about her mental well-being.

'How are things? Have you thought about taking a break at all?'

'No.' She tried to meet his gaze but found herself looking away. 'I don't need a break. I'm fine. In fact, I may be on to something.'

'Oh yes?'

'Just a theory at the moment but I'll let you know very soon if it's a runner.' She had said more than she meant to, but the urge to build herself up into a credible, worthy detective was all-consuming in the face of the pitying looks of her superiors.

Preedy frowned. 'What kind of theory?' He held the door open for a nervous-looking teenage girl who nodded her thanks. Ronnie couldn't decide if his gesture was a symbol of human kindness or stifling patriarchy.

'I'll tell you later. I just need to find out if there's any mileage in it.'

'Fair enough.' An elderly man was struggling with the door and Preedy held it open again, causing Ronnie's patriarchy theory to crash and burn. 'I look forward to later.'

With what looked like a wink, he turned to leave, letting the door swing shut behind him. Ronnie watched him take the steps two at a time before disappearing around the corner. The truth was she couldn't make up her mind about Matt Preedy. Normally, she was firmly a believer in leopards and spots. Once a misogynist, always a misogynist. Once a bully, always a bully. You could insert any word you liked, because history seemed to show that being over-hopeful about human nature only brought disappointment. Then again, she wanted to believe in redemption. If she didn't, then what was the point of anything? Why educate people if not to change hearts and minds? Life was a pretty dark and empty experience if there was no growth or change. She should embrace that and give the man a chance. After all, wouldn't she want to be given the same chance if the tables were turned?

She trudged up the stairs with a heavy heart. The reason she couldn't do it was because she wasn't ready. Simon's departure had left its scars and the thought of letting someone do that to her again filled her with unease. On top of that, a nagging doubt festered in the back of her mind about his role in the Met dismissals. For all his reassurances, she wasn't entirely sure there wasn't more to it. He'd been keen to reiterate that all the loose ends had been tied up when it came to getting rid of the rogues in their midst, but that was easy for him to say, as the architect of the operation. It was like marking your own homework.

Overton was waiting in her office when she arrived. 'I saw you out of the window, sarge. Figured you'd only be a minute so thought I'd wait here. Hope that's OK.'

'Sure. What have you got for me?'

'Well, you were right about the vehicles. Transit vans to be precise, one of which came through Dover at the weekend, one a week before that. We're still cross-checking the other numbers with previous weeks to confirm the correlation with the code in the texts.'

Ronnie felt her brain engage and come to life. Her theory was fast becoming a reality, which gave a sudden sense of urgency to her day.

'And if that works out, we should have one of them coming through today, right?'

'Just had sight of that one, sarge, currently en route from Kent by the looks of things.' He opened his tablet and slid it across the desk to her. On the screen was a blurred but legible image of a numberplate.

'Where did you pick it up?'

'M20 just outside Maidstone.'

She sank into her swivel chair and spun one way, then the other, turning a pen between her thumbs and index fingers.

'Who's the vehicle registered to?'

'A hire company down in Kent. They've rented a few vehicles to the same clients over the last few months. All of them have been registered on cross channel ferries from Calais, this one early in the morning, a few hours before it was spotted on the motorway.'

'Can you check out the hirers? I presume they had to provide names and addresses – or more importantly driving licences which would give us a shortcut to both of those.'

Overton smiled the smile of the pupil who has done his homework early. 'They have a copy of the driving licence which we followed up with DVLA, but then, the bad news.' His smile disappeared. 'It's a fake.'

'That's all we need.' Ronnie threw the pen onto the desk and put her head in her hands to gather her thoughts. There was now an undisputed link between Adam and criminal activity, but the chances were they were just scraping the surface. The next steps would have to be handled carefully to ensure they didn't lose the trail. 'Presumably the address they gave matched the one on the licence. Is it worth checking out the address anyway?'

'Officers are on that now, sarge, and should have news very soon. It's an address in south London, tenanted, apparently.' He hesitated. 'Can we go to Preedy now? Sounds pretty watertight.'

'I think we bring Adam back in first,' said Ronnie, pulling on her jacket. 'And find out who lives at that address. And then I promise.'

CHAPTER THIRTY-SIX

Adam Lloyd looked as if he hadn't slept for weeks. He opened the door and held it for Ronnie and Overton to enter. 'I presume you have a warrant.'

Ronnie regarded him for a second before stepping across the threshold and wiping her feet.

'We don't need one.'

'What is it now?' He blinked a few times, as if they might be a figment of his imagination.

'It's bad news, I'm afraid Adam.' Ronnie used his first name, possibly for the first time and simultaneously wondered what had led her to do that. He was the fox hunted by the hounds, now cornered and helpless. Something pathetic about his demeanour made her break off. She took in the scene before them, more lived-in than it had been during their last visit, but lived in by someone who had gone off the rails. A mass of takeaway bags and Tupperware cluttered the worktops, several empty beer bottles stood on the floor by the bin and a pile of dirty plates sat gathering mould by the sink. In one corner above the kitchen cupboards, a tiny red light was just visible. She'd have missed it if she hadn't been looking exactly there, as the plastic unit containing it was the same colour as the walls and ceiling. Her heart missed a beat as she realised what she was looking at.

'Go on, I'm on the edge of my seat.' Adam looked

anything but. He was swaying slightly, his eyes moving slowly from one of them to the other.

Overton opened his mouth to speak but Ronnie put her hand on his arm and fixed him with a look. 'Please can you come with us, Mr Lloyd?' She regretted her earlier deviation from formality. Everything must look routine, to the letter. 'Now.' She hoped the sternness of her tone covered up her nerves.

Adam made as if to protest, but was manhandled into the hallway and out of the front door before he could make sense of what was happening. On the doorstep, Ronnie gestured for him to be quiet and put the door on the latch, pulling it shut without locking them out. She glanced around the eaves of the roof that overhung the front elevation of the house.

'Any more cameras out here?'

'Any *more?*' Adam seemed to have suddenly come to life. He jerked his arm away from Overton, who looked to Ronnie to see how he should react. She nodded, indicating Adam could be released from his grasp for now.

'In the corner of the kitchen ceiling by the sink there's a camera watching everything you do in that room. By the look on your face I'm guessing you didn't know it was there.'

'What the fuck?' He had found his voice. It seemed that surveillance was much more of a threat to him than the possibility of arrest by the police. Overton's eyes widened. He hadn't noticed either, then.

Adam cocked his head and frowned. 'You mean

the burglar alarm sensor? Doesn't work, never has. They came to replace it under the management contract for the flat but I'm pretty sure it's obsolete.'

Ronnie took in his demeanour. He clearly had no idea what a burglar alarm looked like. He might be a solicitor but he was looking less and less intelligent by the day.

'Look, Adam. It's time to be honest with us. We've found information on your phone that led us to a vehicle hire company in Dover. Whoever hired the vans, whose registration numbers were listed on your text messages, gave a false driving licence, and the whereabouts of those vehicles are currently unknown. We thought you might be able to help us fill the gaps.' Her eyes didn't leave his for a second. She needed to see his reaction to every word, but so far he was giving nothing away. His face had turned a ghostly white and his fists were clenched at his sides.

'I don't know anything about any van hire firm,' he said eventually.

Ronnie watched him for a few seconds, pondering her next move. 'But you knew about the times and dates those vehicles were coming through the port of Dover, didn't you? Someone has been feeding you the information. There are blue ticks next to the messages so we know you read them. That brings you firmly into the picture, whether you like it or not.'

Adam unclenched his fists and put both hands on the back of his head, eyes heavenward, appealing to an invisible deity.

'I need a solicitor.'

Ronnie smiled. 'I thought you were a solicitor. Or have you given up on that line now? What was in those vans, Adam?'

His eyes met hers. 'I want to see my solicitor before I answer any more questions.'

'Fine.' Ronnie exchanged glances with Overton, gesturing to the car. 'Let's take him back to the station. Adam Lloyd, I'm arresting you on suspicion of the murder of Hannah Lloyd. You do not have to say anything, but it may harm your defence if you do not mention when questioned something which you later rely on in court. Anything you do say may be given in evidence.'

CHAPTER THIRTY-SEVEN

Front desk said they hadn't seen Preedy all afternoon and he wasn't answering his calls, so it fell to Ronnie and Overton to interview Adam. His solicitor, when he finally arrived, seemed flustered. A good sign, Ronnie thought, and they would have a lot more to be flustered about when they got the full story. She texted Tilly to warn her she'd be late home. It was going to be a long night.

Once the formalities had been dealt with, Adam sat in his plastic chair, nearly falling over backwards.

'Careful.' Ronnie couldn't help herself. Automatic mummy-mode when it came to looking out for accidents.

He pulled his chair in and clasped his hands on the table in front of him, fixing Ronnie with a stare. His solicitor leaned over and whispered something she didn't catch but she could guess what it was. A no-comment interview was probably Adam's best bet at this point. She just hoped he'd be angry enough at being caught to override any sensible advice.

'As you know, Mr Lloyd, we have found information on your phone, messages from an untraceable number, containing the registration details of several vehicles and their dates and times of arrival in the port of Dover. Do you have anything to tell us about that?'

'No comment.' Damn, he was going for it.

'The transit vans are registered to a leasing company and when we asked them for information on the hirer, it turned out that the hirer had supplied a false driving licence to the leasing company, which carries a ten-year prison sentence, but you would know that, wouldn't you, Mr Lloyd, being a lawyer yourself.' She saw his chest rise and fall as he breathed deeply in response to her words.

'No comment.'

Ronnie smiled. 'I see. We traced the vehicles to see where they went, using our magical powers... I mean automatic number plate recognition. We found one of them this morning, would you believe, heading up the M20, and it's just been spotted on the M25 heading this way. On its way here perhaps?'

'No comment.' A sigh this time, a (more careful) lean back in the chair, arms folded. He felt invincible. Ronnie liked it when they got cocky. It usually meant a slip-up was imminent. The trick was to look anxious, as if you realised you'd been beaten. He'd take that as a sign of victory and he'd relax, take a risk maybe. She moistened her lips and blinked, glanced at Overton who was on high alert, staring at Adam as if he'd just landed from space.

'Mr Lloyd, who was it who hired the vans? Was it you?'

'No. Comment.' He separated the words, half a smile playing on his lips.

'Well, we are investigating that now, getting the CCTV from the hire office, so we'll see who it was that came in.' She looked down at her notes, giving him room to panic silently if her last comment had worried him at all. 'And we have officers going to the address provided on the false licence, as well as analysing the origin of the hire contract.' She looked up and smiled, almost kindly, at Adam who was looking more and more uncomfortable. 'We have ways, you see, of determining the IP address of the person who made the booking online. Amazing isn't it?' Beads of sweat were appearing on his brow, glistening in the harsh strip lighting of the interview room. 'Anyway, my next question for you, Mr Lloyd, a question which you may or may not answer, as you feel appropriate is this: Was it your job to make sure those vehicles came through customs without being checked? Because it looks very much as if that was the case. And if it was, you might also want to tell us what was in the back of the vans, before we find out and charge you with smuggling drugs. Or firearms? You tell us. The last border force officer to get done for that got twenty-five years.'

'No!' His fist came down on the table.

Ronnie smiled and raised her eyebrows. 'Do you mean it wasn't your job, or it wasn't firearms you were smoothing the path for?'

The sweat was building now, and his right hand, the one that had thumped the table, began to shake uncontrollably. The solicitor frowned and asked for a moment with his client and Overton summoned a uniform to escort them next door. Shutting the door behind Adam, he turned to Ronnie and shook his head, as if in disbelief.

'I'm impressed, sarge. You're doing a great job.'

'He's making it easy for me. I can read him like a book.' She glanced at his phone. 'Any news on tracing the truck? And the driving licence? I'd like to know who the asshole was who's masterminding this smuggling operation.'

Overton flicked through his notifications. 'Nothing yet, sarge. Unless. Hang on.' He used his thumb and forefinger to enlarge the print on the screen and passed it to Ronnie. 'A message from uniform, the ones checking the address on the licence.'

She looked at the words he was pointing to, then looked up at him in confusion. 'What? I don't understand.' But she did understand, because it said it there in black and white. The IP address of the booking didn't link back to Adam, and the house the driving licence was claiming to be registered to was owned by none other than DCI Matthew Preedy.

***

When Adam and his minder returned, Ronnie was still shaken up. She had had a feeling that all was not OK with Preedy, but hadn't been able to pinpoint why. There was something he wasn't telling her, and now here they were, with him at the centre of a murder enquiry, if it came to that.

The solicitor interrupted the interview before they went any further.

'I'm afraid I still see no link whatsoever between the allegations you are making and the murder of my client's wife, and I believe I have serious grounds to doubt the lawfulness of the arrest.' He pushed his glasses up his nose and chewed his cheek, waiting for their response.

'It will all become clear,' Ronnie said in what she hoped was a reassuring voice. 'If you'll just let us conclude our questioning.' She turned to Adam, who didn't look any different from before his break. 'What was in the back of the truck, Adam?'

They sat for what must have been seconds, but felt like minutes. Adam blinked and looked up at the ceiling. 'I don't know.'

'You don't know?' Ronnie's voice rose to a new level. 'You don't know? You mean you agree to get involved in the illegal import of goods into this country without even knowing what they are? Do you have no conscience at all? Don't you care?'

Adam exchanged glances with his solicitor who was shaking his head, clearly having been kept in the dark about most of it. Ronnie continued. She felt so close to the truth now she could almost taste it.

'Adam Lloyd, I put it to you that on the afternoon of Sunday 24th October, you called your wife on the phone and during that call you overheard the voice of Alison Tremaine, and inferred from the words that you heard that Hannah was about to divulge a secret relating to your illegal activity and you needed to stop her before she did that.'

'No. That's not what happened. I didn't kill my wife.' Adam's voice was pleading, desperate. He shrank back in his chair, looking at Ronnie with fear in his eyes.

'I don't know if you meant to kill her. Perhaps we will never know, but you went round to her flat, and finding her alone, threatened her with the knife on the table. I'm assuming that things escalated, Hannah staggered backwards and went over the balcony, falling to her death.'

'No.' The table shook under his fist once again. The solicitor touched Adam's arm to get his attention and muttered something under his breath.

'So if I'm right, then the exposure of your secret, Adam, would have had serious consequences. The kind of consequences you'd kill to prevent. And I think you know what you were having waved through at the port. I think you know exactly what was in the back of that transit and I think you're going to tell us.'

'I don't know. I'm telling the truth. They don't tell me.'

Ronnie let it sink in. He'd said it. She had him. Overton leaned forward and she nodded, indicating he could take over the questioning.

'Who don't tell you, Adam?' His voice was suddenly more authoritative than usual. Adam looked terrified. His bravado had melted and he was nothing but a simpering wreck of a man, hardly able to get his words out. The solicitor was staring straight ahead now, powerless, wishing himself somewhere else.

'*They* don't. They say it's better I don't know.'

'*Who* gives you your instructions?'

Adam screwed his eyes tight shut, folded his arms and hunched himself forward, all the body language of a frightened animal bracing for the hit.

'He's called Wolf. He calls himself that. He's the one who sends the messages. We don't meet. He uses a voice changer on the phone if we speak.'

'How much does he pay you to do his dirty work?'

Silence.

'How much was it worth to you, Adam? How much did you need to fund your political campaign? Must have been a tricky decision, wondering how you'd get away with corruption inside a government department, or was that a prerequisite for the application? Here's all my relevant previous experience...' Overton was on a roll. Ronnie wasn't sure how it was going to go down but she liked his style, irreverent, taking things to the limit.

'Nothing. He pays nothing. You can look at my bank account.'

'Don't worry. We will.' He looked at Ronnie, who nodded her agreement to taking over again.

'There's only one other scenario I can envisage then, Adam, and that's that you owe them money, and this is how you're paying them back. That makes me wonder how much you owe them, and how long the payback is for. Maybe there's no limit on it. Maybe...' She broke off, pretending to rack her brains for the words, but they were right there on the tip of her tongue. 'Are you being blackmailed?'

His face changed then. That was how she knew. It was as if a burden had been lifted from his shoulders. His whole body seemed to let go, relax, sink back into the chair with gratitude. It was often like that, Ronnie had found over the years. Holding onto a secret under pressure was more stressful than most people could bear, and the release of that stress, whatever the consequences, was almost life-giving. He had come back from the dead. There was expression in his face. Emotion. A desire to cooperate.

'Do I take that as a yes?'

Adam looked from Ronnie to his solicitor, who just raised his eyebrows, waiting for the next bombshell.

'Adam, what is it that you've done that's so bad you have had to become a pawn in a cross-border smuggling gang? Because it must be pretty horrific if you're willing to put your life and freedom on the line, not to mention your son...' She paused just long enough for the meaning to sink in, 'to protect your secret.'

The dam broke. Any vestiges of self-possession were washed away in the torrent of what came next.

'It was just the once, the risk was minimal, and if it meant that I stayed out of trouble, and got to keep my son, I'd have done anything. Wouldn't you?' Ronnie didn't answer. There was so much more to come. 'The first time was supposed to be the only time. A tip off to the guys at the port and nothing more. I had no idea who they were, what was coming through. I didn't need to know. Knowing would have made things even worse. Can't you see that? I didn't want to know. Didn't ask. Delivered the message straight to the front line myself, told them some crap about sensitive cargo and to let the vehicle through to be checked by the NCA, that it was above their pay grade.'

'They believed you? Who was it you communicated with at the port? What reason would they have to abandon protocol for the instructions of someone on the legal team? I find that hard to believe, unless of course he or she stood to benefit financially, or you had something on them that would convince them to do your bidding. Which was it?'

Something between anger and fear filled his eyes. He was a cornered animal, snarling to keep them at bay.

'There was money, alright?'

Ronnie smiled and took a second to enjoy his slow capitulation. 'How much?'

'Enough to persuade the guy to run with the line to his colleague. Told him it was orders straight from the minister. It wouldn't be the first time we had instructions to carry out that skirted on the thin ice of the legal pond.'

'But surely, whoever it was that was blackmailing you could have gone straight there. Why bother with a middleman?'

'He needed someone on the inside, someone who had their finger on the button, a link in the chain. And, I'm guessing, why not use a middleman if it gives you another layer of disguise?'

'Why not indeed?' Ronnie nodded, exchanging glances with Overton. 'A keen and eager go-between with a reputation and a family to protect would be even better. Which brings us back to the question on everyone's lips, Adam. What was it that you did that brought you into contact with this depraved member of the criminal underworld? You're going to have to tell us eventually. Why don't you save us some time and get it over with.'

Adam looked at his solicitor who gave him an empty smile. He couldn't help him now he'd dug himself into a hole this deep. Ronnie almost felt sorry for the guy, for both of them, clutching at the last splinters of the raft as they hurtled towards the waterfall. Perhaps he needed more persuasion.

'Was he holding evidence of some kind that you had committed a crime? Was it that?' She studied his face and noted the swallowing motion in his throat. 'Did he have footage, a recording, a video that he was threatening to go public with? To tell Hannah about?'

This time she was prepared for the fist on the table and sat back a split second before it came down. His anger was directly related to his lies. It was the connection she had established in their previous encounters and now she was testing it to the limit. This time, the fist was on its way to the table before she had finished the sentence. She was right about the secret. Someone had something on him. But whether he'd killed Hannah was another question.

'Is that why you killed her?'

'I didn't kill my wife. I may be all sorts of things but I'm not a murderer.' His words were spoken quietly with none of his former rage.

Ronnie nodded. There it was, the truth in all its raw beauty. Adam Lloyd had committed crimes but *not that one*. There was every chance he had gone along with his illegal activity to prevent Hannah finding out what he'd done in the past, but apparently he hadn't killed her. She gave Overton a long look, wondering what he was thinking. But if it wasn't Adam who had killed Hannah, who was it? If he was telling the truth, then the whole theory that he had overheard something on the phone that sent him round to her flat in a panic would hold no water at all. They'd be back at square one. Unless of course someone *else* was worried about the truth getting out. Presumably Adam's blackmailer, the criminal mastermind running the port behind layers of disguise, also had a secret to keep. Was he more closely involved with Adam than she thought?

Was it *him* that overheard part of the phone conversation between Hannah Lloyd and Ali Tremaine?

She looked at her watch. 'This seems the right time for a short break. I have an officer outside who will look after you for two minutes while my colleague and I step out of the room.' She got up and Overton followed her to the door which clicked shut behind the uniformed officer who replaced them. It was a security measure but the custody suite was mercifully empty and there was no need to seek out an empty room. The corridor would do for what she had to say.

'I need to run something by you. My brain can't process what I'm thinking fast enough to make a coherent argument out of it.'

'I know what you mean, sarge. I'm struggling to know what to believe, but I think we've got the wrong guy for the murder.' He looked at her unsurely, as if he might have jumped to one conclusion too far, but she smiled back. He was learning fast.

'So if there's still anything in overhearing that phone call being the trigger for the attack on Hannah, and if it wasn't Adam...' she began.

'Then he wasn't alone during the call,' Overton finished.

'And we know he puts all his calls on speaker. We know that.' Ronnie imagined the scene. Adam making the call from his flat, phone face up on the table, speaker mode, his hands on his hips, perhaps one running through his hair as he tried to negotiate the timings for the rest of the weekend. He must have had a lot on his mind, what with the blackmail, the uncertainty of whether his man on the ground would do as he was asked, whether someone would come looking for answers. He'd have been pacing the floor, his blood pressure rising.

'So who could have been with him? A woman? Delilah? We never got to the bottom of what was going on there.'

'Delilah was at Hannah's flat. In any event, she could never have made it to Adam's in time, and there are cameras with footage of her on the bus she took home.' Ronnie closed her eyes. 'I'm trying to picture the scene.' She brought it back again, this time with more background, a dripping tap, the oppressive central heating, the dirty plates by the sink and the half-open cupboards. That was it. 'Oh my God. Mike. He wasn't with anyone.'

'What? Then why are you smiling if your hypothesis is a no-go?'

'Because...' Ronnie took a deep breath and let it out slowly, feeling the tension melt away. 'Someone was watching. The camera. Watching, and listening. The phone number he was making repeated calls to, the one that rang unanswered. I think that's our man. He's got something on Adam.'

It was all falling into place. Overton was nodding and rubbing his hands together. 'So what's the plan?'

'I want you to set something up for me. You'll need authority from the DI. Possibly the chief super. Don't go to Preedy. Not yet.'

Overton frowned. 'That's going to lead to a few raised eyebrows, sarge.'

'I'll risk that. Now what I want you do is this...'

***

Back in the interview room a few minutes later, Ronnie took up the questioning again. She'd have to rely on her gut as to whether he was lying, but it hadn't let her down yet.

'As you know, there was a surveillance camera in

the kitchen of your flat. Do you still maintain you were not aware of that fact?'

'Of course I bloody wasn't. I'd have smashed it up. That was never part of the deal.'

Ronnie nodded, looking down at her notes. 'But it makes sense to assume that whoever put it there thought there was perhaps a little more to the deal, or at least felt in need of insurance?'

'It makes sense to assume that, yes, detective. Go to the top of the class.' Adam's sarcasm was back on track, which was good to see.

'So for now let's assume that the person who put the camera in place is the same one that was putting the pressure on you.'

'Blackmailing me. Don't pussyfoot around. Call it like it is.'

As he spoke, Overton pushed the door open and entered, armed with a box which he proceeded to unpack, plugging a laptop into a socket and attaching a series of cables. Ronnie turned her attention back to Adam.

'Blackmailing you.' She watched him squirm inwardly at the words as if he had swallowed some nasty medicine. 'Blackmail is a nasty business, but I don't need to tell you that.' She made a note on her pad. There was one more thing to mention to him, but it needed building up to if she was going to tease the next chapter out of him. 'Listen, Adam. If you are concealing his identity, you are withholding information from the police that would be instrumental in solving a murder, and possibly a whole smuggling operation. The consequences for you, never mind him, aren't worth it. If you co-operate, on the other hand, things could go a lot easier for you.' She paused as Overton took his seat and the room fell silent again. 'Where can we find this man?'

'I don't know who it is, but I suggest you take a long hard look at your own doorstep.'

Ronnie stomach lurched, but she held it together and stared him out. 'What's that supposed to mean?'

'What do you think it means? Haven't we had this conversation before? There you all are, sitting behind the safety net of public service...'

'As were you, in case you've forgotten.'

Adam ignored her interruption. 'And yet it's public knowledge, *public knowledge*,' he repeated in disgust, 'that the police force is a hotbed of corruption, racism, misogyny and fuck knows what else. How you and your lot stayed in your jobs I have no fucking idea.' Sarcasm and swearing now; he was back to the old Adam.

'What do you know about this subject that we don't, Adam? You sound like you've been affected by it personally, wouldn't you agree DC Overton?' A surprised Overton gave her a nod and turned his attention back to Adam.

'Believe me, I'm as furious about it as you are, more so in fact.' Ronnie looked at Adam with genuine compassion. 'It's a disgrace that police officers have got away with abusing their positions as public servants, that they have not only brought their own prejudice and hate-think to the job but shared it, spread it around, propagated it until it was endemic, a disease in the ranks. I have thought about leaving the police, but what would be the point of that? Don't they need the good guys to stay on, keep the numbers up?'

'What do you want? A medal?' His eyes narrowed. There was more work to do but it might have to wait. She tapped her pen on her pad. Time was marching on. She decided to cut her losses.

'I'm going to accept that you can't identify your blackmailer, for now.'

Adam nodded. 'There's a but coming.'

'I think you suspected that he might be responsible for Ali Tremaine's disappearance, and that you went to her house to do your own detective work on that. The suitcase story, although a good effort, let you down a bit.'

'It was worse than that. He told me I had to go there or a woman was going to die. He left the key, the key he'd taken off her, on the wheel hub of my car. Probably just wanted to set me up. Probably knew you'd be waiting. You could have done me there and then. Why the hesitation?'

'We hadn't deciphered your vehicle reg codes, hadn't linked those plates with vans coming through Dover, hadn't put two and two together. The stakes weren't high enough. We needed cooperation.'

Adam hung his head, silent.

'And now I need to know where that van is

headed.'

'What makes you think they'd tell me that?'

'I don't think you know. But I think you can help us find it.'

'How?' He looked simultaneously baffled and disgusted. Ronnie made a note to perfect the look next time the twins asked her for an advance on their allowance.

She reached into the evidence bag on the table and pulled out his phone.

'I want you to call your man.'

Adam blanched. She could almost feel the thump of his racing heart across the table. 'What, now?'

'Once we've plugged it into the system. We'll trace the location of the phone you're calling and we'll know where to pick him up.' She watched the panic rise in his face. She needed him calm. 'Don't worry about repercussions, there won't be any once he's under lock and key. But the consequences for you, and Max...' She paused again. 'Let's say this will put you in a very favourable light in court.' She turned to Overton. 'Good to go?'

'Good to go.'

She slid the phone across the table to Adam, who stared at it, white-faced. 'What if he doesn't answer? What if he works out he's being recorded or whatever you're doing?'

'He'll have no idea. Trust me. And if you're his right-hand man, I see no reason why he wouldn't answer. You might have all sorts of news for him, like the police being on his tail, for example. I'd answer, wouldn't you?' She glanced to her left and Overton nodded.

Adam seemed reassured. 'What should I say? It's normally him calling me. He'll think something's off.'

'Exactly, so he'll answer because he'll know something's gone wrong. That's what you're going to tell him. Specifically, I want you to say you think you've been caught out, that you've been told not to go back into the office but to call the minister immediately. You're calling for advice, and he'll know he has to calm you down, reassure you he'll protect you, to stop you revealing his identity.'

'He knows I don't know who he is. How can I reveal his identity?'

'He doesn't know that. Even if he's sure you don't, there will be a shadow of doubt. He'll need to make sure. If he's monitoring your flat, he'll know you're not there, so tell him you're walking the streets, afraid to go home. You're wondering whether to turn yourself in. Let him take as long as he likes persuading you not to.'

Adam seemed to accept the plan. 'How long do you need?'

Ronnie looked at Overton. He was the expert on the technology. 'A minute, the longer the better to pinpoint the location. If he's on the move, we may be able to pick up a route that will give us the intel to work out a possible destination. If he's in the vehicle we're following, then cross-referencing with ANPR, we can make do with even an approximation.'

She turned back to Adam, who had his eyes screwed tight shut. 'Adam, all you need to do is stick to the plan. You're pounding the pavements, it's not safe to go home, you're thinking it might be better to cut your losses and go to the police. You can't ID him and you've never met, so he's safe, and you're doing him a favour by giving him time to make his own escape if he has any worry at all that we'll be onto him.'

'You don't know who you're dealing with. He'll be worried alright. What about Max? How do I know he won't take revenge on him?'

'Max is with Meghan right now,' Ronnie began, but seeing his reaction, reached out to calm him with an outstretched hand on the table between them. 'She doesn't know everything, but she's ready to bring him in, in the unlikely event that something goes wrong and we need to get you and Max to safety.'

Adam nodded mutely.

'What we're doing is drip-feeding him information about what's already happened, but making sure he's a few steps behind. False honesty. He'll think you're telling the truth and he'll have no idea you're already here. DS Overton, please check with the officer on duty to make sure we don't get disturbed.'

Overton jumped to his feet and opened the door, murmuring instructions to the uniform outside. The door fell shut again and the room was silent except for the almost inaudible whirr of the electric lighting.

'Ready?'

Adam nodded, his pulse visibly slowing as his

shoulders relaxed. He picked up the phone. Overton gave a thumbs up as he pulled the laptop to where both he and Ronnie could see the screen.

Adam's index finger touched the call button and he held the phone to his ear, but before it began to ring, Ronnie pointed to the phone and the table. 'Speaker. That's what you do, isn't it?'

Adam nodded and put the phone on the table, pressing the speaker button just as the ringing tone started. Ronnie held her breath. The slightest noise might arouse suspicion and she couldn't risk anything jeopardising the plan.

After four rings the line went dead. 'See. I told you he wouldn't pick up.' Adam looked at Ronnie defiantly.

'Text him,' she said without hesitation. 'Ask him to call you. Say it's urgent.' She walked around the table to check the words he was typing. 'No funny business.'

It felt like a matter of seconds later that Adam's phone rang. He accepted the call, putting it on speaker. 'Hello?' The voice that spoke next was muffled, deep, distorted.

'What's the problem? Why are you calling?'

'I'm sorry to call. I know it's not protocol. It's just, I think they're onto me.'

'Explain.' Minimum words. It made sense. Ronnie's eyes flicked to the screen where flashing lights indicated an ever-decreasing zone that, if given long enough, would shrink to show them exactly where their caller was.

'I've been told not to go back into the office. To

expect a call from the minister tonight on a matter of serious misconduct. I don't know, but if they're hunting me down...'

'Are the police involved?'

'I don't know. I'm thinking... maybe I should hand myself in.'

'NO!'

Ronnie jumped, suddenly feeling the consequences of what she'd started. She thought about the twins at home cooking pasta and watching TV, Frank chatting to her mother on the phone, reminiscing about Fred's poker nights – anything to ground her. Adam was staring at her, wide-eyed in panic. She made a calming sign with her hand and gave him what she hoped was a reassuring smile.

'I don't think I have any choice.' He was doing well, the triangulation software was closing in. Overton was nodding encouragement.

'Where are you now?'

'Outside, walking the streets. If I go home they'll come for me. I know they will.'

There was a pause. Deafening silence in the room. Ronnie suddenly knew what was coming next and was already on her way to the window. How could she have been so stupid?

'Doesn't sound like outside. Can't hear traffic.'

'I'm down a side-street. Didn't want to call you in public, did I?' Adam sounded suitably angry. He was going for an Oscar at this rate. He caught Ronnie's eye as she pushed the window open and the sounds of the street, as well as a sharp rush of cold air entered the room.

'There, happy?' Ronnie gave him a thumbs up.

The alien spoke. 'You know the rules, Adam. Say nothing. Do nothing. They have no proof of anything.'

'I don't know. They must know something, or how is this happening?' His voice was rising. Ronnie couldn't have done a better job herself.

'I've got to go. I'm in the middle of something. Keep quiet. Delete your call log. Get rid of your phone. And don't fuck it up. I'm doing it myself now, can't trust the drivers to keep them alive after last time.'

The line went dead. Ronnie looked at Overton. 'Did we get it?'

'We did better than that. He's on the road. Only a few miles away.' He turned the screen towards her.

'Let's get unmarked cars on his tail, low profile. I'll brief the DI.' She opened the interview room door and asked the uniform to step in.

'Am I not coming with you?' Adam asked.

'I don't think that's a good idea, do you?' Ronnie replied, pulling on her jacket. 'We'll see you back here in a while, hopefully with news.'

CHAPTER THIRTY-EIGHT

Lydia drew her chair closer to her desk and regarded them with a more serious face than Ronnie had ever seen. They didn't have long, but this meeting wasn't a step of the process they could easily skip.

'You turned down the offer of some time off, and now you're coming to me to tell me that DCI Preedy is involved in a trafficking offence?'

She took her glasses off and looked from one of them to the other, waiting for an answer. But she didn't seem shocked enough, and Ronnie didn't know whether to be worried or pleased about that. Did she have her own doubts about Preedy? That might explain his absence from the station all day, if there were investigations going on. Her head was beginning to pound with the stress of processing all the possibilities.

She showed Lydia the land registry print-out. 'Well, it's an assumption that wasn't hard to make. The connection is there in black and white. He owns the house. The address is the one given to the van hire company. The van was waved through customs thanks to Adam and his puppet-master.'

'Whoever he is.' Lydia's face was glum.

'I'm not saying it's Preedy, but he's linked to what's going on whether we like it or not.'

Lydia nodded slowly and picked up the narrative.

'And Adam's puppet-master is currently being tailed through the streets of suburbia by our unmarked cars.'

'We have a live track on all the surrounding ANPR as well, so we should be getting regular updates. In fact, here's an image of the van just coming into Wakehurst.' Overton handed his phone to Lydia, who zoomed in and out again before handing it back.

'What's the plan for intercepting the van? I take it you've done a risk assessment to cater for the possibility of firearms?'

'Not exactly, with the time pressure as it was...' Ronnie trailed off. Lydia had a point. She stared at the screen and used her thumb and forefinger to magnify the image to its maximum size.

'Do we need ARV on standby?' Lydia was still blinking her disappointment, or disbelief, at Ronnie, at Preedy, or both. It wasn't clear.

Ronnie was about to reply when Overton almost yelped with shock. 'They've got it. The A342 from Wakehurst heading south. Pulled over in a petrol station. One of our cars has carried on past and another's pulling onto the hard shoulder before the garage ready to take over when they're back on the road.'

'That's only two miles from here. If they need back-up, be ready.'

'We should head off that way now.' Ronnie looked up at Overton who was already nodding and reaching into his pocket for the car key.

'You need to call the DCI.' Lydia's tone was blank.

Ronnie considered the idea. He'd have to be involved at some point, and if anything, it would be wiser not to go behind his back and raise the alarm. It might actually be better for him to assume nothing was amiss.

'Of course, ma'am.'

'Sound as if you mean it.' Lydia met Ronnie's eyes and held her gaze.

'As long as you don't think it might put the operation in jeopardy.'

'We have no choice. At the moment the connection is tenuous. What a landlord's tenants get up to isn't the responsibility of the landlord, yet. One day maybe, if the government legislates personal autonomy right out of existence.'

It wasn't Lydia's usual style, commenting on politics.

'I realise that, ma'am, but if it was anyone else, we'd most likely be onto them, and the police shouldn't be exempt from that kind of follow-up.'

'You're referring to Operation Maslow.' Lydia smiled. 'And you're quite right. The new rules are quite clear on it. We can't be seen to be overtly condoning, or even accidentally overlooking the suspicious conduct of a colleague.'

'So, where does that leave us?' Overton wanted clarification. Ronnie was grateful it wasn't her asking all the questions.

'As SIO on the case, DCI Preedy is in charge, and unless we have an extremely good reason to withhold information from him...'

'How do we decide when it's an extremely good reason?' Overton wasn't going to let go of this one, but Lydia had an answer for him.

'I decide.'

Overton's shoulders visibly slumped. 'Yes, ma'am,' he managed.

Lydia smiled. 'I will take the flak if necessary.'

'Let's hope it doesn't come to that.' Ronnie pulled on her jacket. 'What happened in the end with Operation Maslow? Is it ongoing?'

Lydia shrugged. 'They say it's done and dusted. I can only take Preedy's word for it. The details were never widely shared. It was a covert operation that started at the Met but ended up with a much more far-reaching remit. Information went around on a need-to-know basis.'

'A bit like the photos on the WhatsApp groups,' Ronnie quipped. Lydia gave her a look.

'I feel as furious about it as you, Veronica, believe me. It sickens me to think how many officers, because it was never just a handful, were acting without thinking for an instant of the danger not only to themselves, but to the reputation of the police force and not only at that time, but going forward, possibly indefinitely. Public trust has been lost. God knows how long it will take to get it back.'

Overton took a deep breath. 'Well, nobody's ever tried to bring me in on anything like that, if it helps – for the record...' He drifted off uncertainly.

'I'm glad to hear it, Mike. So are we agreed on how to proceed?'

'We'll phone Preedy from the car. And we'll call in with updates of course.' Ronnie was halfway out of the door when Lydia called after her.

'Oh, and DS Delmar, one more thing.'

'Yes ma'am?' Ronnie had one hand on the door frame as she turned to see Lydia smiling a half-smile, the sort a mother might give a child going off to a new school.

'Be careful.'

CHAPTER THIRTY-NINE

The rain was back with a vengeance, sheeting down on the windscreen and compounding the bad visibility that darkness had brought. Ronnie turned up the phone volume to maximum as Overton switched the wipers to top speed. It rang five times before a voice answered.

'Preedy.' There was background noise – traffic perhaps. She held her breath. *Please let it not be you.*

'Sir, it's Delmar and Overton here, following a lead and wanted to put you in the picture.' She chose her words carefully. Worst case scenario, Preedy might call ahead to warn them off, whoever *they* might be.

'What kind of lead? Why haven't I been informed before now?'

Ronnie hesitated and Overton stepped in, raising his voice for impact. 'Tried you, sir. They said you weren't available. DI said to call you from the car.' The cat was out of the bag. He'd know they were on the road now, but it would never have been a secret for long.

'So who are you going after?' Preedy's voice had changed, as if the car door had slammed and shut out the noise. They had his full attention.

'We don't know, yet. Could be nothing.' Overton slowed for a red light as he spoke.

'Well, call me again when it's something. I'm on my way back to the station now.'

'Roger that.' Overton ended the call just as the radio buzzed into action, telling them the suspect was heading north-west out of town.

'What's up that way? Why would they come off the A road only to head back towards it minutes later?' Overton pulled away as the lights turned green. 'Doesn't make sense.'

Ronnie looked at the maps app on her phone and frowned. 'I've done that route a few times recently. Avoids the roadworks on the slip road and sends you a few miles out of your way.'

'I thought the roadworks were finished now.'

'They are. I drove straight in this morning. Maybe these guys don't know.'

'Maybe.' Overton didn't sound sure. 'Puppet master doesn't sound like the kind of guy not to know stuff, that's all, given that he can install secret cameras, record phone conversations, use voice distortion, bribe a civil servant...'

He accelerated into the fast lane and Ronnie gripped her seat. She should have insisted on driving. She was a hopeless passenger. She tried to picture this man, or woman, come to that, who might be capable of all those things, who might even, having overheard Hannah's conversation with Ali Tremaine, have felt so panicked about their secret being discovered that they rushed to the Lloyds' flat and whether or not it was their intention, ended up committing a brutal murder. If that was still the theory, and they had no others to go on at the moment, then what on earth did he overhear that sent him on the rampage? She still didn't know.

'Not to mention smuggle fuck knows what into and out of the port.' Overton finished his sentence as the traffic thickened again amid a cacophony of honking horns. Someone had chosen the wrong lane and was blocking an entire queue of traffic trying to turn left.

'Out of what?' Ronnie wasn't sure she'd heard right.

'Out of the port,' Overton shouted above the hooting.

'Oh my God, maybe that was it!'

'What?' The rain and the bottleneck were too much for Overton whose impatience was getting the better of him.

'Was that what Adam's blackmailer misheard? Ali said she'd call from the airport. He heard port, assumed she was onto him.'

He glanced over at her. 'I see where you're coming from but it feels like a long shot. Too tenuous for such a violent response, I'd say.'

'You're right.' She closed her eyes. Right now she needed to rewind her thoughts and play them back on half-speed. What else could Ali's words have sounded like, and how could whoever was spying on Adam have been so certain of what it meant? It would have to be a matter of life or death to react like he did. Or she. There was no reason to preclude a woman's involvement, given her last two major cases. Her head began to thump again with the pain of thinking. The radio buzzed again but the voice was unclear. Overton asked them to repeat the message, and then slapped the steering wheel in frustration.

'What do you mean you've lost them? You were on their tail. It was in the bag.'

Ronnie put her head in her hands. *Shit shit shit*, what could they do now? Uniform were requesting instructions – the van had vanished and there had been no camera sightings since they lost the trail. They needed to come up with something. It couldn't have disappeared into thin air.

'Mike, pull over. Let's look at the map again.'

He swung across two lanes into a parking layby and killed the engine. 'Not sure what good that's going to do.' A car raced by too close, making the vehicle shake. Heavy rain slamming the roof. Too loud. Too dark. Ronnie flicked the light on.

'Look. Here's where they were headed.' She traced the road leading off the dual carriageway and northwards into the countryside. 'It's mostly fields, a few farm tracks leading off the road, easy for a van to get down I imagine. Some of them link up pretty decent roads, if you can bear the bumps.'

'So you're suggesting we get them to go bouncing down every dirt track on that route?'

'No. Of course not.' But she wasn't sure what she was suggesting.

'What's around there? Go on street view.'

Ronnie didn't need telling twice. Street view was her go-to when it came to scrolling through Rightmove on a Sunday night, on the odd occasion she allowed herself to imagine moving to the countryside, or winning the lottery and buying a second home. It allowed her to explore the whole area around the house she was looking at, and more often than not what looked like her dream home turned out to be let down by its location in a second-rate street or next door to a run-down B&B.

The screen quickly filled with the image of grey tarmac stretching through green fields. Clicking on the arrow, she navigated the road in hundred metre leaps, following it as it meandered through farmland and alongside the woods, past a boarded-up gate to what looked to have been an impressive stately home. She handed the phone to Overton.

'How often do these maps update? I'm sure I've driven that way but I've never seen that place before.'

'God knows. Could be months ago.' Overton zoomed in with thumb and forefinger. 'What are you thinking?'

'I want to know what's behind the gate.' She moved the cursors backwards and forwards but to no avail.

'Looks like that's a step too far for the app.' Overton started the engine again and checked his mirrors. 'There's only one thing for it.' He pulled out into the slow-moving traffic and swung across to the fast lane. 'Let's go and take a look.'

The rain was easing off, just the odd gusty spatter on the windscreen, easily cleared with a swish of the wipers. 'Come off at the next junction.' Ronnie had her eyes on the map again. 'We're less than a kilometre away from where they lost the van.'

Overton did as he was told, sharing his location on the radio and checking whether there had been any more sightings.

'Now left at the roundabout,' Ronnie said.

'This really is the arse end of nowhere. Get me a road number if you can.'

The speed they were going at reminded Ronnie of Joel and George and the speed awareness course. There was something you had to do to keep awake and aware at the wheel in times of stress. 'A high hedge, a narrow road, no white lines, a blind bend...'

'What are you muttering about?'

'Nothing, it's just something someone said, *say what you see.*'

'Fair enough. Carry on, if it's going to help.' He took the next bend too fast and Ronnie held onto the seat. A dilapidated sign came into view for a split second, half-hidden by the hedge as they raced past it.

'Fayre Court Hall,' Ronnie said under her breath.

The radio crackled into life again as she spoke and Overton put his hand to his ear. 'Airport what?'

'Fayre Court Hall. The hotel.' She broke off, suddenly realising what had just happened. 'The one they've been converting for the last six months or so. That was the side entrance. Oh my God. That's where they are.'

'I don't follow.' Overton slowed to a legal speed and threw her a confused look. 'Where do you want me to go?'

'Keep going, down here, and it's up on the right-hand side. It's the place we were trying to get a view of behind the hedge. It's also the name that Adam's surveillance overheard on the phone.' It was sinking into place, partially at least. She replayed Ali Tremaine's voice in her head, imagining how it could have sounded when heard not only down the phone line but through a basic camera microphone.

'What was it she said again?'

'"Let's have a catch up when I've met the girls at the airport. Call me."'

'I'm losing you, sarge, sorry.'

'Fayre Court Hall. Airport. Call...' Ronnie held her breath, knowing that its release would set a whole procedure in motion she needed all her energy for. 'Whoever it was thought Hannah Lloyd and Ali Tremaine were onto them.' Ronnie's mind raced through the possible scenarios. She pictured the crumbling building, guarded by scaffolding, and a scowling gatekeeper in a portacabin. She imagined the vans being waved through customs, racing up the motorway and peeling off into the Surrey countryside to deposit their human cargo in a derelict hotel before handing them over to whoever paid the highest price. Her stomach turned over at the thought of it.

'Put your foot down. We're less than a minute away. I'll call for back-up.'

CHAPTER FORTY

Dusk had fallen and the rain had eased to a spit as they pulled up at the main entrance, and without the benefit of street lighting, the darkness was almost stifling until their eyes adjusted. The barrier was down, blocking the driveway to the hotel and the cabin that guarded the entrance was empty. The house itself was in darkness apart from a few lights in the top floor rooms, the same ones she'd seen on her way back from work. Ronnie climbed out and shut the car door, scanning the building with a shiver. Something wasn't right. It was eerily quiet and there was no sign of the van they were looking for, but she remembered the car park at the back on the left of the gardens. She looked back at Overton.

'Leave the car. Let's check out who's around.'

'Back-up's five minutes away. Shouldn't we wait?'

'Not if it might mean losing our prey. We've come this far.'

Overton lifted his hands in resignation. 'You're the boss. But I don't want to be the one telling Lydia when this all goes tits up.'

'Don't worry. I'm used to that job.'

Ronnie was heading for the house before he'd finished, staying close to the right-hand wall. She stopped at the corner before the drive circled left and beckoned for Overton to come closer. 'The main entrance is on the south side. Car park's across to the left but there's a big gravel area between the house and the gardens. They could be anywhere.' She put her finger to her lips and listened. Nothing but the wind in the trees, the drip of rain off leaves and the distant hum of traffic. She crept forward and shone her torch around the corner away from the house, where a broad expanse of grey stretched into the blackness, then followed the edge of the gravel until it met the stone façade. Still nothing, and her eyes were taking too long to get properly used to the dark. Overton pulled out his phone and switched on the torch, pointing it in the opposite direction towards the car park, then bringing it slowly back to meet Ronnie's.

'Nothing. We've missed them,' he hissed.

'No, wait. I hear something.' She closed her eyes to sharpen her other senses. 'Listen.'

There was a muffled banging sound, barely detectable in between the gusts that shook the bows of the chestnut trees, sending another flurry of leaves scattering to the ground. 'Over there.'

'Got it.' Overton's torch shone ahead of where she was pointing. 'We weren't looking high enough. Now what?'

The van stood against the hedge, its roof just a foot or so above the wall that separated car park from garden, sticking out like a child hiding behind a tree trunk in hide and seek. She crept towards the wall, glancing backwards to check Overton was with her, then back at the house to check for movement around the front door which still stood firmly shut. Beyond the wall an area of potholed asphalt faded into mud. The van had been parked at an angle, in a hurry. The number plate matched the vehicle they had been following and the driver's door was ajar. Whoever it was wouldn't be gone for long.

'Can you hear it now?'

Overton stopped to listen, just as an outdoor light came on and a male voice shouted something unintelligible. Was it even English? There was no time to wonder. She pulled Overton down to the ground and shuffled backwards on all fours into the undergrowth. Whoever it was had a torch and was heading towards them. She held her breath, thinking of their car at the entrance blocking the way. Anyone trying to leave the premises would work out they had company at Fayre Court Hall. But the immediate concern was the footsteps crunching on the gravel that were heading their way.

As the man approached, the banging from inside the van became more frantic. Plaintive, panicked female voices calling for help, but it was the intonation of help rather than the word itself. From her vantage point in the brambles Ronnie could just see a silhouette round the corner and head towards the van. More banging, a scream this time, as if a life depended on it. Ronnie debated whether to break cover, but thought better of it. She put a hand on Overton's arm, to say they should stay hidden a few moments longer.

The front door of the house still stood wide open,

now with a light from the hallway pouring out onto the gravel that encircled the building. The silhouette turned back and shouted something that was lost in the wind, but whoever he was calling must have heard, or was on their way, because another figure emerged and broke into a run towards him. She called his name. Matt? The flatness of the 'a' in the single syllable sent her heart into double time.

Please let it not be you.

He was too close for comfort now. One flash of a torch and they'd be seen. Ronnie held her breath and let it out slowly, desperate to move even just a fraction to stop a stone digging into her knee but not daring, just in case. It was a long time since she'd last felt this fear, but it was beyond certain now that this was their man, the one blackmailing Adam into facilitating what she could only assume was people-trafficking. The same man who had installed surveillance cameras in his house, who was ready to kill to stop his secret getting out. She wasn't in any hurry to confront him. At least not until she heard what he said next.

Perhaps the wind had dropped or changed direction, but his words were as clear as if they'd been whispered in her ear. In that moment, Ronnie felt the incredulousness that was normally resolved by waking from a dream, but this, as she realised when she *didn't* wake up, was real. Horribly real. The man stood with one arm raised, ready to open the van doors, as the woman rounded the corner, panting slightly.

'You took your fucking time. Get in there and

untie them.'

Ronnie froze. There was no mistaking him.

'Sorry. They just called. Wanted to know how long till we bring them.'

'How long will it take to scrub them clean and get them dressed?'

'Depends on how bad...' Ronnie didn't hear the end of the sentence as the van doors were yanked open. 'Oh my fucking God.' The woman screamed as a body practically fell on top of her from inside, landing with a thump on the tarmac. 'What the fuck? What's the matter with her? Why's she shaking like that?' The body on the ground, tied at the wrists and ankles was convulsing violently. The woman climbed into the van, shouting orders at someone and then another girl was climbing down, sobbing through a blindfold and reaching out with both hands. .A shove from her captor sent her reeling backwards.

'Don't you go near her. You fucking hear me?'

'What do we do now?' Overton's hot breath in her ear made Ronnie shiver and pull away, detaching herself from a bramble that had gripped onto her hair.

'Wait. Not yet.'

'But the girl. She's dying over there,' he hissed.

Ronnie held him by the shoulders. 'Listen to me, Mike. She's having a seizure. There's nothing even a doctor could do until it passes, except stop her injuring herself.'

Overton sank back down in the leaves, losing his balance in the process and letting out a small yelp as his hand went into a bed of nettles. At the same time, the girl on the ground stopped shuddering and silence fell again. Ronnie held her breath as the man turned in her direction and pointed his torch at the woods.

'Shhh,' he ordered. 'I heard a noise.'

'It'll be a fox. Let's get the girls indoors before she has another fit.' The woman had two of the girls under her control now, both of them tied at the wrists and blindfolded, ready to be herded like cattle back to the house.

'A human noise.' They both stopped this time, the woman turning to look where he was pointing. 'Helen, we've got company.'

Ronnie froze. His gun and the woman's torch were trained on her where she crouched in what had been darkness. She raised her hands to her head, not taking her eyes off his.

'You certainly have got company.' A voice from the depths of the blackness behind them. 'Put the gun down. Put your hands where I can see them.'

The man spun round to face the direction of the voice. DCI Preedy's voice. His hands went up behind his head. So did the woman's. Helen. He'd called her Helen.

'Check them for weapons.' Preedy again. The armed response team made themselves visible around him. Overton was already running over and patting down pockets. He removed a set of keys and threw them to Ronnie. 'Clear.' He straightened up.

Ronnie was too stunned to move for a second.

She'd prayed for it not to be Preedy, but never in her wildest nightmares had she imagined the alternativeIn the torchlight, there was no mistaking his familiar form, the Barbour jacket and checked waistcoat.

'Frank?' She wasn't sure if she said it or thought it. His first words had identified him beyond question, but she hadn't wanted to believe it. Not her Frank, not the one who fixed things, made things better. Not him. She staggered out of the bushes, brushing wet leaves off her jacket.

'Frank?' Louder now, so he could hear. She walked around to face him and stood inches from his face, staring into his eyes as if she'd find out it wasn't him, if she looked hard enough. It was a lookalike, a robot. Anyone. Anything but Frank Reilly.

'DS Delmar. We meet again.' His expression was impossible to read in the inky darkness, but she hoped it was fear, regret, shame.

'Helen?' She turned to the woman, then back to him. 'Helen?'

He nodded, the crack of a smile on his lips. 'Elyena, to be precise. I like to remind her she lives here now, can't be going round with a foreign name or she'll put people's backs up.'

Ronnie might have done something she regretted if she hadn't felt Preedy's hand on her shoulder just then. 'Let us take it from here. Check the vehicle.'

'Yes, sir.' Ronnie could hardly hear her own voice. A third girl climbed down from the van, then a fourth, bewildered and dishevelled, shielding their eyes from the torchlight. One by one they let themselves be led away by uniformed officers. Ronnie shone her torch around the interior which was empty now apart from a scattering of empty water bottles, padlocks on chains and a bucket in the corner covered with a lid. She felt the vomit rise in her throat again and stepped back to the ground, taking lungfuls of damp night air.

'Frank Reilly I am arresting you...' Preedy was reading out the caution when reality landed like a brick. Within seconds, Frank was handcuffed and being led to the patrol car. Another team had followed the uniforms and the girls to the house. Ronnie was about to follow them when Preedy reached out a hand to hold her back.

'Good job. And calling for back up. Not like you, Veronica, I've heard.'

Ronnie tried to avoid his gaze. 'I've had my moments of deluded heroism, like anyone else.'

'And you've been quite the hero today, I'd say.'

'Just doing my job.'

'Not just doing your job, but uncovering a human trafficking operation as a sideline to a murder investigation.'

'It's not a sideline. They're connected.' She looked at him quizzically. 'Of course they are. We've just found Adam Lloyd's blackmailer. That's the link.'

'No proven link yet.' He looked almost apologetic. 'Nothing that the CPS will accept. He won't be charged with Hannah's murder. We have no evidence that he was at the flat, remember.'

'Give me time. Let me interview him. I'll find out

the truth.' It sounded like a line from a film, but if she couldn't do it, who could? Surely after all they'd been through, Frank owed it to her. He'd been caught red-handed, didn't stand a chance of being released without charge.

Overton and the others had gone on ahead. Armed response had been dismissed. She and Preedy were alone. She stopped, took a long slow breath in and out and turned to face him. 'And one of our own.'

Preedy grimaced and held the passenger door for her. 'I'm getting rather used to it, I have to say.'

'But a scene of crime officer, leading the murder case and running a smuggling ring on the side?'

Preedy was about to shut the door but pulled it open again and stared at Ronnie in disbelief. 'A SOCO?'

Ronnie frowned. 'Of course. You know that. He was the lead on the Lloyd investigation. They'd finished before you were put on the case.' She paused. How did he not know this? 'You'll see – it'll be in the file.'

His hands went to his head and he began pacing up and down next to the car. 'I've read the file. I know it back to front. The crime scene manager on the case was Pete Knowles. He signed off on the report.' Ronnie frowned. None of it made sense. 'What made you think it was Frank Reilly?'

The seconds it took her to answer felt like hours. In her head, a flashback of her arrival at Mulberry Court played out in slow motion. The floodlit expanse of tarmac below Hannah's balcony. Approaching the tape, having it lifted, ducking under, heading for the main door with rain in her face and the misery of working on a Sunday on her mind, and then seeing the white suit walking towards her. Frank's delighted face under the hood, behind the mask, pleased to see her, the interruption by Overton.

'I don't understand. He came out of the block of flats just as I got there, wearing full PPE.'

'You met Knowles inside, surely. Pete Knowles?'

Ronnie groaned. 'Of course. I just presumed, because I'd always known Frank as crime scene manager. Fuck.' She never swore. Life was too full of minor annoyances, but this was more than that. This was an absolute catastrophe of an assumption. 'I can't believe I did that.'

'Easily done.' Preedy was quick to reach out for her hand. She let him take it. 'Confirmation bias, don't they call it?'

She pulled her hand away. 'I shouldn't be making mistakes like that.'

He held her gaze. 'We all trust our friends. That's normal. That's pretty much all we have.' He waited a beat for the moment to pass. 'When was that exactly?'

'Late. Almost nine I think. But only a few hours after the incident.'

'The last time I saw Reilly was on his last day at work at the Met. Not his choice. He'd have stayed. Thought we'd cut him a deal with the information he gave us but we had to disappoint him on that one. He certainly wasn't going to be getting another job in any area of police work. We made sure of that.'

'Maslow?'

Preedy nodded. 'He was our man on the inside. Gave us names, screenshots, recordings, you name it.'

'So why get rid of him? If he wasn't involved?'

'Because he *was* involved.'

'I don't get it.'

'He couldn't be part of that behaviour cult without joining in, and once he'd joined in, he was as guilty as the rest of them. Our fault, not having envisaged how the whole thing would play out, but when we went through his computer, we found things that pre-dated his undercover mission. Ironically, that's what had made him such a good spy.'

'What things did you find?' Ronnie felt the heat rising inside her. How could she have missed this? Her brain refused to process what she was hearing. Was Preedy talking about another Frank Reilly? Surely they couldn't be the same person?

'You'll find out, eventually, because he's more than breached the terms of our agreement.'

'What agreement? You made some sort of compromise not to tell?'

'Something like that. Everything would be shut down, we had eyes on his online activity. He'd never work for the force again but we wouldn't press charges for the sex offences.'

Ronnie waited for what seemed like an eternity.

'Frank Reilly had set up a website, subscription-only, and several of his customers were police officers or otherwise affiliated to the Home Office in some way.

The material on the site was bad – young girls, fourteen-year-olds, doing things I don't need to tell you about right now. We got the subs list and there were prosecutions, mostly out of the public eye, but there are a dozen or more of them doing time right now.' He looked at Ronnie to gauge her response, but she gave nothing away. 'All of them handed over by Reilly. They would have assumed he got the same treatment, although they never knew his identity.'

Neither did I, thought Ronnie. Neither did anyone. 'You gave him new ID?'

'That wasn't an option. It was a one-off. Nothing like this had happened before. We were making it up as we went along, but trying to do the right thing.'

'I suppose I can relate to that.'

Preedy inclined his head towards the hotel. 'Anyway, we'll hear the full story when he's had a chance to stew in a custody cell. The rain's stopped. Looks like uniform are waving us over. Let's go and see what's been going on inside.'

It wasn't as bad as it could have been, Ronnie told Susie later on the phone. There were fifteen girls crowded into the two locked rooms on the top floor, all alive, but thin and frightened. One of them spoke a little English and was able to give them some information about where they'd come from, what they'd been promised and descriptions of the ones who'd already been taken away. They had been removed from their families in a rural part of northern Georgia, but their captors had met with no resistance at all. 'Everyone grateful to leave,' the hollow-eyed girl said. 'Competition for a place on the truck. My sister go last year and write me to say very happy in UK. I want to follow her, then I find she not here. The letter not from her, just to make me come. The same for others.' She indicated the frail young bodies around her. The 'men' who drove them off in the middle of the night had laughed as they picked them off one by one for a 'special time', telling them afterwards that they would just have to hope the English men waiting for them didn't mind having spoiled goods.

Susie was lost for words for a minute. 'The worst thing of all is that this stuff is officially sanctioned. If we can't rely on government departments to do the right thing then what hope is there?'

'But we did the right thing,' said Ronnie. 'In the end.'

CHAPTER FORTY-ONE

Frank Reilly sat with his arms folded, empty-eyed. His solicitor took a sip of water and pushed a plastic cup his way. He ignored it, stated his name and address and completed the formalities. Preedy launched into the questioning.

'Mr Reilly, please explain your connection with Adam and Hannah Lloyd.'

Frank's hands clenched together in front of him. 'Shouldn't you be asking him that?'

'I'll repeat the question.'

'It wasn't a question.' A wry smile played on Frank's lips. 'But I'll oblige. I know what you want to know, and I don't mind telling you, now that he's proved himself to be the scumbag we all knew he was.'

He took a long drink of water. Ronnie sat up in her chair. If he was going to talk in riddles, she wasn't going to let any of it get past her.

'Adam Lloyd was one of my, how shall I put it, one of my best customers. Came online when I'd hardly been up and running a month applying for an annual recurring subscription. Someone who really knew what he liked and where to find it.' His smile spread a little wider as he went on. 'New stuff went on the site, he wanted to see it. Must have been harbouring desires he'd kept under wraps for a long time, I thought. My ideal client, there for the long haul.'

Preedy glanced at Ronnie who nodded, her eyes fixed on Frank who was spinning his empty cup between thumb and forefinger now.

'He wasn't on the list you gave us, when we had our, what did we call it? Exit interview?'

'No. I don't believe he was.'

'And why was that?'

'I was never going to deliver the whole package to you, was I? Gift-wrapped lambs to the slaughter. Always keep a little back for yourself, that's what I always thought.'

Preedy took a second to absorb this. Ronnie imagined how he must feel, having his shortcomings exposed in front of her, effectively a junior officer. In some strange parallel universe she wanted to give his hand a squeeze, tell him it was easily done, that nobody would have acted any differently in the circumstances.

'Did you ever meet him?'

Frank let out a laugh. 'Meet him? How much of an idiot do you think I am? I knew him well enough, I'd been into his flat, set up the camera, had a tracker on his car, I knew about his every move. He was mine. Which was lucky, when you think about it, because I had nothing after you dumped me from a great height, took me off the job once you'd got what you wanted.'

Preedy made as if to interrupt, but Frank was fully charged now, not letting go of the baton just yet. 'I had him over a barrel, and he knew it. I'd had to close the site down. I knew the Met were decent on the tech and would have found me online at some point, but there are other avenues.'

'Trafficking women into the country?' Ronnie found her voice. 'Sex-trafficking?'

Frank sat back in his seat, the triumphant teacher whose student has just experienced the lightbulb moment. 'A lot of demand for it these days, as I found out. And our Adam, not only trying to curry favour with some figures in politics with a penchant for a good party, but with his finger on the pulse of Border Force... well, I couldn't really turn that down, could I?'

Preedy made a show of looking at his notes, but the facts were in all of their heads. Ronnie knew what was coming next.

'How did he make it happen on the front line? As a lawyer, he wasn't in control of searching vehicles.'

Frank shrugged. 'Don't know. Don't care. That wasn't my problem.'

Ronnie glanced at Preedy for approval to take over the questioning. It was one of those looks you understood but couldn't describe, the kind of silent communication between detectives that said *I've got this next bit.* Preedy nodded and sat back, hands clasped behind his head to show where the power lay.

'Tell us about the cameras, Frank. You had Adam's flat under surveillance. We've looked at the devices and they are top of the range. Obviously we'd expect nothing less.' Frank didn't react, so she continued. Might as well go all the way with it. 'Did you overhear a conversation between Adam and Hannah

Lloyd, and make an inference from it?'

'Inference, nice word. Good work, Veronica.' Ronnie felt sick but held his gaze. 'You're right about that. I acted on that, a little too impulsively, perhaps. But there was a risk she was onto me. I had to shut it down.'

'By shut it down, you mean kill her?'

'If you put it that way, but as you can see now you have all the facts at your manicured fingertips, it was a big deal. I had a lot to lose.'

'You didn't.' It came out too quietly, but he heard, and leant forward towards her, his brow creased with a frown she didn't like. Preedy was leaning forward, taking notice. She'd promised him this. And now she was delivering the goods, word by guilty word.

'What are you saying? Hannah knew something. Adam had clearly got wind of what I was up to, was trying to escape my clutches, and I can't blame him for that.'

'Hannah didn't know anything. Nothing. Nada.' Ronnie's voice rose in a crescendo of fury. 'What you thought you heard and what her friend actually said in the background were two different things. You heard "Fayre Court". She said "airport".'

There was a long pause. The colour drained from Frank's face. Eventually he spoke in a half-whisper. 'Hall. I heard "hall", she practically recited the address.'

'She said "call" not "hall". It was "when I'm with the girls at the airport, call me".'

Frank's face had turned from blank shock to a

manic grin. 'Well, it seems I must be going a little deaf in my old age.'

The rest of it was a formality. With an admission of trafficking underage girls from Georgia, one of whom was his 'wife' Elyena, the abduction of Ali Tremaine and the murder of Hannah Lloyd, there was nothing more to get out of Frank Reilly. Preedy terminated the interview and had him taken to the cells overnight. 'We won't have a problem with the CPS on this one. I reckon we can sleep easy tonight.'

Ronnie held the door for him, enjoying his look of surprise. 'I still don't understand it. He's a family friend. Why didn't I pick up on it? I never doubted him for a second. Not ever.'

'He was pretending to be a lot of things. Probably believes his own lies, seems to think everything was justified, and it was in his eyes. Makes you think.'

'He was coming out of the flat, dressed as a CSI.'

'Have you seen the number of spare suits they take in, just in case of contamination?'

'So he hid in the flat until they came, and managed to get into a white suit and escape as if he was one of them. That's why we had one extra person coming in that we couldn't trace coming out. We assumed we'd miscounted the CSIs going in.'

'Not that hard, when you think about it. They all look the same.'

Ronnie pondered this. He had a point, but she felt ridiculous nonetheless. 'He made this big show about moving to the suburbs with his new wife.'

'Some of that would have been true. It's the best way to lie, mixing it up with the truth so thoroughly nobody knows the difference.'

'She was supposed to be disabled, this Helen. I went to their house. It was all set up with ramps and lifts and everything.'

'Did you actually see her?'

Ronnie shook her head. 'And there was something else I assumed. Not sure if I should tell you, but now we are where we are...'

'What's that? I can take it.' Preedy put up his hands in resignation. 'Do your worst.'

'I thought you were involved. There were a few things, like the van used in the trafficking registered to a house in your name, the way you had no part in the interview with Adam, when I assumed it would be protocol for it to be the SIO, when we were so close to a charge.'

'No longer protocol. Interviewing is best left to the experts. Anyone with Reilly's contacts can get hold of a fake driving licence. Using my address was all part of his smokescreen, or his little game, depending on how you see it. And as for our Adam, call it a kneejerk reaction. Border Force aren't my favourite government department, not since, well, for a while now.'

'Since what?' He'd said something that was knocking on the door of her memory but that she couldn't quite grasp.

'Since my wife left me for one of their number.' He turned to give her a knowing look. 'No sense to it.

Just makes me – I don't know – lose my impartiality. Better to stay out of things like that.'

'Why did you let me into the interview with Frank, then? Surely you could find a conflict of interest there?'

'The other way round though. You had him down as a friend. He needed someone who'd seen his good side, and if even you were having second thoughts about his innocence.'

'Fair enough.' Ronnie wondered whether to reveal the rest of what was on her mind, and decided she probably had nothing more to lose by sharing it. 'It also occurred to me, at one point when I suppose nothing was out of the question, that Baz Munro might have something to do with it.' She closed her eyes in anticipation of his shock at her words. But Preedy threw his head back and laughed out loud.

'Baz Munro? Possibly the last man on earth, if you don't count Overton, to be involved in something like this. We're not all bad, Ronnie, there's no need to punish the whole of the male race for the sins of a tiny minority. Have more faith. Otherwise there's no hope.'

Ronnie nodded. 'Yep. I have to admit I'm a little inclined to make assumptions, but safer that way than the other.' She yawned. 'Now isn't it time we called it a night?'

CHAPTER FORTY-TWO

When the duty sergeant found Frank's lifeless body the next morning, he called the DCI in a panic. Preedy took the stairs two at a time and arrived in the custody suite grim-faced. The other staff didn't need to know the details of his background with the prisoner, but there was a good chance Reilly had tried to pin this last act on his old enemy. Ronnie wasn't far behind Preedy. It was as much her case as his, and a witness was always a bonus when attending a scene like this one. She'd learned that the hard way.

'What happened?' Preedy turned to the custody sergeant. 'Is it suicide?' They were standing in the doorway of the cell. Frank's body was curled on the bench that served as a bed, facing the wall.

'The doc thinks it's almost certainly suicide. First time we checked on him, we thought he was asleep, then one of the staff called me in because they couldn't wake him. I called the doc. He confirmed no pulse, but there's no obvious cause. Paramedics were already on their way. We're about to cordon off the whole custody suite as a crime scene and they're coming to speak to me and the other staff.'

Ronnie felt a strange wave of relief pass through her, then glanced around the room. 'He was asking for pen and paper last night. Did he get it?'

'I authorised it,' Preedy sighed. 'Thought he could do with writing a confession in his own words. It does save us some trouble sometimes. I presume someone collected it, whatever he wrote?'

'I gave him a sheet of paper and a pen but he wanted the pen from his jacket. It was only a pen...' The custody sergeant checked his notes. 'I'm not sure what he wanted to write. The night sergeant hasn't recorded any collection of anything.'

'Could be in his pocket,' Preedy said. 'Gloves on, let's move him.'

Frank's body was heavier than Ronnie expected. She avoided looking at his face – it was all still too much of a shock – but she managed to feel around in his jacket pockets while Preedy held him up.

'Got it.' She pulled out a neatly folded note, with writing on both sides. 'Where's the pen?' she asked, getting to her feet. 'Not in the pockets.'

'I see it.' The custody sergeant pulled a glove on and plucked something from the line where the floor tiles met the wall. 'There you go.'

Preedy turned it over in his fingers. 'Nice pen. Not the usual sort you find in a desk drawer.' He passed it to Ronnie. 'What do you think?'

She unscrewed the barrel. 'I think there's a reason we don't hand out pens like this.' She looked at Preedy. 'Bic biros only, last time I checked.'

The sound of the buzzer and slamming doors announced the arrival of the paramedics. Two young men in hi vis jackets pushed their way into the room and

Ronnie stepped outside to give them space. Preedy followed, while the custody sergeant secured the door to the unit.

'What's your theory?' Preedy took a seat at the custody desk and motioned for Ronnie to do the same.

Ronnie was still screwing the barrel back onto the pen, more as a distraction than anything else. 'It was in here, whatever it was he took.'

'A suicide pill?'

She nodded. 'I'm sure forensics can examine the inside for traces of drugs, and the post mortem will confirm it, but that's my hypothesis.'

Preedy put his head in his hands. 'His last act of revenge.'

'Nothing we can do now.'

'Except re-educate the desk sergeants. I don't imagine it will go down well with the commissioner though.'

They sat for a moment, watching the men remove Frank's body on a stretcher. As the doors swung and clicked shut, Ronnie unfolded the piece of paper she had retrieved from Frank's pocket. 'Shall we go back up and find a space to read this?'

Preedy got to his feet and headed for the door. 'I can hardly wait.'

CHAPTER FORTY-THREE

The handwriting was rounded and even, a far cry from the rantings of a disturbed mind. Ronnie cleared her throat, resisting the temptation to glance ahead to the ending. They would hear this together.

I expect to be dead by the time you read this. The pill I'm about to take is a lethal dose of cyanide which is supposed to lead to painless death within twenty minutes, so you don't need to worry that I suffered. It was always a contingency plan, if things got out of hand, which they clearly have. I don't think that's up for debate. And it's not a life I've enjoyed much so I don't expect I'll miss it, wherever I find myself next.

If there's therapy in the afterlife, no doubt they will pinpoint the loss of my Jess as a trigger for acute PTSD, and then they'll reframe all of my subsequent behaviour so they can attribute it to some sort of general disregard for any other young women's lives. That would be a fair assessment – if she couldn't live, then why should anyone else's daughter? I was out to punish the world for taking her from us. At least that's what I thought I was doing. But one thing led to another and I found myself in too deep and too addicted to the adrenaline rush. I was overwhelmed by the demand for the videos, and to start with I convinced myself there was nothing really wrong with any of it. The girls were underage but they looked old enough. They weren't children. I'm not a monster. And from a business point of view, I was responding to market forces. As time went by, I dared myself to do more, go further, take more risks. Being close to being caught was the only thing that made me feel alive, but the first time I was found out, I realised I wasn't ready for it. Not then.

Veronica, a message for you. An apology, but I'm not going to hang around for your forgiveness. When your father needed bailing out, for the third or fourth time, if I remember correctly, he wouldn't let up trying to find out where my money was coming from. I gave up pretending, in the end, thought that he'd keep a secret. Told him about the website, even offered him a free membership. I didn't give him the whole picture, not the whole ugly truth about how old they were and where I was getting them from. But Fred didn't want to keep it to himself. He was going to go to the police. I had no choice, in the end. It was my life or his.

You may remember two years ago, almost to the day, we met in a bar. I'm not sure you'd have recognised me. I did a decent job of a disguise, spiked your drink, tried to get you into a cab but some asshole cop got in the way. So I put in a complaint to the police about your behaviour bringing the force into disrepute. Thought that might get you out of there, out of the police, less chance of you ever uncovering what happened to Fred. But you're a hard nut to crack, Ronnie. Should have known you were your father's daughter – a bit of a maverick – but an irritatingly good person at the end of the day.

Inventing Helen was the fun part. She was already there as a character in my new life narrative after Preedy kicked me out of the Met. One of my early imports from Georgia and utterly reliant on me to keep her family back home alive and fed. Hadn't banked on you being so keen to meet her, hadn't banked on bumping into you at all, but at least I had my story straight there.

Luckily the police don't take any notice of who's on what

job and the SOCOs themselves can't recognise each other in those suits. If they had done, I'd have said they were a man down and I'd been shipped in from another area. When I saw you walking towards me in that car park I had to think quickly, but it made things a lot more interesting. You trusted me implicitly, fed me information which I used to mis-direct your investigation. I've never had so much fun in my life. Poor Giselle. I hope she gets her son back soon. I'd say poor Ali Tremaine, but she gave as good as she got. That was an unexpected challenge… I might as well have got beaten up by the gangsters I blamed for it.

I think that's it – enough for you to tie up your loose ends. At least I will be with Jess now, assuming I'm right about heaven and hell. Desk sergeant shouldn't have allowed the pen though, and the buck stops with Preedy on that one. I'm only sorry I won't be around to see how they punish him.

'Is that it?'

'That's it.' Ronnie folded the letter up, put it in an evidence bag and pulled off her gloves. Her heart should be raging against the man who had just admitted to killing her father, but she felt strangely calm. 'Everything makes sense now.'

'I'm so sorry, Veronica. I can't imagine how it must have felt reading that.'

Ronnie looked up, surprised at the sudden expression of sympathy but still unmoved. 'I feel nothing at all. I suppose it won't have sunk in yet. What's the plan for Adam? I take it someone's told him?'

'We haven't finished with him obviously, but with a confession, a guilty plea and good behaviour, you never know, he might be out in ten.'

Ronnie thought about little Max. Preedy read her mind.

'The uncle and aunt will take the boy. Best thing for him, I think. He can even help with the new baby. They found Hannah's will, by the way.'

'What did it say?'

'Everything in a trust for Max, with her brother and Meghan as his guardians, so they won't be short of cash for his education.'

Ronnie took it all in. 'So she changed that in time then, thank God. And we can tell Ali Tremaine she's safe to go home.'

'Indeed we can. Delilah might face some questioning over her involvement in turning a blind eye to Adam's dubious practices, but that's going to take more investigation.' He stood and came closer to her, leaning on the desk. 'Why don't you take the rest of the day? We'll tidy up the rest. You've done a terrific job.'

'Thanks.' Ronnie got to her feet. 'I might just do that.' She turned to go, then with one hand on the door handle she looked back at Preedy, whose expression was all concern. She'd been so wrong about him, so wrong about Frank. But none of that mattered right now. Things had worked out for the best. 'And Matt?'

'Yes, Ronnie?' He smiled, eyebrows raised in amusement at hearing her use his name.

'If you're still up for it, I'd love to go for that dinner.'

ABOUT THE AUTHOR

Lucy Martin grew up in London and Brussels and after gaining a first-class degree at Oxford in French and Russian became a lawyer working mainly in central Asia, before retraining as a languages teacher and eventually settling into a less frenetic life of French tutor and thriller writer. She now lives in Devon and London with her partner, dog and occasional visits from five grown-up children.

Lucy has written four novels including Stop at Nothing and The Choice, which are the first and second in the DS Ronnie Delmar trilogy leading up to Last to Leave, and published by Welbeck. The thread running through the three books comes through loud and clear in Ronnie's character – an uncompromising quest for justice alongside a fierce commitment to female victims of crime. Like her creator, she's not afraid to push a few boundaries, take risks and break the rules, not always with the result she imagines...

ACKNOWLEDGMENTS

There's never enough room here to thank everyone that needs thanking, but let's have a go. Firstly, my fellow authors – what a smashing group of chums you are, especially our SW London group and the Harrogate gang – always there with a whoop and a cheer when required.

Talking of festivals, it's been a joy to meet in real life some of my favourite thriller writers including Louise Doughty, Elly Griffiths and Vaseem Khan. Thank you for being so friendly and approachable. Graham Bartlett – you were a huge help when it came to checking police procedure and sorry for calling you Stephen. David Penny, thanks for your top marketing tips. Charlotte Graham, Lorraine Stevens, thank you for keeping me company and sane, and Heather Fitt – I have never been so outlasted at the bar. That award goes to you.

Thanks to all those who have taken the time to read the Ronnie series and give their quotes – TM Logan, Helen Fields, BA Paris, Louise Mangos, Eve Smith, Greg Mosse, Emma Christie, Penny Batchelor, Philippa East, Claire Dyer, Sarah Clarke, Alex Chaudhury, Simon McCleave, Marion Todd, Victoria Dowd, DE White, Paul Gitsham, Jacqueline Sutherland and Joy Kluver. Your time and input are a real gift and reading your enthusiastic soundbites keeps me going in times of self-doubt.

Big thanks to my editor Liz Ward and cover

designer Matt Davies for their tireless work and for coping with my endless revisions, and to Anne Cater and all the bloggers for making some noise and making the launch go with a bang.

And finally – a huge shout out to everyone who has bought, read and reviewed my books. I wouldn't be here without you. Don't ever stop reading!

Printed in Great Britain
by Amazon